AF783680

Jürgen Backhaus (Ed.)

The Reformation

The Reformation

As a Pre-Condition for Modern Capitalism

edited by

Jürgen Backhaus

LIT

Gedruckt auf alterungsbeständigem Werkdruckpapier entsprechend
ANSI Z3948 DIN ISO 9706

Bibliographic information published by the Deutsche Nationalbibliothek
The Deutsche Nationalbibliothek lists this publication in the Deutsche Nationalbibliografie; detailed bibliographic data are available in the Internet at http://dnb.d-nb.de.

ISBN 978-3-643-10737-4

A catalogue record for this book is available from the British Library

Fresnostr. 2 D-48159 Münster
Tel. +49 (0) 2 51-620 320 Fax +49 (0) 2 51-922 60 99
e-Mail: lit@lit-verlag.de http://www.lit-verlag.de

Distribution:
In Germany: LIT Verlag Fresnostr. 2, D-48159 Münster
Tel. +49 (0) 2 51-620 32 22, Fax +49 (0) 2 51-922 60 99, e-mail: vertrieb@lit-verlag.de

In Austria: Medienlogistik Pichler-ÖBZ, e-mail: mlo@medien-logistik.at

In Switzerland: B + M Buch- und Medienvertrieb, e-mail: order@buch-medien.ch

In the UK: Global Book Marketing, e-mail: mo@centralbooks.com

In North America by:

Transaction Publishers
New Brunswick (U.S.A.) and London (U.K.)

Transaction Publishers
Rutgers University
35 Berrue Circle
Piscataway, NJ 08854

Phone: +1 (732) 445 - 2280
Fax: + 1 (732) 445 - 3138
for orders (U. S. only):
toll free (888) 999 - 6778
e-mail: orders@transactionpub.com

The Reformation as a Pre-Condition of Capitalism

01. August 2010

Prof. Dr. Dr. h. c. Jürgen Backhaus Lic. jur.
Krupp Chair in Public Finance and Fiscal Sociology
University of Erfurt
Nordhäuser Straße 63, 99089 Erfurt
POB 90 02 21, 99105 Erfurt
Phone: 0361/737-45 50
Fax: 0361/737-45 59
E-mail: juergen.backhaus@uni-erfurt.de

Summary

General discourse discusses reformation as a spiritual or cultural phenomenon. Recently, the issue comes up in the context of integration policy. The difficulty of integrating Islamic immigrants into Western society is seen as consequent to the lack of the Islam having undergone a reformation. Three generations ago, discussions in the social sciences and, indeed, the news media, were more advanced. Religion was seen as a necessary element of the fabric of any society, and hence, different religions were discussed in terms of how they could together form the social fabric of modern capitalism.

Keywords: Capitalism, Reformation, Religion, economic systems, Johannes Calvin (1509-1564), Martin Luther (1483-1516), Werner Sombart (1863 – 1941)

J.E.L.-codes: B15, H82, O15, P1

The Reformation as a Pre-Condition of Capitalism

Contents | Page

Frontispiz: Martin Luther (Stamp, 1961)

BUNDES
DEUTSCHE
POST
Luther
15

Introduction

Jürgen Backhaus

General discourse discusses reformation as a spiritual or cultural phenomenon. Recently, the issue comes up in the context of integration policy. The difficulty of integrating Islamic immigrants into Western society is seen as consequent to the lack of the Islam having undergone a reformation.

Three generations ago, discussions in the social sciences and, indeed, the news media, were more advanced. Religion was seen as a necessary element of the fabric of any society, and hence, different religions were discussed in terms of how they could together form the fabric or texture of any society to come. Clearly, religious movements can stagnate, and they can also through reformation spark larger developments in society, even in economic processes. Of course, economic processes follow a certain calculus, but whether and where they happen is dictated by different considerations or circumstances. Consider the importance of religiously caused emigrations and immigrations and what they brought about. Can, for instance the ascent of the Chicago School in Economics be described without discussing forced emigration and immigration into the United States?

When Martin Luther in Erfurt in the Monastery of St. Augustine pondered the freedom of a Christian soul, he certainly could not foresee, let alone intend, what forces he would unleash with the reformation. The basic hypothesis of this book and his contributions is that the reformation is a pre-condition for the development of modern capitalism.[1] It is a sufficient, but not a necessary condition.

---

[1] See Backhaus, Jürgen, (ed.). 1996. *Werner Sombart (1863-1941) - Social Scientist*, 3 vol., Marburg: Metropolis.

One could have imagined a largely agrarian society in Central Europe even after the reformation. That might have been a much more peaceful scenario compared to the catastrophy of the Thirty-Years-War. However, what might have been is not the focus of this book, rather what has emerged and why.

The Weber Hypothesis[2] connects the spirit of capitalism with the teachings of the reformers Luther, Melanchthon, Calvin, and Zwingli. This is a somewhat narrow view, since the Weber Hypothesis was put up of a research program cooked up in long discussions in Heidelberg and shared by Sombart, Weber, and others. Sombart took up the part on the Jewish spirit in *Modern Capitalism*.[3] The haphazard activities of the Iranian president Ahmadinejad bring home a more basic insight. Without reformation, neither Christian, nor Jewish spirit would ever have allowed the basic institutions of modern capitalism to spring up.

The essays collected in this book reflect this basic hypothesis in various ways. Helge Peukert emphasizes those aspects in Luther's thinking which come close to modern economic thought. Gerrit Meijer emphasizes John Calvin as a reformer and Hans Frambach looks at the impact on the work ethic of the thought of the reformers. Reginald Hansen traces the roots of the modern Social Market Economy all the way back to the time of the reformation and

---

[2] Max Weber, Max, 1904, 1920², *Die protestantische Ethik und der „Geist" des Kapitalismus*. Dirk Käsler, ed., Munich: C. H. Beck. 2004, 2006².

[3] Werner Sombart, 1911. *Die Juden und das Wirtschaftsleben*. Leipzig: Dunker & Humblot. English translation, 1913. *Jews and Modern Capitalism*. London: Unwin. Reprint 1969. New York: Burt Franklin; see also the introduction to the American edition by Bert F. Hoselitz (1951) to: Werner Sombart, *The Jews and modern capitalism*, Glencoe, Ill: Free Press; and 1916², 1987. *Der moderne Kapitalismus. Historisch-systematische Darstellung des gesamteuropäischen Wirtschaftslebens von seinen Anfängen bis zur Gegenwart*. [Modern Capitalism], 3 vol., Munich/Leipzig: Duncker& Humblot. Reprint 1987: München: DTV.

this is critically discussed by Enrico Schöbel. Eugen Dühring was a controversial economist and a social philosopher in imperial Berlin and must clearly be seen as a late intellectual product of the reformation. He questioned everything which he turned his thought to. While James Gay looks at Eugen Dühring's work in terms of documenting what this polyhistor made of the reformation – During was almost a-religious –, Benito Arruñada takes the modern theory of rent seeking and applies it to the practice of confessions. He then looks at a second chapter at the protestant work ethic in the tradition of John Calvin. Weber's, Sombart's, and Müller-Armack's thought are likewise late intellectual products of the reformation and Günther Chaloupek traces this with respect to the different theoretical concepts of economic style, economic system, and spirit. His contribution is commented upon by Ringa Raudla. Alexander Ebner explores Max Weber's thoughts on capitalism, Protestantism, and democracy. Inspired by the presentation by Erik Reinert at the 18th Heilbronn Symposion, Hans Frambach comments on the impact of the Reformation on Veith Ludwig von Seckendorff,[4] whose handbook for the chancellor of a model state (Teutscher Fürsten Stat) became a classic on good governance. Remarkable is the life of Georg Anton Veth, who started out a priest and after his conversion to Protestantism became a hard-working farmer. Hans Esser presents Veth's biography which survived as it has been commissioned by his friends after his death.

The essays presented in this book were originally discussed at the 18th annual *Heilbronn Symposion in Economics and the Social Sciences*, June 16 – 19, 2005. We are grateful to the Lord Mayor of the City of Heilbronn and the City Council for their generous hospitality and support.

---

[4] Compare Erik Reinert, 2005. „A Brief Introduction to Veit Ludwig von Seckendorff (1626-1692)." *European Journal of Law and Economics, 19: 221-230.*

References

Backhaus, Jürgen, (ed.). 1996. *Werner Sombart (1863-1941) - Social Scientist, Vol. I: His Life and Work*, Marburg: Metropolis.

Backhaus, Jürgen, (ed.). 1996. *Werner Sombart (1863-1941) - Social Scientist, Vol. II: His Theoretical Approach Reconsidered*, Marburg: Metropolis.

Backhaus, Jürgen, (ed.). 1996. *Werner Sombart (1863-1941) - Social Scientist, Vol. III: Then and Now*, Marburg: Metropolis.

Reinert, Erik. 2005. „A Brief Introduction to Veit Ludwig von Seckendorff (1626-1692)." *European Journal of Law and Economics*, 19: 221-230.

Sombart, Werner. 1911. *Die Juden und das Wirtschaftsleben.* Leipzig: Dunker & Humblot. English translation, 1913. *Jews and Modern Capitalism.* London: Unwin. Reprint 1969. New York: Burt Franklin.

Sombart, Werner. 1951. *The Jews and Modern Capitalism.* Translated by M. Epstein, with an introduction to the American edition by Bert F. Hoselitz. Glencoe, Ill. Free Press.

Sombart, Werner, 1916^2, 1987. *Der moderne Kapitalismus. Historisch-systematische Darstellung des gesamteuropäischen Wirtschaftslebens von seinen Anfängen bis zur Gegenwart.* 3 vol., Munich/Leipzig: Duncker& Humblot. Reprint 1987: Munich: DTV.

Weber, Max,1904, 1920^2, *Die protestantische Ethik und der „Geist" des Kapitalismus*. Dirk Käsler, ed., Munich: C. H. Beck. 2004, 2006^2

Martin Luther: A first modern economist

Helge Peukert

1. Introduction

In the following text we will not deal primarily with Luther´s ´general theory´ and life[1] or his criticism of perverted rules of the catholic church (e.g. the sales of indulgences, see Luther 1962b /1541). We will primarily interpret Luther´s most important contributions on economic problems (especially *Von Kaufshandlung und Wucher*, 1983/1524, also included in the Calwer edition, see Luther 1965, and WA [Weimarer Ausgabe] 1966b). It may be mentioned in passing that Luther´s initial critique of the sale of indulgences had to do with the amalgamation of the medieval church with the spirit of capitalism, i.e. an improper mix of religious and financial or commercial matters. Albrecht of Brandenburg became archbishop of Mainz in 1514, he had to pay high duties for confirmations in addition to the costs associated with his problematic possession of the dioceses of Magdeburg and Halberstadt. The fiscal solution for his problems was a 50% share of the Peter´s indulgences sales. Indirectly Luther also castigated the grand monopolists like the Fugger´s. They were involved in the indulgence system so that the credit debts of the church were paid off. Also Luther´s social concerns are obvious: Those who have money to give to the church should give it to the poor and they should not finance expensive churches like St. Peter.

---

[1] See e.g. the short overview by Kunst (in Kunst (ed.) 1982, 13-60), and Friedenthal (1967).

These facts already reveal Luther´s general attitude on economic institutions and problems. It is not so easy to extract his points of view because Luther was a somewhat unsystematic thinker, he mostly dealt with case studies and did not elaborate abstract systems of thought. Some interpreters have even found some apparent contradictions in his writings. This necessitates the application of the principle of hermeneutical charity. In our view the ´contradictions´ are mostly due to his endeavor to formulate a new theology as part of an interpenetrating society (see below). In so far, they transcend his reflections conditioned by the times (Aland 1983, 406-408). As will be seen, his ethical proposals for the good merchant can still be applied today and show more or less up in the more recent debates on business ethics.

In addition, we will include his other main articles on the economy which are much more restricted to the discussion on usury: *An den christlichen Adel deutscher Nation* [At the Christian nobility of the German nation] (1962a/1520, WA 1966a), the *Kleiner Sermon vom Wucher* [The minor lecture on usury] (WA 1966d/1519), *Eyn sermon von dem unrechten Mammon* [A lecture on the evil mammon] (WA 1966c/1522), the *Großer Sermon vom Wucher* [The major lecture on usury] (WA 1966e/1520), and *An die Pfarrherrn wider den Wucher zu predigen* [At the ministers to preach against usury] (WA 1967/1540). It should be mentioned again in advance that in his few writings on economic problems, Luther never tried to develop a concrete or precise political or economic program or statute (also the German secondary literature is not abundant, see Barge 1951, Prien 1992, Pawlas 2000, Hesse and Müller (eds.) 1987, Backhaus 2005). He aims first of all at the economic problem from the religious viewpoint of the Christian conscience.

Luther´s economic writings are few but he almost always included economic aspects in his predominantly religious writings, e.g. in his major and minor catechism (in Kunst (ed.) 1982, 61-144/1529). In his explanation of the fifth commandment (you shall not kill) he also includes social economic aspects: If you do not give clothing and/or food to the hungry and freezing and they die for hunger or coldness the fact of killing is obvious (Kunst (ed.) 1982, 79). In the 7th commandment (you shall not steal) he includes the wrongdoing and swindling of artists, workers, etc. who exploit the open, free market. "Weltliche Abmachungen verwerfen wir nicht, wenn sie durch gerechte Verträge miteinander zustandegekommen sind – ohne Habsucht und ohne Betrug" (1960, 260).[2] In his religious texts he also develops the anthropological foundations of his reasoning. "(D)ie Natur ist so beschaffen, daß niemand den anderern so viel wie sich selbst gönnt und ein jeglicher so viel er immer kann an sich bringt, ein anderer bleibe, wo er kann" (Kunst (ed.) 1982, 92).

For a Christian he formulates in the catechism a rudimentary business ethics. "Also lassen wir diese Gebote in der allgemeinen Bedeutung bleiben, daß erstlich geboten sei, daß man des Nächsten Schaden nicht begehre, auch nicht dazu helfe noch Ursache gebe, sondern ihm gönne und lasse, was er hat, dazu fördere und erhalte, was ihm zu Nutz und Dienst geschehen kann, so wie wir wollten, daß man uns täte" (Kunst (ed.) 1982, 93). This principle of benevolence is at the root of Luther´s thinking on the economy.

---

[2] „Desgleichen rede ich auch von Handwerkern, Arbeitern, Tagelöhnern, die ihre Willkür üben und nicht wissen, wie sie die Leute übervorteilen sollen, und doch lässig und untreu in der Arbeit sind ... So geht es doch auch mit voller Macht und Gewalt weiter auf dem Markt und in den allgemeinen Händeln zu, wo einer den anderen öffentlich mit falscher Ware, Maß, Gewicht, Münze betrügt und mit Kunstgriffen und seltsamen Kniffen ... übervorteilt, weiter mit dem Kauf überteuert und nach seinem Mutwillen beschwert, schindet und plagt ... In Summa, das ist das allgemeinste Handwerk und die größte Zunft auf Erden ... was stehlen heißt, dass mans nicht so enge fasse, sondern so weit gehen lasse, wie wir mit dem Nächsten zu tun haben" (Kunst (ed.) 1982, 83-84, 86).

Another aspect of this text is to highlight the importance of Luther´s concept for modern Western economies. In contrast to the well-known economic-sociological interpretations (Weber 1975 /1905ff.) which underline Luther´s traditionalism we will argue that Luther had a very modern concept which is still latently prevalent in European societies. In contrast, in Anglo-Saxon countries, especially in the United States, the Weberian Calvinist creed is dominant. The dominant evolutionary path of Western societies is not autopoetic differentiation in Luhmann´s terminology (Luhmann 1997), but interpenetration (Münch 1982, 470-525) in the sense of an overlapping of the Weberian value spheres. In this view the political, cultural (/religious), and economic subsystems interpenetrate: On the one hand, they develop their own internal logic, on the other hand they interpenetrate in real life interactions with the other subsystems, they all extend their area by overlapping. In these zones of overlapping they restrict their internal logic.

So in markets we have the overlapping of e.g. an exchange logic <u>and</u> of universalist societal norms and ties with the political order and law so that we can really perceive unique occidental ´market communities´ as a synthesis (in a certain sense a precursor of the social market economy), an integration of opposite components. It transcends the traditional pre-capitalist order with a strict internal and external moral <u>and</u> pure economic utilitarianism: Luther was one of the first who conceptualized such a synthesis, this was his great merit beyond all specific and time bound proposals. As we will see he accepted the internal logic of politics and the economy but at the same time he did not only call the individual and his/her conscience, he also formulated demands at the public authorities. In the political sphere we do have a certain implicit and at least rudimentary religious legitimization which prevents the full-fledged differentiation of a Machiavellian logic of power.

These interpenetrations are an essential upgrading mechanism of Western societies which is usually neglected in social theorizing. It allows a non-zero-sum-enhancement of the different spheres. In abstract sociological theories, very often differentiation is presented as a general concept with the overall consequence of a cultural-symbolic disenchantment. In this text we will show that Luther´s concepts (see especially Luther 1983a/1525) make interpenetration possible and intellectually conceivable. "Wo sich nur die ökonomische Produktion und der Geschäftsverkehr ausbreiten, ohne die Interpenetration mit der Gemeinschaftssphäre, ohne dementsprechende Auflösung partikularistischer Bindungen und ohne Universalisierung von Gemeinschaftsbindungen, hat der ökonomische Utilitarismus zwar die traditionalistische Ordnung zerstört und Anomie erzeugt, aber keine neue Ordnung entstehen lassen" (Münch 1982, 517). The success, moderation and distinction to e.g. Islamic societies and economies is therefore maybe essentially attributable to the reformation impulse to make a modern interpenetrating society possible in which "(g)leichzeitig … [die] Temperierung des hemmungslosen Strebens nach Gewinn bei Übernahme des Erwerbsprinzips in die Binnenwirtschaft statt[findet]. Das Ergebnis ist regulierte Wirtschaft mit einem gewissen *Spielraum für den Erwerbstrieb*" (Weber 1924, 304). It is an open question in how far catholic modern orthodoxy has not in principle implicitly adopted the same framework.

Another central aspect of the occidental interpenetration concept is the mechanism of inclusion. It means the public participation of actors in different value spheres which are to be brought together by the modern individual. Interpenetrating subsystems cannot be integrated by a concrete functionally differentiated agency or institution (like the catholic church). The cultural effort to integrate the opposing value aspects of the different value spheres must be accomplished by the individual. Culture therefore cannot be confined to the reflections of a specialized caste in society. For Luther, all actors in society are therefore priests. In the next part we will briefly describe some major aspects of Luther´s approach which are relevant for is economic thinking.

2. The social-economic environment

Before we will discuss Luther´s writings it is worthwhile to briefly highlight the social-economic situation at his time (Prien 1992, Irsigler 1983, Lütge 1963, Bosl 1970, Henning 1977). At the beginning of the 16th century still 90% of the population lived at the countryside and worked as peasants. But some developments threw the medieval economy out of its traditional lines of an economy according to need. Besides a secular increase in population, especially in Thuringia and Saxony an intensification in the mining industry took place. Between 1470 and 1680 the so-called price revolution occurred because the low investment rates in the production of goods could not keep pace with the increasing demand so that wheat increased by 260% in the aforementioned time interval and the salaries only by 120%. This surplus was mainly appropriated by the feudal land owners. The stratification of the rural areas consisted of a small stratum of rich farm owners, owners of a farm of half of the average size and maybe 50% consisted of day laborers, small tenants, etc.

Even the more important towns like Wittenberg were still towns dominated by agriculture with no more than 2100 inhabitants in 1513. But in these towns slowly a town democracy (sometimes oligarchy) and autonomy developed and they became centers of commerce. The long-distance trade with massive capital concentrations flourished without energizing the local trade. The crafts and their production for the markets were also at the ascent in some towns, accompanied by the new social question of unguilded craftsmen. A third new phenomenon was a first wave of standardized mass production in the putting out and manufacturing systems, especially the production of textiles, metal products, book printing, and leather goods have to be mentioned. Well-organized grand merchant companies in Augsburg, Nürnberg etc. organized the production and processing of silver, copper, ore, tin, and mercury. Sometimes they almost had modern capitalist organization forms like joint stock companies.

The regular overproduction crises in mining lead to the organization of cartels and monopolies. The Fuggers, Welsers, Höchstetters, and Fürers stood for (German) early capitalism in the form of family and corporate associations. They were engaged in long-distance trade, mass production, and in financial and banking activities. The profits were also used for consumption, the acquisition of real estate, and usury. A close connection existed with the nobility which needed money and therefore conferred privileges to the grand merchants, the prime examples are the feudal ore regalia.

The activities of these rich merchants and their collusion with the feudal nobility was often criticized and many pamphlets castigated the exploitation of the majority. Another component of Luther´s time was the monetary crisis which lasted from 1480-1525. The production of species could not catch up with the increased need for it in exchange even though between 1450 and 1540 precious metals were imported from America and increased the price hikes in this period. So (often illegal) credits with high interest rates interfered in everyday´s and even small exchange activities. Also new minting occurred with decreased silver or gold content. In the lower and middle strata of society all this lead to great aversions against the money economy and early capitalist developments which are obviously apparent in Luther´s writings. As we see, he lived and wrote in a time of conflicts and transition and of profound socio-economic change. "Die sozialen Kosten des wirtschaftlichen Fortschritts waren hoch: Rückgang der selbständigen Handwerkerexistenzen durch Verlagsbildung, Schließung von Zünften, Zunahme unqualifizierter Hilfskräfte. Die Krise des Geld- und Währungssystems verschärfte bei stagnierenden Löhnen die Folgen der langfristig steigenden Preise für Grundnahrungsmittel; betroffen waren vor allem die stark zunehmende Zahl von Lohnarbeitern in den Städten, im Bergbau und auf dem Land. Die Krise des Feudalsystems äußerte sich in wachsendem Druck der geistlichen und weltlichen Grundherrn auf die abhängige bäuerliche Bevölkerung und die unterbäuerlichen Schichten, die sich schließlich 1524/25 im Aufstand des ´gemeinen Mannes´ [äußerten]" (Irsigler 1983, 17).

Luther´s mother came from the middle classes, his father started as a small peasant, he became a face worker in a mine and later rose on the social ladder as a mine master. His job career exemplifies the transition from an agrarian to an early capitalist society. When Luther was young the family was not well-off. Luther had almost no contact with peasants and his vivid criticism of the fraudulent behavior of the peasants can only refer to the owners of full farms. He mainly lived in urban environments in Mansfeld, Eisenach, Erfurt, and the local trade city of Wittenberg. There he made friends with Lucas Cranach, who was a mass producer in a putting out firm, a merchant and a money lender who held the drugstore monopoly. He became the greatest landowner and in 1537 he was appointed as mayor. Luther will have known the economic conditions in Leipzig (the 40% interest rate in Leipzig is a prime example of usury for him) which was a vibrant early capitalist city where the commercial activities of the Fuggers with regard to copper took place.

Luther was surely confronted with economic problems in his pastoral care activities and as curate. His wife Katharina of Bora had to manage the economic affairs of the Augustiner cloister with a pension, student dormitories, etc. In later years he received many inquiries by the town councils how to deal with the interest problem, etc. He personally experienced the problem of increasing prices and the quarrels which may result from giving warranties.

3. The catholic church and the problems of usury and interest

To understand Luther´s contribution it makes sense to briefly highlight the state of the debate when Luther started thinking about interest and usury. The prohibition of interest is one of the few strict economic rules in the bible (see e.g. Dtn. 23,59; Lk 6,35). In the 11th century with the increase of trade and commerce and the increased need for money in productive activities this became a problem but the official church reaffirmed its strict position on usury at the second, third, and fourth Lateran councils (1139/1179/1215) and at the councils of Lyon and Vienne (1311/12). The arguments were (1) the duty for charity, that (2) money is unproductive and (3) only a medium of exchange. It is therefore unethical to get something for nothing. The only two factors of production are land and work. One main function of the prohibition was to save people who need a consumption credit from excessive exploitation by exuberant interest rates. An accompanying aspect was the fight against monopolies and their extreme prices. Thomas of Aquin delivered the central arguments which to a high degree also show up in Luther´s reasoning.

A certain relaxation of the strict interdiction happened in 1425 by Martin V, and in 1455 by Kalixt III. Now a difference was made between usury and credits with interest in general and a specific form of risk sharing was introduced (risk sharing was later appreciated by Luther as we will see): profit on share. This so-called *Zinskauf* (credit on participation) which came up in the 15th century was a modified mortgage. As already pointed out by Schmoller (1860, 557), it could take numerous forms: "1. Der Zinsmann überläßt das Grundstück dem Zinsherrn zur Nutzung. 2. der Zinsmann bestellt das Grundstück selbst und überläßt dem Zinsherrn den Ertrag. 3. Der Zinsherr erhält nur einen bestimmten Teil des Ertrages oder eine feste Geld- oder Naturalrente als Zins. Dabei gilt das

Grundstück für den Zinsherrn als Sicherheit für den Fall, dass der Zinsmann die Rente nicht zahlt. 4. Die Rente wird nicht auf ein bestimmtes Grundstück, sondern auf den Gesamtbesitz eines Schuldners oder eines Gemeinwesens gekauft. Im Schadensfall haftet dann der Zinsmann mit seinem gesamten Besitz. Diese gefährliche Form nannte man „blinden Zinskauf“[109]. 5. Es ist zu unterscheiden zwischen Zeit- und Leibrenten. Leibrenten dauerten bis zum Tod des Zinsherrn, Zeitrenten eine vorher festgelegte Zeit“ (Prien 1992, 62-63). Especially the fourth variant makes it possible to decouple interest from landed property.

Many pamphlets interfered in this debate. The most advanced was Eck´s position, a theologian who belonged to the school of Tübingen. He argued in 1514 that a 5% interest rate for investment capital was reasonable because capital could only be directed in productive purposes with the aid of the work of the merchants. Eck was financially supported by the Fuggers. The official church could not make up its mind. The solution of the problem was open when Luther entered the scene. The fifth Lateran council in 1514 reaffirmed the interdiction of interest but in fact let the problem unresolved.

It should be mentioned that the catholic church had an interest in interest. In fact, the church often needed the capital of the merchants as much as the nobility. What enraged Luther was this hypocrisy of rejecting and willingly taking capital gains at the same time. For example, in the northern Italian banks a lot of money was invested with interest by the Vatican, the money came from the donations for the crusades. The Vatican eagerly took the interest of these financial investments. By this money accumulation and increase of the east-west trade as a consequence of the crusades the church influenced the emergence of early capitalism (Strieder 1925).

4. Some aspects of Luther´s general theology

A good starting point to correct some prejudices about Luther is his analysis of the free human will. His view of the human free will and the role of reason (Luther 1961) should not be confounded with the message of the humanists. In his debate with Erasmus of Rotterdam (who at the time supported the view of the catholic church) Luther explicitly *denied* the free will of man. Maybe overinterpreting some sentences in the Bible (e.g. Joh. 3,27: "Der Mensch kann nichts nehmen, es werde ihm denn vom Himmel gegeben") Luther states that before the advent of Jesus humans have not known the way of salvation and therefore were not able to do so by their own reasoning. If it would have been possible the crucifixion of Jesus would not have been necessary. Luther strongly favors an antithetical argument: What is outside the grace of Jesus and God belongs to the realm of darkness, error and the opposite of truth. Man is totally sinful, god´s grace is absolute.

Evil dominates the merciless world which needs uncompromising hope. Our condemnation is sure and cannot be influenced by ourselves what is needed is total faith. He ridicules the free will as apparently a free floating thing in the middle, neither good nor bad in itself, neither right nor wrong, neither belonging to Christ or Satan (1961, 319-321), i.e. an impossibility. Flash, the body and blood are not the bad mortal or animal parts of man in contrast to human will and reason but they all together belong to the sinful and fallen part of man (1961, 323). Not optimism but resignation has the upper hand in this elaboration. Total faith could lead to totalitarian political solutions but we will see below how Luther cushions this result in his teaching on the two empires.

"Sünde hängt nicht äußerlich an der Haut und den Haaren, sondern gerade an der Vernunft und am Willen. Da Johannes aber die ganze Welt dieser Sünden schuldig spricht und man aus Erfahrung weiß, dass die Welt diese Sünde ebenso wenig wie Christus kannte ... ist klar, dass der freie Wille mit seiner Vernunft und seinem Willen durch diese Sünde vor Gott als gefangen und verdammt erachtet wird. Darum, solange er Christus nicht kennt und nicht an ihn glaubt, kann er nichts Gutes wollen oder anstrengen, sondern dient notwendigerweise der Sünde, eben da er jenen nicht kennt" (1961, 324-325). This is a very extreme thesis on religious bounded or almost non-existing rationality. But how can man get out of the realm of sin if his nature is bad from the beginning and if reason and will are not capable of changing the human mind?

"In dieses Reich gelangen wir nicht aus eigener Kraft, sondern durch die Gnade Gottes … wenn wir ihm [dem Reich Satans] nicht durch göttliche Kraft entrissen werden" (1961, 326-327). The devil is much stronger than man so that salvation totally depends on god´s grace and compassion and mercy. Not our good intentions, reason or hard work can surpass the evil but we totally depend on mercy. God chooses us not depending on our efforts and achievements – "nicht durch das Verdienst unseres Werkes, sondern durch die Huld seiner uns verheißenen Barmherzigkeit" (1961, 327). This is an obvious predetermination by god which became a major point in Calvin´s teaching and which was toned down in Luther´s later writings. We do not have to be nervous about our being chosen, in the sense that we have to perform well or that we need special proofs of being chosen – the assurance of his mercy gives us security. A side aspect of this is our *un*knowledge of the reasons of his actions and e.g. with regard to justice or the problem of the theodicee.

"Aber da Gott der Wahre, der Eine ist, dazu ganz unbegreiflich und unzugänglich für die menschliche Vernunft, so ist es billig, sogar notwendig, daß auch seine Gerechtigkeit unbegreiflich ist" (1961, 328). The theodicee problem has an economic aspect: Why are bad people rich? "Die Hütten der Gottlosen haben die Fülle" (Hiob 12,6; 1961, 329). Our knowledge is too limited to answer these questions we only know that there will be a life after death and that "dieses Leben nichts ist als ein Vorläufer oder vielmehr Anfang des künftigen Lebens" (1961, 330). In summary "ist die Vernunft selbst gezwungen zuzugeben ..., dass es einen freien Willen weder im Menschen noch im Engel, noch in sonst einer Kreatur geben kann" (1961, 331). This allegation is in stark contrast to interpretations that Luther and the reformation liberated and empowered the human mind.

We know that Luther liberates the human being from the dictates of the catholic church but we see here that he does not erect the ideal of elucidated human will and reasoning in the humanist tradition. He develops a strict predestination principle. Our innerworldly activities are more or less irrelevant for god´s grace. The life in the hereafter is much more important than our stay on earth. In contrast, Erasmus (for the Luther-Erasmus debate see Friedenthal 1967, 549-569) held the ideal that man could be educated and elevated and transform himself into a reasonable personality. The catholic church rejected the free will at the council of Ephesus in 431 but e.g. Thomas von Aquin gave way to a certain (little) margin of freedom of the human will which was at some times considered as heresy by the catholic church. Erasmus also shared the position of a limited free will, he was a so-called "Semipelagriner." Luther was more orthodox than his opponent but his basic message survived: Only faith, no deeds; only pity, without intermediaries.

In his contribution *Von weltlicher Obrigkeit* [On the worldly authorities] (1983b/1523, see also 1962a, 1966a) Luther tries to show that the worldly power of rights and the use of the sword are exercised through god´s will and order in the world right from the beginning of public authorities in history. A main reference is Röm. 13,1-2: „Jedermann sei untertan der Obrigkeit, die Gewalt über ihn hat. Denn es ist keine Obrigkeit ohne von Gott; wo aber Obrigkeit ist, die ist von Gott verordnet. Wer sich nun der Obrigkeit widersetzt, der widerstrebt Gottes Ordnung; die aber widerstreben, werden über sich ein Urteil empfangen" (1983b, 10).

Luther does not qualify the governments: any government has god´s approval to use the sword.[3] A right of resistance does not exist. “(U)m des Evangeliums willen darf man keinen Aufstand erregen, um Widerstand zu leisten, sondern muß alles erdulden” (1960, 193).[4] At first sight this seems to be a very pre-modern, authoritarian and undemocratic approach. He also justifies the death penalty in case of murder. In the following Luther presents the thesis of the two empires: human beings belong to the empire of god and to the worldly empire. Good Christians do not need neither a king or prince nor the power of the sword. The function of law and power is to prevent the non-Christians from committing crime, to punish them and to protect the well-intentioned. According to his skeptical basic view the large majority has not the right Christian spirit so that a public authority is essential to prevent chaos and anarchy and to keep peace. That is why god ordered the two regiments. Because “alle Welt böse und unter Tausenden kaum ein rechter Christ ist, würde eines das andere fressen, daß niemand Weib und Kind aufziehen, sich nähren und Gott dienen können, wodurch die Welt wüste würde. Deshalb hat Gott die zwei Regimente verordnet: das geistliche, welches durch den heiligen Geist Christen und fromme Leute macht, unter Christus, und das weltliche, welches den Unchristen und Bösen wehrt, dass sie gegen ihren Willen äußerlichen Frieden halten und still sein müssen“ (1983b, 15).

Luther rejects all hope to install a Christian regime in the world, „denn die Welt und die Menge sind und bleiben Unchristen, ob sie

---

[3] „Die Obrigkeit ist ein Zeichen göttlicher Gnade ... Denn sonst ließe er’s alles hingehen unter Türken und anderen Heiden als Anarchie, so richteten sie sich selbst zugrunde“ (1960, 179).

[4] But we also read in Luther: „Ein Christ ist durch einen doppelten Gehorsam gebunden: gegen Gott und gegen seinen Fürsten. Und dieser zweifache Gehorsam wird nur aufgelöst, wenn der Fürst befiehlt, was gegen Gott ist. Denn dann muß man Gott mehr gehorchen als dem Menschen“ (1960, 191).

gleich alle getauft (sind) und Christen heißen“ (1983b, 16). No revolutionary consequences do follow from these considerations. “Christus kümmert sich um politische oder wirtschaftliche Fragen nicht ... In einer und derselben Person muß sorgfältig der Christ und der Staatsbürger unterschieden werden ... Ein Prediger darf sich nicht in staatliche Dinge einmischen” (1960, 180, 183). The power logic of the political system is accepted but in his personal behavior the good Christian should internalize a different behavioral code. The thesis of the two empires allows Luther to be very radical and pragmatic at the same time. The good Christian does not obey the authorities in his own interest because he does not need the authority, in case of chaos he would deliberately give away his possessions. The reason why he accepts the authority is the regard of the interests of his neighbors, their protection of live, property and peace. “(S)o ergibt er sich aufs allerwilligste unter des Schwertes Regiment, zahlt Steuern, ehrt die Obrigkeit, dient, hilft und tut alles, was er kann, das der Gewalt förderlich ist” (1983b, 18). The citizen - as a general and strict law (1983b, 26) - should not revolt and e.g. pay the taxes, but the motive is the love for our neighbors.

So far Luther´s concept seems to be extremely authoritarian and even totalitarian. But in the second part he discusses the limits of the exercise of power and authority. The worldly power only has to refer to external things like the protection of the body, the absence of violence, the distribution of reputation, the economic conditions, the professions, the estates, etc. (see the analysis in Vogt 2001, 42-45). But it has no right to interfere in the world of thinking and belief, i.e. what the human soul is concerned. This radical split demarcates a sharp difference to the practice of the catholic world which wanted to dominate the worldly power and which tried to define what is good for the human soul and define the contents of their beliefs. This radical dichotomy foreshadows Kant´s realms of spiritual freedom and natural necessity, it is an essential precondition of our hypothesis of Western interpenetrating societies because it opens the door of freedom in the realm of the spirit. "Das weltliche Regiment hat Gesetze, die sich nicht weiter erstrecken als über Leib und Gut und was äußerlich auf Erden ist. Denn über die Seele kann und will Gott niemand regieren lassen als sich selbst allein. Deshalb: wo weltliche Gewalt sich vermisst, der Seele Gesetze zu geben, da greift sie Gott in sein Regiment und verführt und verdirbt die Seelen" (1983b, 29).

Bishops and princes are fools if they try to administer by law or force what the people should think or belief. These considerations go hand in hand with his harsh attack of the catholic church: We are baptized for Christ and not for bishops, the human soul is taken out of the hands of human beings and is submitted directly under the merciful power of god (1983b. 30-31). This again shows Luther´s double strategy: On the one hand we are sinful and intellectually weak and need god´s mercy to be saved but at the same time the human spirit is liberated from institutional dictates.

Finally, Luther argues against the tyranny of the catholic church in their endeavor to be superimposed on the worldly authority, and on the other hand the worldly regiment is accused of imposing high taxes and interest, etc. Again Luther has a double strategy: We all know that the worldly regiment will always be unjust but at the same the public authorities are measured against the standards of a good Christian government. Here Luther even justifies the bad characters in politics to a certain degree, "denn es sind Gottes Stockmeister und Henker, und sein göttlicher Zorn gebraucht sie, die Bösen zu strafen und äußerlichen Frieden zu halten" (1983b, 36). But in the third part Luther also talks about good governance of a Christian authority which may occur in rare cases.

Luther refrains from elaborating rules for the good republic. He only considers the state of mind of the ruler who should be motivated by Christian love. He must have the sword in his hands but in specific cases he can be lenient and he should always have the interests of his subjects and not primarily his own in mind. He should also have critical confidence in the proposals of his advisers and prevent war if possible (1983b, 47). Luther also mentions the principle of non-violence of the subjects in case of obvious wrong behavior of the ruler. In this case the Christians should not resist with violence but tell the truth in the open. “Denn der Obrigkeit soll man nicht mit Gewalt widerstehen, sondern nur mit Bekenntnis der Wahrheit” (1983b, 47).

At the end the text also contains a message for adequate behavior in the economy. Luther takes the example of borrowing: Good Christians should always pay back debts among themselves (Luther leaves out the interest problem in these passages). They should also always pay back their debts to non-Christians. Interestingly, a good Christian should also always presume that the non-Christian will repay his debts. Luther sets the ethical standard very high: When the creditor is rich and the debtor is poor and cannot pay back without difficulties no general rule applies. As a rule, the debtor should repay as much as he can, his basic standard includes his house, nutrition, and clothing for himself, his wife, and the children (or the larger family). The richer the creditor, the more he can dispense (1983b, 49-50). These rules are flexible and make the interpenetration of value spheres possible. The non-Christians have to obey the law, the Christian can behave in an economic rational way but with a couple of exceptions. The concrete decision how much to forego is put in the decision realm of the individual actor and is not predefined by a public or religious authority. So ethical standards and the logic of the system can work side by side.

To understand Luther´s texts of the economy a brief look at his theory of the three estates which was to a certain degree a common view in Medieval theology seems warranted. Estates are first of all broadly defined by Luther, they include groups of people like virgins, social estates like peasants and e.g. the group of monks (see Vogt 2001 for the details). The most important distinction are the following three institutions or hierarchies: the state *(politia)*, the church *(ecclesia)*, and the economy (*oeconomia,* comprising marriage and family). These estates are given by god they represent the natural order. They are all necessary to preserve peace and law. They are universal in all cultures.

They are not mere copies of reality. Luther for example criticizes self-chosen estates like monks and nuns which are inferior compared with the most modest crafts. No estate should be considered as inferior, they all have the same value. So in whatever estate a human being is put: All men and women are equal. For god´s evaluation it is important that we all should carry out our jobs very conscientiously. The conservative element in Luther´s thought is that e.g. a peasant should not try to become prince or priest, i.e. change his basic estate. This would cause anger and chaos. A person who became a Christian should or need not change his/her profession. “Es gilt nicht also, daß man um des christlichen Glaubens willen das äußerliche Leben wolle ändern; sondern das äußerliche Leben soll bleiben. Bist du berufen ein Ehemann, Ehefrau, Knecht, Magd etc., so bleib darinnen bei Gott , worinnen du berufen bist“ (cited in Vogt 2001, 49, LSS 13,1613).

As mentioned, the revolutionary consequence is that a good Christian need not change his estate. God “fordert nicht, daß der Knecht nicht mehr Knecht sei: sondern läßt den Hauptmann Hauptmann und den Knecht Knecht bleiben. Damit zeigt er an, dass sein Reich das weltliche Reich und die äußerlichen Stände auf Erden nicht zerstöre. Alle Stände, so von Gott geordnet und geboten sind, sind gut, und dass man ein Christ werde, da bedarf man keines äußerlichen Standes zu. Es ist nicht vonnöthen, daß Mann und Weib von einander laufen und in ein Kloster gehen, auf dass sie Christen werden und Gott dienen; sondern können in ihrem Stande und ehelichen Leben Christen sein und Gott dienen, ja bessere Christen sein und Gott mehr dienen, denn wenn sie ihren Stand fahren ließen“ (cited in Vogt 2001, 48, LSS 13, 1609-10). Luther directs human orientations to the innerworldly activities and rejects a separate religious life in e.g. monasteries which absolutely looses its religious exclusiveness and superiority.

Those who work for the church as the third pillar of his estates are not better than those working in the other two, there are no first and second class Christians.[5] A good Christian can perform as a Christian in his profession, because after Luther it is a duty given by god ("Ein jeder soll sein Amt, das ihm von Gott befohlen ist, fleißig und getreu ausrichten", in Kunst (ed.) 1982, 373). Luther accepts social stratification but he equalizes their religious qualities. For a work ethics this concept has important consequences (see also Pawlas 2000, 43-83): We praise God in our work ("Es ist eine andere Sache, Besitz haben und dem Besitz dienen", in Kunst (ed.) 1982, 377). The central motive force should not be A. Smith´s self-interest but benevolence. In Luther´s view A. Smith´s (elucidated) self-interest motivational bias is an expression of the wrong world of sin. "Wenn Du merkst, daß Du allein Deinem Nutzen dienst, dann ist Dein Dienst falsch" (in Kunst (ed.) 1982, 418). Modesty is a central value against emulation and conspicuous consumption. "Wenn wir uns prächtig kleiden und uns der Vergnügungssucht hingeben, bezeugen wir vor allen, daß wir das Böse, dem wir entrissen sind, wie auch das Gute, das wir empfangen haben, vergessen haben" (in Kunst (ed.) 1982, 408). In summary, we should not get our identity from work and innerworldly activity but our identity should be first of all shaped by the fact that we are sinners in the

---

[5] „Ein Schuster, ein Schmid, ein Bauer, ein jeglicher hat seines Handwerks Amt und Werk, und doch sind alle gleich geweihte Priester und Bischöfe, und ein jeglicher soll mit seinem Amt oder Werk den andern nützlich und dienstbar sein, so dass vielerlei Werke alle auf eine Gemeinde gerichtet sind, Leib und Seele zu fördern, gleich wie die Gliedmaßen des Körpers alle eines dem andern dienen" (1962a, 162).

face of god. The consequence is a certain indifference what the importance of our work is concerned.

Even the most dirty work is valuable in god´s eyes. Everybody should work. "Von der Arbeit stirbt kein Mensch; aber vom Ledig- und Müßiggehen kommen die Leute um Leib und Leben; denn der Mensch ist zur Arbeit geboren wie der Vogel zum Fliegen ... Gott will keine faulen Müßiggänger haben, sondern man soll treu und fleißig arbeiten, ein jeder nach seinem Beruf und Amt" (in Kunst (ed.) 1982, 375, 416). But work should not be in the center of our thoughts and efforts. Work becomes a spiritual component in Luther but it is also devalued as only secondly important. "Ein Mensch hat zweierlei Brot. Das erste und beste Brot, das vom Himmel kommt, ist das Wort Gottes. Das andere und geringere ist das zeitliche Brot, das aus der Erde wächst. Wenn ich nun das erste und beste Himmelsbrot habe und lasse mich davon nicht abbringen, so wird jenes zeitliche Brot auch nicht fernbleiben“ (in Kunst (ed.) 1982, 378).

Further, to be rich does not make happy. "Viel Reichtum tröstet nicht so sehr wie ein fröhliches Herz ... Besitz wird nicht darum gegeben, dass man darauf bauen und seine Zuversicht setzen soll – es ist nichts und nur eitel – sondern dass man ihn brauchen, genießen und anderen mitteilen soll" (in Kunst (ed.) 1982, 424). Luther argues that our success in business does not directly depend on our achievement and effort, that it does not make us happy and that we nevertheless have the right to enjoy it - in the limits of taking care of others. Luther does not preach asceticism. "Unser Herrgott gönnet uns wohl, daß wir essen, trinken und fröhlich seien. Deshalb hat er auch so viele Dinge geschaffen ... (Christen) ist es nicht untersagt, Schauspiele aufzuführen, weil darin von der Liebe die Rede ist und zuweilen sogar Zoten vorkommen. Sonst dürfte ein Christ aus dem gleichen Grunde auch die Bibel nicht lesen“ (1960, 264-265).

The conservative element is often modified, e.g. when he positively mentions that an ambitious person is able to climb up the social ladder (es "geschehe oft, das ein person steigt durch alle stende bis oben hinauff", WA 37, 170). For Luther the average Christian belongs to all three estates at the same time because due to the abolition of the celibacy and the integration of the minister into civil life the sociological difference between the estates vanished.

The minister and preacher in general should be courageous and not care about power relations. He should "frei reden und niemand scheuen, ob er gleich mancherlei Leute und Köpfe sieht, und kein Blatt vor den Mund nehmen, weder gnädige noch zornige Herren und Junker, weder Geld, Reichtum, Ehre, Gewalt noch Schande, Armut, Schaden ansehen und nicht weiter denken, als daß er rede, was sein Amt fordert" (in Kunst (ed.) 1982, 167). The preacher does not interfere directly with worldly institutions but in his judgments he is absolutely independent and without any consideration for personal consequences. So a peasant belongs to the economy as producer and head of a family (the family is the basis of social life and the estates), as a citizen he belongs to the policy, and as a Christian he belongs to the church. Luther It should not be forgotten that Luther also strongly advocates clear distinctions between the estates.

5. Luther on commercial activities and usury (*Von Kaufshandlung und Wucher*, 1524)

Luther´s contribution was influenced by Eck´s disputation in Bologna in 1515 where Eck legitimized moderate but general interest rates. In addition, since 1517 Ulrich von Hutten, who became a friend of Luther in 1520, had raised some criticism against the Fugger´s monopoly. In 1522 Jakob Strauß changed from Basle to Wittenberg, he became preacher in Eisenach in 1523. At the time many people were put into fiefdom to the church authorities. Strauß argued against interest in principle. He urged the debtors not to commit a sin and pay back the credits with interest. Luther shared his criticism but he urged good Christians to pay the interest and only tell the creditors that they are wrongdoers (WA.B 3, 177-178). The church asked duke Johann, the brother of the elector, to intervene. He ordered to reduce the interest from around 12% to 5%. The son of the duke asked Luther to give his opinion on the subject and Luther in a letter to elector prince Johann Friedrich in accepted an interest rate of 4-5% as a transitory solution.

Luther will have influenced the Eisenach 5% interest rule, he supported the ´Eisenach rule´ in similar cases. But he underlines that the natural tithe would be a better transitory rule and it should be kept in mind that Luther recommended to the council of Dresden not to abandon interest abruptly - this did not prevent its abolition in the longer run (WA.B 3, 485). It should be kept in mind that Eisenach was the first town in Germany with a publicly fixed maximum rate of interest.

A second major influence on Luther´s reasoning was the antimonopoly movement, a broad movement of merchants, entrepreneurs, parts of the nobility, the clergy, and craftsmen. They were oriented against high monopoly prices and commodity speculation of the the grand merchant associations (mainly in Augsburg) which operated much more aggressively than the merchants of the Hanseatic League. Already the Cologne-Trier imperial diet in 1512 interdicted the cornering of the market *(Fürkauf)*. But the law could not be enforced so that the diets in 1521 and 1523 had to discuss the topic again. The much milder agreements in 1524 at the diet in Nürnberg surely made Luther even more angry because they were due to bribes (the Habsburger had a large amount of debts and could hardly repay them to the Fuggers). Luther therefore thought that he had to discuss the question of usury in the broader context of merchants activities.

The text under consideration here starts with the very fundamentalist allegation that a trader can hardly live without sin (1983a, 263, in the following we will skip the year of publication in this section). Bad trading habits prevail but some Christian people exist who prefer to be poor with God instead of being rich with the devil (263). Luther clearly has the opinion that a certain contrast exists between a true Christian and commerce. According to this starting point trade, commerce and exchange may be bad for Christians in principle. This would generate an outworldly ecclesiastical orientation. But Luther continues that selling and buying are necessary things which also Christians cannot dispense. Already the patriarchs exchanged cattle, milk, corn etc. (264).

Examples of the bible are always his prime references to substantiate his claims (Luther often neglects examples in the Bible which show the opposite). But Luther to a certain degree restricts this legitimate trade, the goods for the daily basic needs are especially mentioned.[6] He contrasts this with the long distance trade with e.g. India of gold, spices, and silk. These products have no utility and only serve for emulation. This trade should not be allowed. It only leads to an outflow of coins and cultivates bad habits (guzzling).[7] Already in this first two pages an interesting moderate or intermediate viewpoint is presented: Trade and money have a problematic natural drift (greed) but they are accepted as necessary. At the same time Luther distinguishes between basic needs commodities and luxuries, he distinguishes between good and bad consumption. Moderation and modesty are best for the soul.

---

6 „Das kann man aber nicht leugnen, dass Kaufen und Verkaufen ein notwendig Ding ist, das man nicht entbehren und gut christlich brauchen kann, besonders in den Dingen, die zum täglichen Bedarf und in Ehren dienen“ (264).

7 „... der ausländische Kaufhandel, der aus Indien und dergleichen Ware herbringt (wie solch kostbares Seiden- und Goldwerk und Gewürz), die nur zur Pracht und keinem Nutzen dient und Land und Leute das Geld aussaugt“ (264).

Luther also propounds a position of voluntaristic resignation: His writings will be almost in vain, only some few people will respect his teaching, so that it nevertheless makes sense to argue (263-264). Luther accepts the state of the world, he has only limited hope in its improvement but he does not give up and tries to change it. In general his thinking has an eschatological aspect in that he thought to live shortly before the Day of Judgement and general fraud and usury proof it ("yn dißer letztenn feierlichen zeytt", WA 1966e, 51). He also limits the range of his considerations. The concrete institutional framework must be worked out by lawyers, economists and others, as a theologian he will only talk about sins and misuse (of the merchants), in so far as they refer to conscience (265, "soweit es das Gewissen betrifft"). He therefore accepts the differentiation of the value spheres and supports a specific interference of religion with regard to the normative setup.

As mentioned, Luther accepts exchange but at the same time he castigates the logic of maximum profit by exploiting what the market will bear until the margin. This argument is put forward with reference to the merchants but it surely holds in general. On the one hand he criticizes the general viewpoint that a right exists to sell a good for as much money as possible. This is the motivational expression of avarice. The situation of the other market side (our neighbor) is totally disregarded (265). The setting of a maximum price is especially not acceptable in two situations: The buyer is poor or the other market side urgently needs the product, i.e. asymmetric powers to withhold exist. In the last case the merchant can increase the price above the normal price, the price increase directly depends on the want and need of the neighbor. This scarcity cannot be accepted as a price determining factor. Implicitly, in the case of a poor person (Luther underlines: A person who is not responsible for being poor) the basic needs goods should be sold at a lower rate. Luther accepts the laws of supply and demand only to a certain degree. In a first approximation the natural price depends on its value and on the producer´s effort and danger/risk.[8] This market price is legitimate but not necessarily the price which the market will bear. Questions of right and justness creep in. Law and conscience should set limits so that our neighbor has no disadvantage. From a religious point of view, exchange is acceptable when it is good for our neighbor ("ein Werk …, das du gegen deinen Nächsten übst", 266). His situation should be more important than our profit.

Interestingly, Luther rejects the administrative fixing of maximum prices as a response to the question what the just price would be. The reasons are often changing qualities, transport costs, weather conditions, etc. (266). No fixed prices should be set by the princes but he nevertheless offers a formula: The merchant´s price should include his costs, his effort, his work, and risk. The best solution would be for the worldly regime to fix for a certain period of time the commodity prices depending on these circumstances so that the merchant would have a decent living (267). He also mentions that in some towns the prices of wine or fish are in fact fixed. But Luther argues that the Germans are so busy that they cannot deal with this (his argument is not really clear). The second best and pragmatic solution is to let the market determine price, "daß man die Ware gelten lasse, wie sie der allgemeine Markt gibt und nimmt, oder wie es Landesgewohnheit zu geben und zu nehmen ist" (267).

---

[8] „Denn wo das Schalksauge und der Geizwanst hier gewahr wird, dass man seine Ware haben muss, oder dass der Käufer arm ist und seiner bedarf, da macht er's sich zu Nutzen und Gewinn. Da sieht er nicht auf den Wert der Ware oder auf den Dienst für seine Mühe und Gefahr, sondern schlichtweg auf die Not und das Darben seines Nächsten, nicht um denen abzuhelfen, sondern um diese zu seinem Gewinn zu gebrauchen, seine Ware (im Preis) zu steigern, die er sonst wohl ungesteigert ließe, wo des Nächsten Not nicht da wäre. Und so muß durch seinen Geiz die Ware soviel mehr kosten, wie viel mehr der Nächste größere Not leidet" (265).

If the factors mentioned above determine prices Luther seems to accept the working of the market forces. He implicitly includes a certain normal profit because merchants also may incur losses so that overall they will not have a very high income including normal profits. He rejects the definition of a general normal profit rate (e.g. 50% or 30%, see 267). If the price of a commodity must be set for the first time the costs mentioned, our conscience, the non-cheating of our neighbor and a principle of sufficient nutrition should be regarded.[9] In Luther´s view we are not able to exactly determine this just price, but in the world we are not without sin and unwilling slight deviations are not so problematic (268), they are unavoidable sins (he discusses a deviation of two or three per cent over the year). To fix his wage (work load) he should take the time and amount of work and compare it with the wage of a day laborer. But this does not lead to a more or less precise labor theory of value because effort, risk and time for transport are mentioned again (269). He finally accepts that his description is somewhat imprecise but he reasserts that it cannot be made more precise. Again his outlook is a moderate one with many obvious implications, e.g. that a laborer should not earn less than the average cultural level of subsistence. As a general rule, Luther accepts the market forces, but he is an advocate of a tamed market society with upper and lower limits.

He explicitly rejects the highest level of Christian behavioral rules (his approach of the three degrees) as impracticable: That we let other people take our possessions without any resistance ("Wer dir den Rock nimmt, dem laß auch den Mantel", Matt 5,40). Only the perfect Christian would behave like this. But it must be admitted that if people would act according to this principle much less mi-

---

[9] „Darum musst du dir vornehmen, nichts als deine ausreichende Nahrung in solchem Handel zu suchen, danach Kosten, Mühe, Arbeit und Gefahr rechnen und überschlagen, und alsdann die Ware selbst festsetzen, (im Preis) steigernd oder erniedrigen, auf dass du solcher Arbeit und Mühe Lohn davon habest" (268).

suse in trade would occur. But he also underlines that much less traders would be busy because human nature and reason are oriented against this principle. The second and less tough Christian rule is to give to the needy free of charge. But also this behavior is very rare, a good Christian belongs to the most seldom animals on earth. So Luther does not expect the world to adopt to the more strict Christian rules and he makes no proposals how the world can come closer to them. He has no general systematic ameliorative aspirations, he knows about the logic of the human mind, (human) nature, and the world. He does not become neither nihilistic nor does he propose a worldly revolution to bring the world closer to the religious ideal.

The third way is to lend money to other people without interest and not ask to get it back in the case that the money is not repaid. If this were the rule, trade and commerce would be tremendously curtailed and depressed. Because the world and human nature are bad these excellent Christian principles cannot be realized, fraud and chaos would result because only a small fraction of the population is really Christian minded. "Ja, auf diese Weise würde kein Handel auf Erden bleiben, würde einem jeglichen das Seine genommen oder abgeborgt werden und den Bösen, Faulfräßigen, deren die Welt voll ist, die Tür aufgetan, alles zu nehmen, zu betrügen und zu lügen" (271).

Luther is a real pessimist in this regard and in the following he introduces his thesis of the two empires. Because very few real Christians exist a worldly regime is absolutely necessary. "Darum ist in der Welt ein streng, hart weltlich Regiment not, das die Bösen zwinge und dringe, nicht zu nehmen noch zu rauben und wiederzugeben, was sie borgen ..., auf dass die Welt nicht wüst werde, der Friede untergehe, und der Menschen Handel und Gemeinschaft ganz zunichte werde, welches alles geschehen würde, wo man die Welt nach dem Evangelium regieren und das Böse nicht mit Gesetzen und Gewalt treiben und zwingen sollte ... Deshalb muß man

Straßen (von Räubern) reinhalten, Frieden in Städten schaffen und Recht in den Landen handhaben und das Schwert frisch und getrost auf die Übertreter hauen lassen ... Es soll und muß das weltliche Schwert rot und blutrünstig sein“ (271-272).

Borrowing and lending among Christians would not be difficult but lending to non-Christinas necessitates the enforcing power of the worldly authority. It is not the task of a Christian to enforce the outstanding amounts. Luther also holds a moderate position with regard to the total amount of lending and alms. A Christian is responsible for his family or enlarged household and he should give as much as he can live without. The necessary needs are not defined it, they depend on the definition of the individual.

A Christian should also not expect counterfactually that most people do not make mistakes and behave in a fraudulent way. In exchange relations, good sense demands to be paid in ready cash (273). In harsh words Luther describes the tricks and cheating of the merchants which will thereby undermine their own position in the longer run. In contrast to A. Smith who argued that self-interest and the free working of the market forces will lead (under specific circumstances) to the best allocation for society (invisible hand) Luther argues against the motive of self-interest which leads to dysfunctional avarice and that the search for maximum profit is contrary to a good society.

Luther describes further unacceptable practices like speculative purchases in the sense of cornering the market and selling goods for a higher price as usual. Somewhat surprisingly he also includes interest for credits which in modern minds conforms with unusual business practices (275). A further critique refers to monopolies and monopoly pricing. Luther does not discuss natural monopolies here. He is concerned about ´artificial´ monopolies or oligopolies. He castigates the oppression of the entrance of new firms into oligopolistic markets by temporary dumping to keep out competitors.

The worldly authority should throw them out of the country.[10] Luther here urges for a rudimentary anti-monopolistic policy. In the same context he later discusses the large long distant trade companies which have almost the status of monopolies: they can manipulate the price (they are nor the ideal price takers) and they can suppress the small merchants. They have a power almost similar to god´s power (281) which is an unacceptable presumption. Luther´s arguments here resembles the ordoliberal focus and critique of powerful price setters.

A further trick is to fool a foreign trader and exploit arbitrage. The foreign trader asks for a certain commodity and the home merchant sells it for a higher as the usual price at his home market. The home merchant can even use the money of the foreign trader to buy the commodities which he will sell to the foreign merchant (Luther is not exact here in his description). In Luther´s view this arbitrage profit is not acceptable because the home merchant had absolutely no risk, he did not invest any effort or work. Another questionable expression of avarice is to offer a merchant - who is urged by banks to repay money but who holds a considerable amount of high quality commodities - a lower price for his commodities. If he does not accept the merchant sends another person who offers an even lower price. Luther here castigates collusive action to disinform the debtor about the market value of his commodities and to exploit his difficult situation as a debtor.

Another practice is collusive action when a small number of merchants holds a (necessary) commodity in their hands and gets a to-

---

[10] „(W)enn etliche ihre Monopole und eigennützigen Käufe sonst nicht aufzurichten vermögen, weil andere da sind, die auch dergleichen Ware und Gut haben, fahren sie zu und geben ihr Gut so wohlfeil, dass die anderen nicht mitkommen können und zwingen sie damit dahin, dass sie entweder nicht verkaufen können oder zu ihrem Verderben so wohlfeil geben müssen wie jene. Also kommen sie doch zum Monopol“ (276).

tal control by introducing a middleman who buys out the market. Here Luther is critical of a deliberate cartel policy.

Luther is fully aware of the detrimental effects of an aggressive debtor policy because an increasing number of defaulting elements in the credit cycle finally backfire at the debtor: If less and less firms are able to pay back their credits the credit crunch impedes the liquidity of all participants (278). Another very questionable action is an alleged bankruptcy when the debtor disappears and hides e.g. in a monastery. In this case the creditors accept the repayment of only 50% and the rest in two years so that the debtor can invest the hidden money in the meantime (279). Luther also rejects all interest payments for credits, a point that will be discussed in more detail in the next section.

An obvious fraudulent behavior is to increase the size or the weight by putting e.g. pepper into a damp cellar. A similar procedure is to put the best quality commodities on top and conceal the products with less quality below (280).

Luther has a very skeptical view of the authorities. They should conduct certain market policies but at the same time he is fully aware that they often cooperate with the wealthy oligopolists. Luther comes very close to the main tenets of the capturing and the public choice approach. Public authorities punish the little swindlers but they enrich themselves by colluding with the rich ("Deine Fürsten sind der Diebe Gesellen geworden", Jes. 1,23, "öffentliche Diebe gehen in Gold und Seide", 282). In a short time the owners of the large companies become so wealthy that they are able to buy the politicians (281). In this case, Luther categorically interdicts the existence of these companies and recommends not to work for them.

As Metzger (1965) pointed out Luther does not give a precise description of an economic order. The application of the Sermon on the Mount and its transformation into laws of the economic order and institutions would lead to chaos. He does not urge for a christianization of the economy but he argues that the individual is responsible before god with regard to his property and his possessions. Not even Christians need or should have communal property because the human soul is too sinful.[11] The Christian has an obligation and duty to perform good in his profession but at the same time his relation to worldly property and money is relaxed because according to Luther it is of secondary importance. "Der Christ dagegen hat ein innerlich gelöstes und zugleich verantwortliches Verhältnis zu Hab und Gut. Er kann sich nehmen lassen, er kann schenken, er kann zinslos leihen, er kann verkaufen ... Eins aber kann er nicht: Gott dienen *und* dem Mammon" (Metzger 1965, 150).

The text *Von Kaufshandlung und Wucher* includes a two page addendum (not published in Luther 1983a) in which Luther comments again the debate of his time (see the overview in Luther 1966b, 279-283). In this short text (1966b, 321-322) Luther rejects fixed interest payments, also in the form of *Zinskauf* (credit on participation): As mentioned, in the most elementary form of *Zinskauf* the debtor transfers the usufruct right to the creditor which he gets back when he pays back his debt (i.e. a concealed interest payment). In conformity with other passages in his writings Luther rejects it because it signifies a one-sided risk bearing, only the debtor takes the risk. This stipulates that the two parties know the future but everything depends on god´s unforeseeable decisions.

To prevent the most exploitative forms of usury he surprisingly accepts the Old Testament institution of the tithe. The creditor gets

---

[11] Die Gemeinschaft der Güter ist nicht dem Naturrecht gemäß. Sie ist nicht etwas Gebotenes, sondern etwas Zugelassenes. Wenn sie gleich ein Gebot wäre, so könnte sie doch wegen der Verderbtheit der Natur nicht beibehalten werden, weil mehr da wären, welche die Güter verzehrten, als die sie herbeischafften, und so würde ein Durcheinander entstehen" (1960, 204).

the 10th part of the produce or yield. The tithe is not in all cases the maximum, it should depend on the situation, also the fifth (= 20%) may be the adequate share (as under Joseph in Egypt). As a rule, the interest should not be too high <u>and</u> both parties should share the risk. Luther mentions the weather etc. as unpredictable circumstances, he does not mention the influence of the debtor´s behavior on the final outcome and does not seem to see a moral hazard problem. Und muste also der zins herr die fahr und gluck eben so wol tragen als der zins man“ (1966b, 321, and 1966d, especially 8).

It is not easy to interpret Luther´s acceptance of the tithe. On the one hand it can be seen as a pragmatic adaptation to the necessities and logic of this world to prevent worse arrangements. It can also be interpreted as inconsequential opportunism which blurs his original message. Or it can be regarded as an intelligent solution: On the one hand real world phenomena are accepted, and the negative effects of interest pure and simple (the development of dependency relations – serfdom, “alle Fürstenthum und Land verarmet und versetzt”, 1966b, 322) are eliminated because the tithe prevents a deepening of dependence of others due to the risk sharing. In general, it is not exactly clear if Luther makes a difference between consumption and production credits. But here it is clear that the tithe is valid for production credits (“Denn wo der zehenden eyn jat wol geriete, so trüge er viel dem zins herrn, Geriete er übel, so trüge er wenig”, 1966b, 321). But it may be asked if the distinction between productive and consumptive credits makes sense in an agricultural environment: Wheat will be used for consumption and production. Is the hay for the cows to be counted as consumption or production? It can also be argued that for Luther the central difference was between credits for those with problems and for those who are not in misery, be this consumers or entrepreneurs in difficulties (Pawlas 2000, 214). His solution can be read as a candid compromise to fuel the economy and prevent dependency structures at the same time.

It is even more surprising that Luther also proposes the adoption of the jubilee for houses and ground. The jubilee implies a redistribution of houses and/ or land after 50 years without compensation ("Das man das hall jar inn solchen sachen hielte und nichts ewiglich verkeuffte", 1966b, 322; see also the Bible, e.g. Leviticus 25). The jubilee was the most severe measure of redistribution in the Old Testament and was therefore probably never applied in real history. It is surprising that Luther combines a pragmatic solution (the tithe) with the most severe proposal of the Old Testament. He does for example not propose the Sabbath year, i.e. the cancellation of all interest payments in the seventh year of the religious cycle. But a connection exists between the jubilee and interest payments for credits: When a person looses his landed property in the context of a credit on participation he may not loose it forever.

Luther reaffirmed this position in many letters to Capito, Count Johann Friedrich, Spalatin and others. Around the 1520s the interest problem was a topic of utmost consideration in the public debates. One point of discussion was if the rules in the Old and New Testament should be considered as direct laws for the worldly order. As mentioned above, this was Carlstadt´s, the Weimar preacher´s Wolfgang Stein´s, and also the opinion of the Eisenach preacher Jakob Strauß who strongly influenced Count Johann. In Luther´s view the Mosaic law should not totally be applied (e.g. Christians do not have to practice circumcision). Strauß rejected any right to take interest and he purported the Sabbath year and the jubilee. The opposite view was held by Eck who argued that in general an interest up to 5% was acceptable. The rumor was that he was open to bribery by rich merchants of Augsburg. In all his radicalism and frustration of the decision of the imperial diet in April 1524 not really to restrain the monopolies, against Strauß´s more radical initial position Luther seeks a compromise.

In the introduction of the Weimar edition of Luther´s complete writings we read: "Dabei ist er mit nicht wenigen seiner erleuchtetsten Zeitgenossen unfähig, den großen Umschwung zu begreifen, der sich damals im volkswirtschaftlichen Leben Deutschlands vollzog, das aus einem Bauernvolk ein Städte- und Handelsvolk wurde und aus der Naturalwirthschaft in die Geld- und Kreditwirthschaft hineinwuchs. Für die Produktivität des Geldes und somit für die Lebensbedingungen des Großhandels hat er soweing Verständniß, wie das kanonische Recht; er hielt an dem überlieferten mittelalterlichen Standpunkt fest, dass nur die Landwirthschaft und daneben das Handwerk ein wahrhaft gottgefälliger Erwerbsstand sei, gegen den Kaufmanns- und Handelsstand theilte er die weitverbreitete Abneigung“ (1966b, 282).[12] In our view this is an extremely conservative outlook. Luther evidently had shortcomings (e.g. his explanation of the rise of the price level) but in his proposals for a good economic order he may have elaborated a first approach of a tamed market order which is still with us. Maybe he saw already the accompanying pitfalls of that order and in so far had a very farsighted view (Marx 1980, 35).

6. Luther again on usury and interest (*An die Pfarrherrn, Vermahnung,* 1540)

Luther´s tract on usury in 1524 seems to have exerted strong pressure on public opinion. In 1529 the subcommittee on coins and monopolies at the second Speyrer imperial diet discussed again the problems of usury and monopolies. In consequence a second accusation was raised against the Augsburg companies at the imperial diet in 1530 in Augsburg with the concrete allegation of illegal

[12] This coincides with Roscher´s harsh (1874, 55), and with Schmoller´s (1860) and Sombart´s (1930, 29) more moderate views that the reformation did not really have a progressive economic impact. Weber (1975, 69) also held the thesis of Luther´s backwardness with regard to the essence of process of capitalist acquisition (see also Troeltsch 1907/08, 214ff.). An overview of the debate: Luther and the economy can be found in Prien 1992, 13-25).

price agreements on spices with the king of Portugal. A special commission could proof market cornering practices. As counter measures the limitation of capital and interest without risk were proposed. On the demand of Charles V the files were sent to Spain before a decision was taken where they disappeared forever. By legal means nothing would change must have been Luther´s conclusion when he started writing the tract in 1539.

Luther mentioned as further background conditions the instant increase of the average interest level up to 30-40% in the last 10-20 years and he located the usurers in the big cities (Leipzig, Augsburg, Frankfort, 1967, e.g. 364, and 421). A drought in 1539 in Wittenberg and a mice plague and the general price increases further aggravated the economic situation for many. Further, in 1539 no more flour was on the market. Luther criticized mayor Cranach for this and he got the reply that the flour was withheld in the Brandenburg Marches by the noble wheat speculators. This explains Luther´s strong focus on the exploitation of crises situations. It can be asked in how far the local politicians and lawyers could abolish the trans-local withholding of necessary basic commodities.

In 1539 (1967) Luther wrote his long warning for the ministers against usury. Luther states that he almost gave up hope but that some Christians respected his earlier expositions. His major point - which he makes clear right at the beginning - is that lending for interest is unjust and one of the major sins. “”Erstlich von Leyhen und Borgen, Wo man Geld leyhet, und dafur mehr oder bessers fordert oder nimpt, das ist Wucher inn allen Rechten verdampt. Darum alle die jenen, so Funffe, Sechs oder mehr auffs Hundert nehmen, vom gelihen Gelde, Die sind Wücherer, darnach sie sich wissen zu richten, und heissen, des Geitzes oder Mammon abgottissche Diener, und mügen nicht selig werden, sie thun denn busse“ (1967, 332-333). Luther does not offer a compromise. Any interest for lending is sinful and should be abandoned. With this verdict Luther is much more strict than the catholic church at the time. He even rejects 5% which were considered extremely reasonable. He again identifies the questionble motive: Avarice. He only accepts interest payments in the two cases of loss compensation *(Schadewacht)* when the creditor experiences a negative impact: (1) The creditor himself has debts which he now cannot repay, or (2) the creditor cannot pursue a profitable transaction because the debtor did not give him back the money in due time. These opportunities must be real and not only hypothetical.

But the basic principle is: A neighbor who lends a bowl does not give it back with interest. Lending without interest is the message of the prophets, Christ, and the rule of many public authorities (1967, 334). The fact that interest is paid everywhere does not count because we know that in the world things are done in wrong ways at large scale but this is unimportant for the preacher and minister. He denies that no more loans would be given if they would bear no interest. He next discusses the argument that another person needs the money and is willing to pay e.g. an interest of 6% so that we do not enforce our will but follow his demand. For Luther this is no argument because the consent of both and a mutual advantage are not enough for ethical judgements: Two persons who commit adultery also act freely and with mutual advantage, nevertheless their action is sinful (1967, 339). Lawyers see the interest problem differently, but the preacher must make clear that they and the public authorities commit sins in this respect. The preacher should make no bones about this.

A central aspect of Luther´s denial of the legitimacy of interest is the fact that the creditor may be lazy, does not work, pursues luxury consumption and gains nevertheless ("faul und müssig, prassen und prangen von andrer Leute erbeit … das ich sitze hinter dem ofen und lasse meine Hundert gulden für mich auff dem Lande werben … on alle fahr und sorge", 1967, 351). In Luther´s view, disposable income should only result from productive activities. He often underlines that the world is ruled by original sins and fraud.

But this is no excuse: Usury must be and is unavoidable but you´ll be sorry if you are a usurer ("Wucher mus sein, Aber wehe den Wucherern", 1967, 354)! In the real world most would-be Christians even adore the rich for their wealth ("Wir Christen aber halten sie inn solchen ehren, das wir sie schir anbeten umb ires gelds willen", 1967, 361). So the unimportant thieves are in prison and the clever money lenders are free ("Kleine Diebe liegen in stöcken gefangen, grosse Diebe gehen inn gold und seiden prangend", 1967, 362).

Luther offers many examples of communities which were confronted with abundant usury, e.g. Athens at the time of Solon, later Rome, etc. Even if the worldly authorities and the cardinals do not fight against it the Christian has no right to organize an upheaval, this is god´s duty (Sodom and Gomorrah, 1967, 356). He cites the testimonies of Moses (1967, 377) and Aristotle. The latter proves that even the non-believers knew the arguments against interest by thinking reasonably. He especially mentions Aristotle´s argument that money is by nature infertile. His positive shining example is Nehemiah who interdicted interest (1967, 363-364). Without a Nehemiah, Germany would surely fall back into serfdom (see also e.g. 1967, 415). In his view the phenomenon of interest is capable of profoundly changing the social structure in the negative.

We will mention in passing, that Luther does not resist some anti-Jewish comments ("rechter Jüdischer, teglicher Wucher", 1967, 364). Luther´s sermon in 1519 had Jews on the first page woodcut on all three editions, also three (out of 12) of the 1520 article editions had Jewish caricatures on the first page. This was due to the editor Johann Grünenberg in Wittenberg who may have wanted to increase the sales. Between 1513 and 1521 Luther refrained from major attacks on the Jews in his attempt to favor their conversion (WA 11, 314-336). Since 1542 he fell back in sinister anti-Semitism (WA 53, 417-552).

In the case of interest, the public authorities should exceptionally not act in a diplomatic way: They should nullify all existing interest bearing contracts[13] and the community should expell them from the Christian institutions, give them no sacraments, notwithstanding if they are little or large usurers (*kleine Wücherlein* versus *Weltfresser*). But it must be mentioned that in some circumscribed cases he accepted the so-called usury in need *(Notwucher)* of widows and orphans. The interest should not be above 5% and the motive should be charity and love of the poor neighbor (1967, 371-372). He strongly criticizes the sophists, and papists, i.e. the catholic church of allowing the non-perfect Christians to take interest and to confine the interdiction to the upper ranks of believers (1967, 379). Luther counters the argument that for poor people a credit with interest is the sole chance to survive that for a poor person the community has the obligation to give food and shelter for free (1967, 373). If the needy really use the credit for nutrition then they would not be able to repay the credit and be left in an even more desolate situation (1967, 374).

Luther strongly underlines that the usury and interest prohibition is a universal principle: It makes no difference if the debtor is a Christian or an enemy. "Du solt jederman, das ist, nicht allein deinem freunde, sondern auch deinem feinde geben, und niemand ausschliessen inn seiner not und durstt (Es sey feind oder freund)" (1967, 381). The Christian should not help any person who claims to be needy. It requires some intelligent judgment on the creditor´s side to distinguish between a really needy person and the many betrayers who only claim to be needy and will not repay their debts. "Solchen zugeben hat Christus hie nicht gebotten, sondern allein

[13] „Denn was wider Gott, recht und natur ist, das ist ein Nullus. Darumb greiffe nur ein Fürst, wer es thun kan, frisch drein, zureisse siegel und brieve, kere sich nicht daran, das er an seine ehre odder glauben gescholten wird" (1967, 366).

den dürfftigen, inn deiner stad oder umb dich …, die nicht erbeiten, dienen, sich neren können, oder ihr trewe erbeit und dienst nicht reichen will“ (1967, 383). It is also in the Christian´s responsibility (he should listen to his conscience, 1967, 393) to decide how much he should give the needy. He should not become poor, to give we first must have. We should give to the needy but keep an acceptable standard of living, i.e. we are not obliges to sell our house for example to feed the many needy. “Sondern, Seiner nottdurfft sol ich mich an nemen, und was ich vermag, ihm helffen, das der arme mit mir esse, und ich nicht mit dem armen esse, oder meinem hausse neme, das sie durfften, und gebe es frembden“ (1967, 385).

A central aspect of the Christian´s help is his motivation, he should give with a pure heart, not summing up the benefits in the future of our deeds, free of all vanity. “… mit einfeltigem hertzen, nicht umb eitel ehre willen, und thu ja, wie er kan, das ers vergesse, als habe er nie nichts gegeben oder wolgethan, Sonst henget sich gar gern dran der teufels stanck, das man sich solcher wohlthat kützelt und gesehen will sein“ (1967, 387). This motivational power is very difficult to share but a very important aspect: A small amount given with a good heart counts more than millions given with vanity. Besides the desire for money the drive of emulation is the most difficult to check in this context.

Luther absolutely parallels donations and lending, both should be practiced with regard to friend and foe (1967, 391). He also mentions the golden rule here. It conforms with pure reason: We should behave in such a way as we would like to be treated by others (1967, 393). He also castigates briefly other misbehavior like charging excessive prices. In his overall behavior the Christians should be servants of each other and not try to bring the neighbor into servitude (1967, 395). Usurers and exploitative merchants try to become godlike and Luther insinuates that they derive pleasure from the hardship of others besides there will to power (1967, 396). This behavior is very common in the real world but the more the preachers, ministers and also the school teachers have to castigate it (1967, 398-399).

The problem not only of his days was the fact that the misbehavior was actively supported by public authorities which claim to be Christian in spirit and by the misbehavior of the large majority of people.[14] Luther again argues that public authorities offer protection ("schutz und schirm", 1967, 403), and that the Christian should not revolt against them and install a new regime ("kein new regiment solten anrichten", 1967, 400). Public authorities in general behave as bad as the ordinary citizens. "... Dagegen wirstu finden gar viel Ratheuser, und noch mehr Bürger, die ja so seer das Evangelion hassen oder verachten, Pfarrher und arme bürger (wo sie können) schinden, plagen und martern" (1967, 405). The nobility is not at all any better (most „bleiben helle brende mit dem Teuffel, und richten leid und unglück gnug an über die Christen", 1967, 406).

Usury leads to price increases. The usurers are located in grand merchant cities like Frankfort or Augsburg but according to Luther they influence the general rise of prices. The are robbers and tyrans, Luther asks for a tough policy against them. "Und alle Geitzhelse verjagen, verfluchen und köpffen, sonderlich die, so mutwillige theurung stifften, wie itzt Adel und Baur thun auffs aller mutwilligst" (1967, 421). Luther does not discuss the economic question why and if they are able to manipulate the price, he takes

[14] „(W)o du einen Christlichen fromen baurn findest, der seinem nehesten armen Christlichen fromen baurn oder seinen armen pfarrher Christliche liebe und trewe erzeiget, mit geben, leihen, raten oder helffen inn seiner notturfft. Da gegen wirstu mehr denn tausent unchristliche bauren finden, die nicht einen pfennig geben, weder Pfarrher noch nachbar, wenn sie gleich hungers not leiden musten, Sondern geitzen, reissen, kratzen zu sich, steigern und ubertheuren, felschen, veruntrewen, nehmen, stellen, rauben, heimlich, wo sie mügen, es sey der Herrschaft, Pfarrher oder nachbar, und kündten sie iderman das blut aussauffen ..." (1967, 404).

it as self-evident and obvious. A market form discussion cannot be found in his analysis. Luther basically holds a relatively simple conspiracy theory of the price level.[15]

7. Conclusions

In this text we could not discuss the question in how far Luther followed traditional and heterodox approaches of his time and in how far his ideas were new. We saw that Luther mainly supported the system of simple commodity production. He tried to force back the grand commercial monopolies, collusion, and high prices. With these measures he at least indirectly supported the preconditions of free market competition. Luther realized the dangers of monopoly and unhindered capital accumulation. He was in favor of money as a medium of circulation but he fought against money in the function of money which gets independent in the form of capital.

Shortcoming may be seen in Luther´s constant combination of lending and borrowing and the context of caritas, so that he did not discuss credits for the use to produce capital. But his critique of credits for charitable reasons are convincing. Also his criticism of high interest rates for consumption credits which lead to dependence and poverty are convincing as well as his allegation that high interest may favor the concentration of wealth.

Luther´s rigorous rejection of interest is much more uncompromising then the flexible late Medieval rules in theory and practice. Luther tried to define new ethical rules starting from the Sermon on the Mount and the love to our neighbors including our enemies. Luther knew about the logic of the market economy but the ethical code of the Christian demanded not to try to get what the market will bear. Usury and avarice are signs of the last days of mankind.

---

[15] We will not discuss Luther (1966c) and (1966e) which do not offer new aspects.

By trying to become independent from social conditions with money man tries to become the master of his existence which implies to liberate himself from the control of the creator, i.e. a denial of god. Luther sees in general a strict antithesis between mammon and god. But he always keeps into account the principle of justness. So he accept under certain conditions interest deals with 5% as acceptable. The worldly regime cannot enforce the Christian principles because this needs good Christians. But it can prevent misuse. If it abolishes interest this should not be done abruptly. In Erfurt he considered 5% as a reasonable compromise. In general, the risk should be shared and depend on the yield. If the interest is higher it should reduce the repayment.

The rejection of the use of power does not lead to innerworldly indifference. The principle of charity is valid and property is needed to help the poor. This justification of private property is not coincident with modern theories on productivity, the division of labor ,etc. He underlines the service character of work for the community and its need satisfaction in contrast to capital accumulation. With his ideal of work as service he transcended leisure as a Medieval value and also prevented a strict innerworldly work ethics.

The worldly authorities cannot follow the Christina rules but Luther demands that they should abstain from tyranny and rule with good reason. They have to regulate markets and control the monopolies, prevent speculation, usury interest payments, etc. and they should be concerned about the problem of poverty.

We interpret him as a first modern economist because his theology paved the way of an interpenetrating society with checks and balances. In so far it transcends the mere discussion of the urgent problems of his time. He does not delineate a precise program for the economic order but he bombards the economy with ethical norms without negating the inner logic of its system. He always considers (economic) problems from two system perspectives:

Within and without the normative-religious and the economic system. His anthropological view is on the one side realistic: Avarice and the motive to dominate are prevalent but from within the normative system the highest ethical and now universal standards confront real life and moral obligations. They must be checked by the responsible individual and individual economic actor, no auxiliary system can perform this duty any more. At the same time the moral and intellectual capacities and the reasoning of the individual are severely limited according to Luther.

Luther frees us from the oppressive institution of a superimposed official church but he also castigates our will to superiority. He motivates us to achieve in our professions but at the same time he makes clear that success does not depend unilaterally on our efforts. The job is a duty but not so important, our identity should not be based on our profession. The principle of predestination restricts the pure logic of achievement and institutionalized individualism. He offers a synthesis beyond traditional morals (with an inside-outside group morals) and economic utilitarianism. The public authorities act according to the logic of public choice but we nevertheless confront them with demands of the common good. His teaching of the two empires prevents open revolt but also sets limits to the public authority and liberates and empowers personal belief and reasoning which cannot be forbidden by the authorities. The logic of power and the logic of a Christian behavioral code are in constant conflict.

His teaching of the three estates is an early compromise between statics and dynamics in society. Luther´s ideal was a small-scale capitalism which was also the ideal of e.g. ordoliberalism which tried via an anti-monopolistic policy to control power and enforce the market form of price takers. Further it should prevent market cornering, fraudulent behavior (wrong weights, etc.), temporary dumping, illegal bankruptcies and many other things.

Luther accepts the stratification of the three estates but at the same time all people are equal before god and no estate has a qualitative superiority. Achievement in the profession is a duty but at the same time modesty should prevail and conspicuous consumption is sinful but we also have the right to enjoy and have a party. We can try to be successful but we are assured that it will not make us happy. Trade and sin are close together, a latent conflict exists between trade, money and being a Christian, but selling and buying are necessary. Luther neither supports revolutionary aspirations nor nihilistic indifference. Money as a medium of exchange is necessary but as a store of value creates dependency relationships.

We may try to use the market forces in our favor but the principle to take what the market will bear is not legitimate. The central motive should always be the interest of our neighbor and not our personal gain. Especially the poor and people in emergency situations need our special care and consideration. Like Schmoller, American old institutionalism (e.g. Commons´s idea of leveling the playing field for labor) and Polanyi´s idea of an embedded economy, Luther opts for a tamed social market economy. Supply and demand are accepted within limits. Income should have a reasonable level, depending on effort, work, risk, danger, and the average wage. The laborer should earn the average cultural level of subsistence. Not (only) our own utility but also the situation of the other should be considered.

In principle, nobody should earn money who does not have to exert work effort or faces risk. Luther is a realist and therefore he does not demand communal property and we must have to be able to give. In his view one-sided risk taking is unjust. In principle he denies the right to take interest but in reality and at least in a transitory phase he accepts moderate interest rates or the tithe.

In our view Luther´s view of the ambivalent interplay of the logic of different orders essentially characterizes our present society: The jubilee for the poorest countries is discussed by the G-8 summit, the salaries of managers are under fire, the legitimacy of different tax rates for productive or financial investments is debated, critical eyes are directed at the more recent luxury fever of the rich, a reduced sales tax exists for basic needs goods, Ackermann´s V is castigated as arrogant, in the Hartz IV debate the question of a humane minimum and care for the unemployed (through no fault of their own?) plays a role, policies of maximizing profits with high external costs (downsizing and transfer of companies in cheaper countries) are questioned, usury laws exist in countries where interest as such is accepted as unavoidable, the question of a 25% profit rate is discussed, high golden handshake fees are questioned, the process of independence of speculative capital and its de-coupling from productive purposes is challenged (proposal of a Tobin tax), and the hedge fonds are described as a plague of locusts. For the beginning election campaign in Germany the problems of justice and uneven burdens of the social groups e.g. with respect to taxes and tax exemptions, are crucial, and also the problem of the acceptable degree of income and wealth inequality pops up.

It seems that the European and especially the German debates on economic policy show this interpenetration of the market and a religious-normative logic which can be traced back to the reformation. The substructure of Luther´s reformation concept of a just economy seems to be deeply ingrained in our cultural heritage today without its explicit original religious connotations. Luther offered western societies a concept of a practicable moral economy or a ´natural economic order´ which is located in the interpenetration zone of economy and morals/religion. It is quite different from Weber´s protestant ethics: Strong public authorities are necessary – they should take the public interest into account, a tamed self-interest coupled with a certain benevolence should be the motivational background of actors, the enjoyment of goods and partys is acceptable but it should not degenerate into luxury fever, full fledged avarice and emulation should be checked, work is important but not the most important thing in life, the payment of moderate interest rates (or better substitutes) are acceptable, income should be earned by productive activities, profits generated without effort or risk are questionable, (especially money) speculation should be curtailed, poverty should be prevented and the poor should be helped, reasonable competition should be established which takes into consideration the situation of others – it is also preferred to unilateral profit maximization and cut-throat competition, as a general priciple: We should never push things to the extreme and always take into account the situation of the others, a certain professional universal ethics is good for everybody (no cheating), we have a certain free will but we should respect the limits of our faculties and we should not play the masters of the universe, the income differential should be within certain limits, monopolies, cartels and cornering the market strategies and (market) power in general should be prevented, wealth is in principle not denied but it should also be used for charitable activities.

The never ending quarrel between the different logic of systems provokes permanent debates and conflicts. This enables the total system to develop along a middle ground. The separation and the interpenetration of the different value spheres may be the most important structure to characterize Western societies. This sometimes has great disadvantages (e.g. the non-resistance of Christians in the time of national socialism in Germany because of the interdiction of political resistance). But compared with many Islamic societies in which a separation of politics and the economy could not take place and the only limited value commitments in e.g. the economic sphere lead to chaos and unproductive strain (or take the United States of America where a comparable takeover of fundamentalism took place in the last years). The central European model with checks and balances may have an evolutionary advantage in so far as it will not experience a regression to the dominance of the economic logic pure and simple in the future. Further, western societies know how to deal with ambiguities and opposing standards in the recent phase of globalization where the modern individual is constantly forced to operate in different systems and to deal with relativizations and the combination of particularism and universalism, in Robertson´s terminology the four elements are national societies, selves, humankind and the world system of societies (Friedman 1995).[16]

“Obgleich also Luthers Aussagen zu Arbeit und Beruf Probleme seiner Zeit spiegeln, überschreiten sie doch diesen engen Rahmen ... [Tatsächlich] bietet seine theologische Grundlage noch für die gänzlich veränderte heutige Situation ein Potential des Widerstands gegen bestimmte Entwicklungen und Einseitigkeiten ... [so] werden doch Christen als Weltpersonen seine prinzipiellen Warnungen vor dem Mammon als Verabsolutierung des Profitdenkens, exzessiven Zinsen und Ausnutzung der Notlage anderer und seinen positiven Ansatz durch die geistliche Auslegung des Dekalogs durch das Doppelgebot der Liebe und die Bergpredigt, konzentriert in der Goldenen Regel, beachten müssen. In Luthers Sinne muß bei wirtschaftlichen Transaktionen immer zuerst nach der Gerechtigkeit gefragt werden. Dem sind die Fragen der Wirtschaftlichkeit, d.h. auch die Frage nach Profit und Zins, unterzuordnen“ (Prien 1992, 232-233).

---

[16] The following tensions are discussed by Friedman: National societies-humankind: Relativization of citizenship, selves-world system: relativization of societal reference, national society-world system: relativization of societies, world system-humankind: Realpolitik – humanity problematic, national societies-selves: Individual-society problematic, and selves-humankind: relativization of self-identities.

References

Aland, K. [„Anmerkungen“]. *Martin Luther: Der Christ in der Welt.* Luther Deutsch, ed. K. Aland. Vol. 7. 3rd. Ed. Göttingen: Vandenhoeck und Ruprecht, 1983. pp. 406-409.

Backhaus, J. „Luther und die Volkswirtschaft“. *Das Ethische in der Ökonomie: Festschrift für Hans G. Nutzinger,* ed. T. Beschorner and T. Eger. Marburg: Metropolis, 2005. pp. 137-147.

Barge, H. *Luther und der Frühkapitalismus.* Gütersloh: Bertelsmann, 1951 ([1]1937/38).

Bosl, K. „Staat, Gesellschaft, Wirtschaft im deutschen Mittelalter“. *Gebhardt, Handbuch der deutschen Geschichte,* ed. H. Grundmann. 9th ed. Vol. 1. Stuttgart: Klett-Cotta, 1970. pp. 694ff.

Friedenthal, R. *Luther: Sein Leben und seine Zeit.* Munich: Piper, 1967.

Friedman, J. "Global system, globalization and the parameters of modernity". *Global modernities,* ed. M. Featherstone et. al. London: Sage, 1995. pp. 69-90.

Henning. F.-W. Wirtschafts- und Sozialgeschichte. Vol. 1. *Das vorindustrielle Deutschland 800 bis 1800.* Paderborn: Schöningh, 1977.

Hesse, H./Müller, G. (eds.). *Über Luthers 'Von Kauffshandlung und Wucher'.* Vademecum zu einem frühen Klassiker der ökonomischen Wissenschaft. Düsseldorf: Verlag Wirtschaft und Finanzen, 1987.

Irsigler, F. „Luthers Herkunft und Umwelt – Wirtschaft und Gesellschaft der Zeit“. *Martin Luther und die Reformation in Deutschland,* ed. Germanisches Nationalmuseum Nürnberg. Frankfurt: Insel, 1983. pp. 17-40.

Kunst, H. (ed.). *Martin Luther: Ein Hausbuch.* Stuttgart: Kreuz-Verlag, 1982.

Luhmann, N. *Die Gesellschaft der Gesellschaft.* 2 Vols. Frankfurt: Suhrkamp, 1997.

Lütge, F. *Studien zur Sozial- und Wirtschaftsgeschichte.* Stuttgart: Fischer, 1963.

Luther, M. *Werke.* D. Martin Luthers Werke: Kritische Gesamtausgabe (Weimarer Ausgabe). Weimar: Hermann Böhlaus Nachfolger, 1888ff. Reprint Graz: Akademische Druck- und Verlagsanstalt, 1966ff. (= WA).

Luther, M. "(Großer) Sermon von dem Wucher". *D. Martin Luthers Werke: Kritische Gesamtausgabe (Weimarer Ausgabe).* Vol. 6. Graz: Akademische Druck- und Verlagsanstalt, 1966e (1888). pp. 36-60 ([1]1520).

Luther, M. "(Kleiner) Sermon von dem Wucher". *D. Martin Luthers Werke: Kritische Gesamtausgabe (Weimarer Ausgabe).* Vol. 6. Graz: Akademische Druck- und Verlagsanstalt, 1966d (1888). pp. 3-8 ([1]1519).

Luther, M. "An den christlichen Adel deutscher Nation von des christlichen Standes Besserung". *Martin Luther: Der Reformator.* Luther Deutsch, ed. K. Aland. Vol. 2. Göttingen: Vandenhoeck und Ruprecht, 1962a. pp. 157-170 ([1]1520).

Luther, M. "An den Christlichen Adel deutscher Nation von des Christlichen standes besserung". *D. Martin Luthers Werke: Kritische Gesamtausgabe (Weimarer Ausgabe).* Vol. 6. Graz: Akademische Druck- und Verlagsanstalt, 1966a (1888). pp. 404-469 ([1]1520).

Luther, M. "An die Parrherrn, wider den Wucher zu predigen, Vermahnung". *D. Martin Luthers Werke: Kritische Gesamtausgabe (Weimarer Ausgabe).* Vol. 51. Graz: Akademische Druck- und Verlagsanstalt, 1967 (1914). pp. 331-424 ([1]1540).

Luther, M. "Eyn sermon von dem unrechten Mammon". *D. Martin Luthers Werke: Kritische Gesamtausgabe (Weimarer Ausgabe).* Vol. 10 III. Graz: Akademische Druck- und Verlagsanstalt, 1966c (1905). pp. 283-292 ([1]1522).

Luther, M. "Von Kaufhandlung und Wucher". *Martin Luther: Von weltlicher Obrigkeit.* Calwer Luther-Ausgabe, ed. W. Metzger. Vol. 4. Munich: Siebenstern, 1965. pp. 115-143 ([1]1524).

Luther, M. "Von Kaufshandlung und Wucher". *D. Martin Luthers Werke: Kritische Gesamtausgabe (Weimarer Ausgabe).* Vol. 15. Graz: Akademische Druck- und Verlagsanstalt, 1966b (1899). pp. 279-322 ([1]1524).

Luther, M. "Von Kaufshandlung und Wucher". *Martin Luther: Der Christ in der Welt.* Luther Deutsch, ed. K. Aland. Vol. 7. 3rd. Ed. Göttingen: Vandenhoeck und Ruprecht, 1983a. pp. 263-283 ([1]1524).

Luther, M. „Vom unfreien Willen". *Martin Luther: Der neue Glaube.* Luther Deutsch, ed. K. Aland. Vol. 3. 3rd., enlarged ed. Göttingen: Vandenhoeck und Ruprecht, 1961. pp. 151-334 ([1]1525).

Luther, M. „Von weltlicher Obrigkeit, wie weit man ihr Gehorsam schuldig sei". *Martin Luther: Der Christ in der Welt.* Luther Deutsch, ed. K. Aland. Vol. 7. 3rd. Ed. Göttingen: Vandenhoeck und Ruprecht, 1983b. pp. 9-51 ([1]1523).

Luther, M. „Wider Hans Worst". *Martin Luther: Der Reformator.* Luther Deutsch, ed. K. Aland. Vol. 2. Göttingen: Vandenhoeck und Ruprecht, 1962b. pp. 22-27 ([1]1541).

Luther, M. *Tischreden.* Luther Deutsch, ed. K. Aland. Vol. 9. Göttingen: Vandenhoeck und Ruprecht, 1960.

Marx, K. *Ökonomische Manuskripte und Schriften 1858-1861.* K. Marx and F. Engels. Gesamtausgabe (MEGA), II, Abt. II, Vol. 2. Berlin, 1980.

Metzger, W. „Vom Wucher [Überblick]". *Martin Luther: Von weltlicher Obrigkeit.* Calwer Luther-Ausgabe, ed. W. Metzger. Vol. 4. Munich: Siebenstern, 1965. pp. 144-150.

Münch, R. *Theorie des Handelns: Zur Rekonstruktion der Beiträge von Talcott Parsons, Emile Durkheim und Max Weber.* Frankfurt: Suhrkamp, 1982.

Pawlas, A. *Die lutherische Berufs- und Wirtschaftsethik.* Neukirchen-Vluyn: Neukirchener, 2000.

Prien, H.-J. *Luthers Wirtschaftsethik.* Vandenhoeck und Ruprecht, 1992.

Roscher, W. *Geschichte der National-Oekonomik in Deutschland.* Munich: Oldenbourg, 1874.

Schmoller, G. „Zur Geschichte der national-ökonomischen Ansichten in Deutschland während der Reformationsperiode". *Zeitschrift für die gesamte Staatswissenschaft,* 16 (1860), 461-716.

Sombart, W. *Die drei Nationalökonomien.* Berlin: Duncker und Humblot, 1930.

Strieder, J. *Studien zur Geschichte kapitalistischer Organisationsformen: Monopole, Kartelle und Aktiengesellschaften im Mittelalter und zu Beginn der Neuzeit.* Munich: Duncker und Humblot, 1925.

Troeltsch, E. „Luther, der Protestantismus und die moderne Welt 1907/1908". *Gesammelte Schriften,* Vol. 4. Tübingen: Mohr, 1925. pp. 202-253.

Vogt, T. „Die Drei-Stände-Lehre bei Martin Luther: Darstellung derselben und Diskussion der biblischen Begründung". *Die vier Schöpfungsordnungen Gottes,* ed. T. Schirrmacher. Nürnberg: Verlag für Theologie und Religionswissenschaften, 2001. pp. 39-83.

Weber, M. *Die protestantische Ethik* I. Hamburg: Siebenstern, 1975 (^{1}1905ff.).

Weber, M. *Wirtschaftsgeschichte,* ed. S. Hellmann and M. Palyi. Munich: Duncker und Humblot, 1924.

Calvin on Economics and Politics: The Reformation and its Impact with Respect to Calvin

Gerrit Meijer

Abstract

The purpose of this article is to expose the main lines of the thinking of Calvin (1509 –1564) on economics and politics. Calvin breaks with the scholastic tradition both with regard to the interpretation of the Holy Scripture and the Classical argumentation with regard to economic and political problems.

His view on earthly life and time are the foundation of his arguments. In this respect his ideas have been conducive to the further evolution and development of economic and political life.

Introduction

The Reformation is characterized by four core ideas:

- *Sola Scriptura* (the highest authority is the Word of God (the Bible), not the Church with her offices);
- *Sola Fide* (salvation is only by belief in Jesus Christ; not by the Church with her offices: indulgence);
- *Sola Deo* Gratia (salvation is only by grace, not works);
- *Sola Deo* Gloria.

"Predestination" is not a core idea of the Reformation (See Appendix).

The Reformation gives rise to another attitude towards Church and State. Most essential becomes the plea for freedom of religion and the connected right of resistance against the State and the Church, with an appeal on the Bible. In the field of the political and economic opinions this of course also gives changes. In this regard there exist to a certain measure differences between Calvin (1509-1564) and Luther (1483-1546). These differences and their background will not be treated in this paper. The purpose of this article is to expose the main lines of the thinking of Calvin. This means that it is not about Calvinism and not about interpretations of Calvin's theology. In the next two sections Calvin's contribution to economic and political thought will be discussed.

Calvin on economics

In this section the ideas of Calvin on interest (usury), trade, labour and profession, luxury, private property, and poverty will be discussed.

We begin with the verdict of interest c.q. usury. (Calvin, 1545); Diepenhorst, 1904, Chapter II, section 4; Elster, 1878). In this Calvin is ahead of his time and of all his contemporaries. He is the only writer on these matters who rejects the verdict of interest c.q. usury. All other writers during his lifetime are following the scholastic tradition, both with regard to the interpretation of the Holy Scripture and the Classical argument (going back to Aristotle) that money is unfruitful.

Calvin shows that the Holy Scripture does not condemn the taking of interest c.q. usury, but also he shows that ethical principles have to be followed in this respect: justice, fairness, truthfulness, etc. He also argues that money is productive. In this respect he sees that time is money, and is a forerunner of Turgot (1727-1781), and for example Böhm-Bawerk (1851-1914).

Böhm-Bawerk (1921, Part I, p. 31) discusses Calvin's contribution and writes: "*Die ersten Vorkämpfer der neuen Richtung waren der Reformator Calvin und der französische Jurist Dumoulin (Carolus Molinaeus)*". (*"The first advocates of the new School were the re-*

former Calvin and the French lawyer Dumoulin (Carolus Molinaeus)" .) Dumoulin lived from 1500 to 1566.

In this respect Calvin distinguishes himself from all other leading figures in the Reformation, who are still thinking in the scholastic tradition. But also from humanists like Erasmus (1466?- 1536). Even the Dutch protestant and Calvinist Grotius (1583-1645: 17th century) did not follow Calvin's exegesis.

With regard to trade Calvin (1999, Part III: section 10; Diepenhorst, 1904, Chapter III) argued that trade was productive and that every profession (*Beruf*) is of a divine nature. He rejected the doctrine of nature and grace. In every activity humans are *Coram Deo.* The life of a monk, bishop, or what else in principle does not have a higher "spiritual" value or has more value viewed from the perspective of the Kingdom of God: *Ora et Labora.* Agriculture and trade have an equal standing in the view of Calvin. This opinion differs from the scholastics and also from his contemporaries. It also differs from the theory of the Physiocrats.

Calvin's opinion in this respect is a corollary to his view on interest. His view on earthly human life and time are the foundation of his arguments. Of course also in this connection Calvin points out the ethical constraints. But in principle according to the Holy Scripture, just like in the case of interest, nothing is wrong with trade; neither is this the case with any other human activity. There also is no difference. Salvation is *Sola Fide.* Activity has to be *Sola Deo Gloria.* He is opposed to asceticism.

In the same mood are his remarks on luxury. Also here he shows that the Holy Scripture does not condemn. Here again he points to moral constraints. He also stresses the importance of saving, as necessary basis for investment, and of entrepreneurship (e.g. instead of the laziness of a leisure class). People have to dispose on their possessions *Sola Deo Gloria* and also to take the position of other people into account.

Calvin also in his quarrels with the Libertines and the Anabaptists showed that there was no ground to be found in the Holy Scripture for "communism" or collective property, and neither for "anarchism". He does not want to throw over the then existing order. He in all his work defends the foundations of the exchange economy which is based on the fact of division of labour. In this respect his ideas have been conducive to the further evolution and development of economic life. He rejects libertine dissoluteness as well as Anabaptist world avoidance.

Whereas in the Middle Ages and also in his time economic life was bound by religious constraints, based on misinterpretation of the Holy Scripture by the most influential persons and institutions, Calvin's influence especially in The Netherlands and the Anglo-Saxon world made new developments possible, not only in economic life, but also e.g. in science, art, and politics.

Calvin also wrote on poverty, its origins, and methods to relieve and avoid it. Besides stressing that labour is a divine calling, rooted in the idea of stewardship and the cultivation mandate, he condemns begging. He attacks every kind of exploitation, and writes in favour of private charity, charity by the church and the (political) community.

He did not only write on this, but did also practical work in this field.

Calvin on Politics

In this section the main lines of Calvin's political insights are discussed (Calvin, 1999, 4:20; De Groot , 1955).

Calvin is positive in his judgment of the state and politics and politicians. This is based on what the Holy Scripture teaches (e.g. Romans 13). Of course, he knows that state and politics and politicians (can) abuse their power.

He defends the doctrine of the sovereignty of God in all fields of human life, also in political life. There is no higher authority than the Creator.

The state (government) is a divine institution, just like the Church, that means instituted by Him and bound to the Holy Scripture (especially the Ten Commandments, the Decalogue).

He writes on the task of government in relation to religion. It is not the task of the state to convert people or force them to adhere to the true religion. The state just has to create the conditions for and to foster the true religion (i.e. not to prosecute or negatively discriminate the true believers).

He distinguishes the task of the church and the state. The Church is not of a higher order than the state; the state not of a higher order than the church. This is lateral subsidiarity *avant la lettre* (sovereignty in its own sphere) (Meijer, 2000). The Church has to preach the Gospel. The state exists because there is sin. The outer consequences of it (theft, murder, etc.) have to be fought by politics. Therefore laws have to be made and enforced as far as possible to restrain people and to limit the bad consequences, and make human society possible.

With regard to the forms of government he prefers aristocracy and rejects the doctrine of peoples sovereignty. Rousseau (1712-1778) is not the consequence of Calvin, they are diametrically opposed. Calvin rejects democracy and believes in the Sovereignty of God. In principle he is teaching theocracy as the form of government. Against monarchy he has no principle objection, but it easily goes astray by neglecting God's sovereignty. Also hereditary succession is not imposed by Scripture. God as the Ruler gives authority to the rulers, and they are bound to rule after His will, and judged accordingly. A special position is held by the magistrates (ephors) in case the monarch does not behave as he should.

The citizens have to obey government, because the governors are servants of God for their well being. They have to live up to the rules of the Kingdom of God. That means that there is a demarcation line. (Illustration: When a Frisian delegate had to go to Spain to "visit" Philip II, they refused to kneel for the King. *"Wy Friezen knibbelje alinne foar God"* was their explanation. The translation of their slogan is: We Frisians only kneel for God). In the light of the Decalogue this was correct behaviour. Another example from the Bible: Daniel and his friends).

With regard to the change of government four possibilities are treated: two changes from within and two from without. From within two possibilities can be distinguished: the right of resistance and the right of revolt. With regard to the right of resistance this was treated already. See above for illustration of the kind of individual resistance.

Revolt is allowed as collective resistance under the lead of the magistrates or ephors. This may even take the form of resistance by force. This happened e.g. in the Netherlands (William of Orange, The Silent (1533-1584)). He justified his action on (interpretations of) Calvin (William of Orange, 1581).

With regard to the change of government from without, there are also two possibilities: Asked for and unasked for intervention of a state in another state. An example of the first possibility is The Glorious Revolution. The Glorious Revolution was justified by a follower of Calvin: William of Orange (1650-1702), grand-grandson of the Silent, King of England (1688-1702) and Stadtholder of Holland (1672 - 1702) , by this conviction as part of his life long (thirty years struggle against two German bishops - those of Münster and Cologne - and the catholic kings of France and England (Meijer, unpublished manuscript; Troost , 2001).

Unasked for intervention, this is outright war, was according to Calvin justified under certain circumstances. These circumstances were elaborated by the Dutch Calvinist author Grotius, whose opinion had its roots in the Holy Scripture, see e.g. Mare Liberum (On Free Seas, 1609; 2004)) and De Jure Belli ac Pacis Libri Tres (1625; 1925).

An extensive book on Politics (Politica) (1603; 1995) in the spirit of Calvin has been written by the German Althusius (1557-1638). His work is still also very important for the theory of federalism. (Gerbrandy, 1944; Friedrich 1932).

Conclusion

Calvin breaks with the scholastic tradition both with regard to the interpretation of the Holy Scripture and the Classical argumentation with regard to economic and political problems.

His view on earthly life and time are the foundation of his arguments. In this respect his ideas have been conducive to the further evolution and development of economic and political life.

Appendix

The thoughts on economics and politics of Calvin have nothing to do with the so-called doctrine of predestination. Weber (1974) and Tawney (1961) relate the development of "capitalism" with the so-called doctrine of predestination which they see as the core of "Calvinism". This is not correct. The meaning of human existence according to Calvin is that of being a creature of God, with a mission on earth. Men live C*oram Deo* and to the honour of God.

The doctrine of predestination, in the form and in the consequences which are connected with that by these writers, is contrary to the Sola Fide, Sola Gratia, Sola Scriptura, and Sola Deo Gloria of the Reformation. The misconceptions about the Reformation that can be found in these works are many. The same is the case with Rüstow (1952).

In the contributions to this conference by Chaloupek, Frambach, Hansen, Peukert, these authors follow these writers without a critical assessment. Moreover they are writing not about Calvin but on Calvinism.

The study of Weber concerns observations in the USA in Calvinistic groups. Tawney's findings are based on observations in England. All these observations are done long after Calvin's lifetime. Müller-Armack (1959, p. 111) correctly remarks: "*Freilich kann diese Identifizierung von geschäftlichem Erfolg und religiöser Erwähltheit nicht für den Frühcalvinismus festgestellt werden". ("Of course, this identification of commercial success and salvation cannot be found in early Calvinism").*

Science made progress by work of Calvinists before the Enlightenment. These people were impressed by the greatness of the Creator and the Creation. Also in the field of art and culture the Reformation had a positive influence, for the same reason, e.g. painting (Kuyper, 1899; Rookmaker, 1960).

The political convictions have had important consequences. In this article a few of these are indicated.

References

Althusius, J., 1995, Politica. An abridged translation of Politics Methodically Set Forth and Illustrated with Sacred and Profane Examples. Edited and translated, with an introduction by Frederick S. Carney. Foreword by Daniel J. Elazar, Indianapolis: Liberty Fund. Originally Politica Methodice Digesta et exemplis sacris et profanes illustrata, 1603, Herborn : Christophorus Corvinus

Böhm-Bawerk, E., 1921, Kapital und Kapitalzins, Teil I, Geschichte und Kritik der Kapital-zinstheorien, Vierte Auflage, Jena: Gustav Fischer

Calvijn, J., 1999, Institutie of onderwijzing in de christelijke godsdienst. Uit het Latijn vertaald door Dr. A. Sizoo, 3 delen, 13de druk, Zoetermeer: Meinema

Calvin, J., 1545, Consilium in Opera X', 245f. Corporus (of Corpus) Reformatorum Joannis Calvini Opera. In French in Diepenhorst, 1904, 129-135. Also in Tract IV (1881) of American Association for Political Education (with Bentham and Danas).

Diepenhorst, P.A., 1904, Calvijn en de economie, Wageningen: Vada.

Elster, L., 1878, Johann Calvin als Staatsmann, Gesetzgeber und Nationalökonom, Jahrbuch für Nationalönomie und Statistik, Bd 30 (Jena)

Friedrich, C.J., 1932, Introduction to the Politica methodice digesta of Johannes Althusius. Cambridge, Ma.

Gerbrandy, P.S., 1944, National and International Stability: Althusius, Grotius, Van Vollen-hoven, Oxford.

Groot, D.J. de , 1955, De reformatie en de staatkunde, Franeker: Wever

Grotius, H., 1609; 2004, Mare Liberum (The Free Sea), Indianapolis: Liberty Fund.

Grotius, H., 1625 ; 1925, De Jure Belli a Pacis Libri Tres, Oxford : Clarendon Press.

Kuyper, A., 1899; 1959, Het calvinisme. Zes Stone-lezingen, Kampen: Kok

Meijer, G., 2000, The Idea of Subsidiarity in Dutch Economic and Political Thought, in G. Meijer, W.J.M. Heijman, J.A.C. van Ophem, B.H.J. Verstegen (eds), ISINI Papers Maastricht, Volume II, 2000, p.415-420.

Meijer, G., The Peace of Munster at the background of the History of Thought (not published).

Müller-Armack, A., 1959, Religion und Wirtschaft, Stuttgart: Kohlhammer

Orange, William of, 1581, The Apologie of Prince William of Orange against the Proclamation of the King of Spain. Delft 1581. Edited after the Englisch Edition of 1581 by H. Wansink. Leiden: E.J. Brill, 1969.

Rookmaaker, H.R., 1960, Reformatorische kunst, in Christelijke Encyclopedie, Deel V, p. 595-596, Kampen: Kok.

Rüstow, A., 1952, Ortsbestimmung der Gegenwart, II, Weg der Freiheit, Erlenbach-Zürich: Eugen Rentsch

Tawney, R.H., 1961;1926, Religion and the Rise of Capitalism, A Mentor Book, New York: New American Library.

Troost, W., 2001, Stadhouder-koning Willem III.Een politieke biografie, Hilversum: Verloren.

Weber, M., 1974, The Protestant Ethic and the Spirit of Capitalism. London: Unwin.

Work and Ethics in the Economic Thought of Reformation

Hans Frambach

1. Work ethics – An old and new topic

Labour has a central meaning for the economy and for society as a whole. Not only because it gives most people the means to earn money, but also because the systems of social insurance depend on the labour markets. The question of how many people have or do not have an income from labour is decisive for financing the systems of social insurance. Furthermore, the fact of having or not having a job determines social position as well as reputation. Issues like the distribution of income and wealth (the precise income distribution, tax tariffs …), the payment of labour (minimum wages, flexibility of wages …), the role of non paid labour (housework, housekeeping etc.), honorary positions etc. are also important.

In contrast to the usual treatment of labour in economic theory – which treats labour as a normal factor related to production – labour assumes a different meaning when it is seen as the <u>human</u> factor of production. Considering labour as human activity, ethical issues quickly emerge.

First of all: work ethics as a singular entity does not exist, nor does a unique ethics of business. There even is no completed theory on morals of work, no theory of work ethics as a constant sum of special virtues. Every ethos of work and the ethics of labour depend on factors like the structure of economic organisation, institutional settings of a society, institutional change, technical progress and so forth, up to concrete situations at the place of work. Ethics of work is not so much of a general attribute people have or do not have, such as diligence or idleness as brazen constants; rather it is the result of a developing process. Ethics of work is subject to change and to distinct historical, cultural and socio-economic conditions, but nevertheless it becoming manifest in the individual.

The fundamental issue of work ethics of the present time may best be described by the publicly discussed loss of morale by workers. One reason mentioned by many economists is a misled incentive to work supposedly caused by payments of too high social transfers. Regarding the loss of work ethics it is more important that the number of individuals is decreasing who sacrificingly devote themselves to work, who work hard, and who see their work itself as their goal, as a duty, as devotion to the community, rather than the earning of money. A decline in the so called secondary virtues such as obedience, duty, reliability, dependability, punctuality, diligence is often noted with regret.

This prompts the question as to why people should obediently, dutifully act when utility is obviously not maximized, and when the message of salvation of the Reformation does not sell? Can the Reformation contribute to answer in the case that modern so called „traditional work ethics“ complains about the loss of bourgeois values and demands its dogma “that only persons who work get satisfaction”? (Noelle-Neumann 1978) Following another work ethics, the „distanced work ethics“, people factually realize labour as necessary for satisfying material needs and sometimes as interesting, but also as strenuous and exhaustive – the negative side of labour, which should be kept at a distance. In other words, it is necessary to keep the attracting and the repulsive side of labour in equilibrium – which is why “distance work ethics” is sometimes called “ethics of equilibrium”. (Strümpel/v. Klipstein 1984) From this point of view, work ethics can be characterised by the contrasts of “accomplishment and disengagement”, “tension and détente”, “active planning of the future and present search for consumption and pleasure”.

Latest studies about values among younger generations (e. g. Shell Deutschland 2002) indicate a current trend towards traditional values such as fidelity, diligence, ambitiousness; even good education and apprenticeship are regarded as important by the younger generations, but primarily in terms of a basis for a successful career, which in itself is necessary to earn the high income needed to have enough money for a life free from cares. Labour is reduced to the function of earning money and seems to have lost its function of imposing meaning to life.

Following these introductory remarks into work ethics, the actual relevance of this paper, "Work and Ethics in the Economic Thought of Reformation", and its central question, “What can we learn from the Reformation?”, should become clear. More precisely: Can advice be given to understand contemporary social and economic issues? Can deficits of modern economic theory be revealed and ways of improvement recommended? Does the Reformation build the basis for the story of success of capitalism and market economy? Can Lutheran tenets help individuals to find orientation in the complex world?

2. Reformation and Protestant work ethics

2.1 Labour in Reformation – relating to its history of ideas

The Reformation was completely built on the grounds of the Christian doctrine and saw life as an indivisible whole. This whole is controlled by the superior and sovereign will of God. God is the connecting link between all areas of life. Theology strongly affects social and individual life, and neither the philosophy of natural reason nor the anthropocentric morality is strong and widespread enough to substitute the pure Christian doctrine. Individuals at the time of Reformation have only one perspective to overcome their life on earth and receive contentment: They have to live according to the letter and the spirit of the Bible, a view of life which is expressed very clearly in the world of labour. (van der Ven 1972, 224)

The Reformation liberates labour finally from the curse of being God's punishment for the Fall of Man. We have to keep in mind that before the Reformation two types of labour were known:

1. The Old Testament states that God created man in his own image. For that reason it follows that the human ability to work is an ability of God as well. That is why a negative interpretation of the notion of labour can be excluded. Furthermore labour is established in the story of Creation because God allowed man to dominate the earth.

> *So the Lord God took the man and put him in his garden of delight, to cultivate and tend it.* (Genesis 2, 15)

Thus, people are allowed to work; they have to thank God for the ability to work. Furthermore, God has told people not only to work; he also has blessed them with work and invited them to participate in his Creation. (Schmieder 1959, 56) According to the bible, labour, in the primordial, paradisical state, is no nuisance and punishment but care for the Creation and also a means of self-preservation.

2. Only the expulsion from paradise made labour a nuisance, bother and burden. After expulsion the whole human race had to work in pain to survive – and this was in contrast to all other creatures. The severity of the work and its conditions is God's punishment for the human sin. As Moses in the genesis said:

> *And to Adam he said, Thou hast listened to thy wife's counsel, and hast eaten the fruit I forbade thee to eat; and now, through thy act, the ground is under a curse. All the days of thy life thou shalt win food from it with toil; thorns and thistles it shall yield thee, this ground from which thou dost win thy food. Still thou*

> *shalt earn thy bread with the sweat of they brow, until thou goest back into the ground from which thou wast taken; dust thou art, and unto dust shalt thou return.* (Genesis 3, 17-19)

The Fall of Man took influence on the conditions of human work – that means, work becomes hard and heavy laden, but work itself has no negative meaning at all. Wenzeslaus Linck, a monk like Martin Luther, his collaborator and long-term friend, saw man before and after the Fall of Man (which includes Eternity) as working on behalf of God and not as following leisure and idleness. Linck said that with the Fall of Man the merry and jolly sinless life changed to painful and embarrassing work. (Elert 1958, 469) Luther also saw work, which was impeded (but not caused) by the Fall of Man, as penance and punishment for the Fall, but also (like Catholicism) as necessary for one's own discipline and restraint. (Vontobel 1946, 8) In the Reformation we find no explanation showing labour as the result of the Fall of Man; the Reformation rather refers to the bible (see Gen. 2, 15, quoted above) people being entrusted to cultivate and tend the earth. Thus, the Reformation knew only one side of work: God has imposed the work on man, it is ordained by God.

The two types of labour were combined by the Reformation, stating that labour is not only a kind of divine command, rather it is a calling. Former hierarchical classifications of human activities, where, for example, rating prayer and contemplation as superior (e. g. in the periods of the classical Antiquity and scholasticism), were abolished: for God all people are the same. For example, Saint Paul worked as an apostle and as a craftsman. Even the scribes were urged to learn a craft profession, helping – by the way – to prevent a separation of people into different social classes. (Hauck 1950, 588) Jesus himself did not emphasize work explicitly. In case he mentioned it, he stressed that work should not become an end in itself and that the true aim in life, listening to the words of God, should never be forgotten. (Luke 10, 38-42; 14, 15-24; Matthew 22, 2-10) In Luke 10 it says that:

> *In one of the villages he entered during his journey, a woman called Martha entertained him in her house. She had a sister called Mary; and Mary took her place at the Lord's feet, and listened to his words. Martha was distracted by waiting on many needs; so she came to his side, and asked, Lord, art thou content that my sister should leave me to do the serving alone? Come, bid her help me. Jesus answered her, Martha, Martha, how many cares and troubles thou hast! But only one thing is necessary; and Mary has chosen for herself the best part of all, that which shall never be taken away from her.* (Luke 2, 38-42)

Jesus was himself a craftsman, a joiner, who called upon his disciples to give up their occupations and to follow him to announce the word of God: „*Jesus said to them, Come and follow me; I will make you into fishers of men. And they dropped their nets immediately, and followed him.*" (Mark 1, 17-18) Even heavy and humiliating work, work as slaves and so on was not felt as disgrace, rather as a service for God and the neighbours.

Luther stressed the equality of people and their work in its independence of the thinking of the estates and said that every work is good when done in the right faith.

> *In this faith all works are equal and one work is like the other, all the differences in work leave, no matter how big or small, short or long, many or little they are. Accordingly the works are pleasant not because of their own but because of the faith, which works and lives in every and all works no matter how much or differently they are.* (Luther, Von den guten Werken. 1520. WA 6, 206, 33-36 a. 207, 1-4)

> *But when you ask a humble housemaid why she washes up the bowl or draws milk from the cows, she can say: "I know that God likes what I am doing, whenever I have God's word and order".*(Luther, Epistel S. Petri gepredigt und ausgelegt. Erste Bearbeitung 1523. WA 12, 337, 18-21)

Already the mystic Master Eckehart anticipated parts of Lutherian thought when refuting the idea that one could receive an advance for Eternity in this world by leisure, contemplation, long fasting, and good deeds and so forth.

> *Verily, if someone thinks to get more by inwardness, deep devotion, sweet rapture and special declaration of divine favour rather than being a slave over a hot stove all day or working in a stable, you do nothing else than taking God, putting a coat around his head and putting him under a bench.* (Eckehart, sermon on John 4, 9)

There is no estate and no way of life in which man can be nearer to God than another man. If a judgement about work will be admitted at all, it can only be the extension to what kind of work is done and whether one serves in the right faith. Luther recognizes that Man cannot contribute by himself to the righteousness of God because the righteousness of God can only be revealed from faith. Human fate only depends on the devout trust in the favour of God which can be seen in the message of salvation of Jesus Christ. All the works of piety are useless, and even wrong and sinful, because they feign people an own fortune, which they do not have – they are totally dependent on God. (Vontobel 1946, 5-6) Work is useful if it is done in the right belief in God, and from Luther's point of view this work represents a kind of service. (Luther, WA 22 (1929), 83) Labour, understood in this sense, is put on the same level with prayer. As Markus von Weida said already about 1500: „*Quite a few people pray less ... but God respects the work of their hands as a prayer.*" (Markus von Weida; here after Conze 1972, 163)

This represents a radical break with medieval philosophy which stressed highly valued activities such as leisure, asceticism, contemplation, prayer etc. as pleasing to God. After Luther there is no longer any difference between religious activities and the lowest of physical works. To put it more philosophically: The distinction between the *vita contemplativa* and the *vita activa* has become invalid and there is no hierarchy between them any longer. Vita contemplativa does not dominate vita activa any longer. Both kinds of activities have an equal value in the face of God.

Martin Luther even condemns the enormous amount of ascetic exercises, the Church's receipt of donations and foundations, the receipt of alms, the costly letters of indulgence etc. as a „parasitic way of life". At the same time he stresses those activities, which were regarded as despicable until that time, as pleasing to God. (Luther, Der Große Katechismus. 1529. WA 30, 1, 153) Luther describes great parts of the contemplative way of life of the clergymen as nothing but leisure and idleness and, therefore, as being a sin against God's order to work as well as a sin against other people. (Luther, Predigten des Jahres 1529 [Predigt am 5. Sonntag nach Trinitatis], WA 29, 442) The life of monks is interpreted as selfish and unkind acts, and as a tool to justify life, albeit being useless in its own right. Every single one should work and live from the return obtained by labour. (Troeltsch 1965, 575) Labour in accordance with one's duty is realized as the best service, and charity to one's neighbour, which evolves from exercising an occupation or profession, is regarded as being much better than charity, which encourages people to beg, making alms a kind of an earning in God. Ernst Troeltsch (1965, 575) – referring to Gustav v. Schmoller's „Zur Geschichte der nationalökonomischen Ansichten in Deutschland während der Reformationsperiode", („Zeitschrift für die gesamte Staatswissenschaft" 1860, 461-716) – speaks about the „obedient duty in one's occupation as the true scope for charity to one's neighbour". There is no normatively substantiated release from work at all, except the work of children, old age and in case of illness. It is not surprising that the Reformation rejected begging, and especially begging for the purpose of "God-loved contemplation".

2.2 Work as calling

Dr. Martin Luther was the first who declared work as a duty towards God; he gave the reason that every work is a task imposed by God. With that Luther radically turned against the Christian doctrine of the Middle Ages and against contemplation as the only true way of life. Luther emphasised the meaning of work in the sense of the calling of Man by God. (The idea of calling or divine summons corresponds to the German notion of "Berufung", which contains the term "Beruf", meaning occupation and profession). Max Weber noted that both the German word „Beruf" and the English term „calling" involve the meaning of a permanent position and a defined field of work and that both terms entail a note of a religious idea. (Weber 1993, 34-35) In the case of German translations of the Bible, Weber pointed out that the term „Beruf" could be traced back to the mind of the translators much better than to the original content.

The idea of work as divine summons the performance of one's duty within all the secular occupations granted unprecedented importance to everyday work and daily duty because work now obtained a religious meaning. This represents the central tenet of all protestant denominations and is most clearly expressed in the term "calling", meaning that is the only means to live a God-pleasing life, and, more precisely defined, refers to knowing how to perform all worldly duties emerging from the personal situation of every single individual. (Weber 1993, 39) Before, those who held a higher position and thus could practise activities known to be pleasing to God –especially the clergy – were regarded to be "called". Now everyone who truly believes is regarded to lead a live in accordance to his calling. Everyone – within the social class he is born into – is called for serving his certain purpose for God and his neighbour. From Luther's point of view, if a humble person has an occupation in which he is "called upon", then he may even perform the most inferior of all activities, and yet this activity is divine. (Luther, Der Große Katechismus. 1529. WA 30, 1, 3-12; Vontobel 1946, 7;)

Knowing that even the most inferior activities are accepted by God and that class differences are ignored, Martin Luther here sees a source for true enthusiasm for one's work: „Sic habet gaudium in labore et hic ingreditur in mediis malis in paradisum". (Luther, Vorlesung über den Prediger Salomo. 1526. Annotationes in Ecclesiasten. 1532. WA 20, 108, 35-36; Der große Katechismus. 1529. WA 30, 1, 153, 3-16)

Thus, Reformation gave labour a hitherto unknown and maybe even unthinkable positive value and brought people into a closer relation to God. Besides this positive reinterpretation of work in the sense of a divine summons, there is another meaning. An individual doing its job can be restricted in its occupation. Within its calling, the individual needs to do what it is instructed to do, no more and no less. Everyone has to live and to endure according to his calling and also according to the social class into which he is born. Following Protestant doctrine, both calling and class are assigned to man by God. Furthermore, because of the tenet of „suffering obedience", man has to be obedient to God. Accordingly, calling has nothing to do at all with free choice. Luther was clearly bound by the medieval system of estates, in which the field of work and the personal situation of the individual was mostly determined by birth. God demands persistence from the Christian, and humble enduring in the work he is instructed to do. Work done with the aim of individual satisfaction, self-realization or simply to pass time is regarded as sinful; the duty to fall into line with the divine assignment dominates. Thus, Lutheran Protestantism stands against the natural striving of people to improve their situation.

People are driven to work by their sense of duty and they have to be conscious about the fact that it is not their work which provides the essentials of life, but solely the compliance with the command to work that raises the hope of being supplied by God. Luther expelled the possibility of any success in the fields of household, politics, and economy without the help of God. Accumulating a great amount of material wealth (or more general: of worldly goods) is regarded as the result of a lot of individual work; but the success must necessarily be preceded by God's favour. In the protestant view it is only God who can create things, not man. God puts man in a certain place in the world, and there he has to endure, to persevere, to bear his fate and to persist in faith. (Luther, Der Große Katechismus. 1529. WA 30, 1, 136, 8-12)

Obviously, Luther separates work and achieving an economic result. Work is an activity resulting from the respect for the divine Commandment. God grants a positive result of work by his favour and mercy. Of course, the favour and mercy of God cannot be created and directed by the hand of man, man can only hope for a mild and gracious treatment by conscientiously following the path of duty.

> *And if you would plough one hundred years and do the work of the whole world you would not be able to get one stalk out of the earth, it is God who is doing all your work while you are sleeping, it is he who makes from a single grain of corn a stalk with many grains, as he pleases.*
> *... One needs to work, but where work is alone and means to feed oneself everything is in vain. Work does nothing, God has to do it.* (Luther, psalm 127. interpreted for the Christians of Riga in Liefland. 1524. WA 15, 366-367, 22-25, 29-2)

2.3 Some comments on the idea of labour and the origin of capitalism

Protestantism combined the performance of work with the search for redemption. As a consequence, calling and work became a religious duty. In the opinion of Max Weber and Ernst Troeltsch this was the prerequisite for the ideal of labour for the sake of labour, which built the intellectual and moral basis to enforce the modern bourgeois lifestyle. (Troeltsch 1965, 654, referring to Max Weber) The combination of the output of work and the search for redemption was driven to an extreme, for instance, by the pietists of the Herrnhuter brotherhood [Herrnhuter Brüdergemeinde] of the Count Zinzendorf; they saw work as the reason for the sense of life: „Man lives for the sake of work and if man does not have anything to work, he suffers or passes away." (Weber 1993, 128, fn. 240)

Luther himself remained in the same settings as the apostle Paul and the old medieval church, regarding the conception of work as a field of activity, not to be abandoned by man. Work was perceived as a means to increase the honour of God and the utility of the neighbour. Calvinism, on the contrary, perceived work not as a given structure for the realization of brotherly love or a proof of faith. Rather Calvinism interpreted work as an arbitrary means enabling love and faith to unfold their impact. Seen from this point of view, calling makes people perform in a different way, it prompts them to be much more effective and efficient to consider the appropriateness and potential of their intended actions. (Troeltsch 1965, 655) God, the tireless worker, calls upon man to work ceaselessly, too. In Calvinism this assertion becomes the quintessence of all virtue, the beginning and the end of all morality. (Schmieder 1959, 77) Specifically, Calvinism demands a stronger asceticism of work, achieved by an increase in individual self-abstention and an altogether flawless lifestyle. The „religious diary" may be a good example for the Calvinistic view: Every well reformed Christian had to continuously record his sins, temptations, the progress in mercy and granted favours in tabular form into a diary. Doing this, he could, as Max Weber put it, “feel his own pulse”. (Weber 1993, 84) Weber called the result of this ethical lifestyle, which Calvinists enforced onto their followers in contrast to Lutherans, an “overbearing Christianization of the whole life“. (Weber 1993, 84-85) For Lutherans people work to the glory of God (and God works through man to his own glory). In contrast, Calvinists refer all human activities to the omnipotence of God, and God rules by force and glory, but without mercy. (Wiedemann 1979, 194)

Max Weber traced the evolution of the “Spirit of Capitalism” to the central tenets of Lutheranism and Calvinism, which demanded that man follows the path of duty in his calling, perseveres and persists in his faith, and, finally, the ideas of worldly asceticism and of predestination. The doctrine of predestination has an outstanding meaning; it is the fundamental doctrine of Calvinism. (Weber 1993, 56-57) Following this doctrine, the fate of man – to be chosen for eternal life or not –already is determined. Accordingly, the inequality of man is ordained by God. Consequently, man has no choice but to be obedient and to accept his fate. (Schmieder 1959, 77) Man can only live in the hope of being chosen, man cannot actively influence the divine decision, which has already been made. Man’s whole efforts are directed towards recognizing his own predestination: and the only means to accomplish this insight is restless and successful work according to his calling.

At this point the question appears as to why people should work at all if they have no means to change their own fate, provided that even heaviest work is useless, because the taint of not being chosen remains? The answer of Calvinism is that restless labour is the very sign of being chosen. Conversely, idleness, i.e. the avoidance of work, is regarded as the unmistakable sign of the lacking divine favour. (Weber 1993, 128) If hard work is a necessary but not sufficient condition for predestination, every Christian has to work hard. Otherwise he certainly is among the non-chosen. In this way, even the rich are forced to work hard, even though there is no "material" necessity, yet owing to reasons of faith. The Calvinist is in a hopeless situation, he needs to work hard to take part in the "divine lottery" despite the fact that the tickets are regarded to have already been drawn. It is important to note that in Calvinism (and in Lutheranism as well) labour and earning are never directed towards the improvement of the individual situation (at least that is what was believed in). Even the owner of capital is just an administrator of the gifts of God and has to use these gifts to increase social welfare. At best he is entitled to withhold a certain part of the returns to cover his existence. (Troeltsch 1965, 720)

3. Conclusion and final remarks

Protestant work ethics contributes to the development of capitalism in two ways: 1. For the sake of its principles of an ascetic and thrifty lifestyle, work ethic is a powerful means to criticize and combat uninhibited consumption, wastefulness, extravagance and luxury because the purposeful striving for wealth and property is perceived as highly reprehensible. 2. Protestant work ethics justifies the striving for wealth as a sign of divine favour, unleashing individual forces. Wealth as the result of hard work is seen as a blessing of God. „That man, to whom God gave wealth and soul to use it well, he has received a special and excellent token of favour". With these words Werner Sombart (1923, 197) summarizes Benjamin Franklin, and gives a telling example of the influence of Protestant ethics on the emergence of capitalism. Both the abstinence and thriftiness of consumption and the release of the acquisitive activities of the individual lead to an accumulation of capital through ascetic compulsion to save. (Weber 1993, 146-147) Thus far a modern argument was given to explain the development of capitalism: high economic growth rates, caused by capital accumulation.

It cannot be concluded that the Reformation had ever intended to build a society which later was described by the terms "capitalist" and "conform to the market". Lutherans, Calvinists, Methodists and Pietists never strived for an increase of material goods and wealth as an end in itself. Rather, they wanted to enforce labour as ascetic duty of each Christian under consideration of the recollection of the Old and New Testament. (Conze 1972, 166) In this sense it cannot be stated, that the modern world was directly initiated and prepared by Protestantism. On the contrary, although Protestantism established and spread new thoughts, it resumed and strengthened the ideal of the ecclesiastical culture of compulsion, even fought the first shoots of a free and secular culture. Furthermore, Protestantism induced Catholicism to put life into its own ideas. (Troeltsch 1911, 44) Troeltsch called it the dilemma of Protestant asceticism that, on the one hand, labour and life were acknowledged in the world, but on the other hand, that they never were provided with an inner essential ethical value. (Troeltsch 1911, 69-70)

With reference to the behaviour of man and the development of modern economic theory one has to state unambiguously that the rules and standards, which are responsible for the degree of self-acceptance and contentment with the results and achievements of oneself and of others, have their origin in the contents and norms of labour ethics. Yet if these contents and norms are attributed to selfishness and opportunism, it is not surprising that attitudes, values and norms of labour are increasingly directed to acquisitive activities. At the same time, other sides of work are disregarded, for example the pleasure of every day work, the pleasure to work together with others, the possibility of self-realization, the endowment of life with labour etc. Economic theory has indeed not considered questions like these, but at least the disciplines of business ethics and an economic theory of ethics could draw attention to them.

The Reformation can convey an impressive image of the impact of norms and institutions. One can easily imagine the impact of institutions and ideologies especially on social and economic life. Of course, Dr. Martin Luther's ideology is Christian faith. Yet much more important is the fact that Luther's ideology put him in a position to move the proverbial mountains. Christian faith feeds his views of sustainable effectiveness and success with understanding and love; it makes the individual the centre of life by demanding people to focus on God and other people. Put in terms of modern economics this is called: "Maximization of individual utility through consideration of the interests of others" – the Nash equilibrium of a prisoners dilemma situation in a non recurrent game can be "solved" by repetition of the rounds of the game. Of course, Gustav v. Schmoller for example, has already expressed a similar fact of the matter more than a century ago; he spoke of the abandonment of short-run interests in favour of long-run interests.

In this paper I am not actually interested in Christian faith but in faith in general. My concerns are benevolence, hope, social interest and commitment, justice and decency. What could economic theory and policy gain if they integrated a view on the future in a way similar that Luther had a view on God?

Bibliography

Werner Conze, 1972. Art. Arbeit, in: Otto Brunner, Werner Conze und Reinhart Koselleck (eds.). Geschichtliche Grundbegriffe. Historisches Lexikon zur politisch-sozialen Sprache in Deutschland. Stuttgart: E. Klett, 154-215.

Meister Eckehart, 1969. Deutsche Predigten und Traktate, 3. eds., München: Hanser,.

Werner Elert, 1958. Morphologie des Luthertums, vol. 2 (2 vols..), repr. Ed. 1931. München: C.H. Beck.

Friedrich Hauck, 1950. Art. Arbeit. Reallexikon für Antike und Christentum, Stuttgart: Hiersemann, Vol. I, col. 585-590.

Martin Luther. Kritische Gesamtausgabe (Weimarer Ausgabe, WA), 65 Vols., Graz: Akademische Druck- und Verlagsanstalt (Weimar: H. Böhlau), 1964-1993.

Elisabeth Noelle-Neumann, 1978. Werden wir alle Proletarier? Wertewandel in unserer Gesellschaft, Zürich: Edition Interform/Osnabrück: Fromm-Verlag.

Eberhard Schmieder, 1959. Arbeitsethos. Eine Einführung in seine Geschichte. Schmollers Jahrbuch für Gesetzgebung, Verwaltung und Volkswirtschaft, 79. Jg., 3. Berlin: Duncker & Humblot, 43-81 (part I); and 79. Jg., 4, 45-78 (part II).

Shell Deutschland (Hg.), 2002: 14. Shell Jugenstudie, Ullstein.

Werner Sombart, 1923. Der Bourgeois. Zur Geistesgeschichte des modernen Wirtschaftsmenschen, 1. ed. 1913, München/Leipzig: Duncker & Humblot.

Burkhard Strümpel and Michael v. Klipstein, 1984. Der Überdruß am Überfluß. Die Deutschen nach dem Wirtschaftswunder, München /Wien: Olzog-Verlag.

Ernst Troeltsch 1911. Die Bedeutung des Protestantismus für die Entstehung der modernen Welt. München/Berlin: Oldenburg.

Ernst Troeltsch, 1965. Die Soziallehren der christlichen Kirchen und Gruppen. Aalen: Scientia.

Frans van der Ven, 1972. Sozialgeschichte der Arbeit, Vol. 2 (3 Vol.). München: dtv.

Klara Vontobel, 1946. Das Arbeitsethos des deutschen Protestantismus. Bern: Francke.

Max Weber, 1993. Die protestantische Ethik und der „Geist" des Kapitalismus, bas on ed. 1920, 1. ed. 1904/05, Bodenheim: Athenäum /Hain/Hanstein.

Konrad Wiedemann, 1979. Arbeit und Bürgertum. Eine Entwicklung des Arbeitsbegriffs in der Literatur Deutschlands an der Wende zur Neuzeit. Heidelberg: Winter.

Religious Conviction, Protestant Work Ethic, and Individual Economic Behaviour: *A Review of the Contributions by Reginald Hansen and Hans Frambach*

Enrico Schöbel

Abstract

Reginald Hansen's historical-institutional analysis of Christian conviction and economic behaviour, "Religiöse mentale Disposition und wirtschaftliches Verhalten in der geschichtlichen Entwicklung", and Hans Frambach's "Work and Ethics in Economic Thought during the Reformation" were presented at the 18th Heilbronn Symposion in Economics and the Social Sciences held in Heilbronn, Germany, in June 16-19, 2005 and are the topic of this review. In addition to critical comments of Hansen's essay and Frambach's chapter to this volume, it provides additional references, and sheds light on recent economic debates of the regulation of professions. In Luther's Protestant Work Ethic, the term "work" is not only a job in the sense of an occupation, but also a calling. This ambivalence poses a challenge to modern economists to take up this topic.

Introduction

Individual economic behaviour is determined by religious values and subjective consciousness. In this way, religion as a part of culture influences both, economic performance and economic development (Jong 2009, 109 ff.; Blum and Dudley 2001, 207 ff.).

Such a social economic, cultural economic and evolutionary economic analysis of religion is rooted in the tradition of Max Weber's sociological study of "The Protestant Ethic and the Spirit of Capitalism" (first published in 1904 and 1905) and Ernst Troeltsch's religious-historical study of Protestantism and the development of modern Western societies (Troeltsch 1906; 1911). Both classical writers in sociology describe the fundamental changes in Christian conviction due to the appearance of Martin Luther (1483-1546), Luther's Reformation during the first half of the 16th century, the appearance of Calvin (1509-1546), and Calvinism in Western Europe in the middle of the 16th century. Weber and Troeltsch demonstrate lasting effects of religion on economic behaviour and economic development and, by these means, they hypothesise that the Protestants pioneered economic development and industrialisation in particular. Max Weber considers religious foundations of law, and examines economic effects thereof. Due to his interpretations of law, economy, and society, he can be considered a classical writer in the discipline of Law and Economics (Peukert 1999).

The so called Weber-hypothesis was critically reviewed not only in economics and the social sciences (e.g. Samuelson 1993; Iannaccone 1998; Barbalet 2008). While some authors agree with Weber's thesis, others abandon it (e.g. Marshall 1982), and yet others argue to the contrary (for a summary see: Pollack 2007, 376 f.). Weber's study was several times corrected for historical detail (e.g. Schwaabe 2006; Lehmann 1996). Later authors enrich to the discussion, for example Becker and Woessmann (2009; 2010) who examine historical data of schools and school enrolment in Prussia and identify effects of Protestantism on education, which is relevant for the subsequent industrialization. The debate about the Weber thesis is continuing. In recent years a number of quantitative and qualitative empirical studies in Economics of Religion appeared, e.g. by Long and Shleifer (1993), and McCleary and Barro (2006), both surveyed by Jong (2008). In their study based on value surveys, McCleary and Barro (2006, 67) found that church attendance has a significant negative effect on economic growth, and that the religious variable "belief in heaven" is insignificant. Other empirical studies get different results.

However, such an analysis of beliefs and values can hardly describe Weber's approach of understanding and, to be more precise, his examination of cultural change, religious foundation of law, economic behaviour, and the economic development. This becomes a. o. obvious in several contributions to this volume, such as the chapter by Peukert (2010), Frambach (2010), and Ebner (2010). According to Peukert (1999, 515), Max Weber is "... one of the last universalists in the social sciences ...", who tried to integrate law, economy, politics, culture, and the later so called social system.

In this essay Reginald Hansen's historical-institutional analysis of Christian conviction and economic behaviour, "Religiöse mentale Disposition und wirtschaftliches Verhalten in der geschichtlichen Entwicklung", and Hans Frambach's "Work and Ethics in Economic Thought during the Reformation" are reviewed. The latter appears as a chapter in this volume. Hansen's long essay is published in: Backhaus, Jürgen G. (ed.), *Religion und Wirtschaft: Die Bedeutung der Reformation*, 2010. Both authors presented their essays at the 18th Heilbronn Symposion in Economics and the Social Sciences in Heilbronn, Germany, in June 16-19, 2005.

In addition to critical comments of Hansen's essay and Frambach's chapter, this review provides additional references, and sheds light on recent economic debates of the regulation of professions. In Luther's Protestant Work Ethic, the term "work" is not only a job in the sense of an occupation, but also a calling. This ambivalence poses a challenge to modern economists to take up this topic.

Hansen's Historical-Institutional Economic Analysis of Law and Religion

In his historical-institutional economic analysis of Christian conviction and economic behaviour Reginald Hansen re-examines the writings by Weber and Troeltsch. In addition, he refers to a much earlier work by Gustav Schmoller (1860) on the history of economic thought in Germany during the period of Reformation (recently reviewed by Fischer 2010, 210 ff.).

Following the three classical writings, Hansen finds the Western civil society deep-seated in Christian religious values and subjectivism. He examines Christian religious foundations of the law in case of the ancient Corpus Juris Canonici. Thereafter, he analyses economic implications of individual religious consciousness as a consequence of Martin Luther's Reformation and Calvinism. He also discusses Catholic values of social justice and finds the German Social Market Economy rooted in generally accepted values in Germany. Thereupon, he states that in Western societies of today such generally accepted religious values have gradually been replaced by divergent individual religious convictions. In his point of view the process of individualisation is anchored in Martin Luther's Reformation and its economic and social consequences. In view of the cultural and, more specifically, religious conditioning of economic development he critically asks what future will hold.

In his introduction, Hansen takes up the example of an international charitable donation to illustrate the religious foundation of economic thinking. Economic behaviour is determined by the particular religious convictions and other cultural differences. He states that Christian conviction can shape the economy, because individuals do not just believe in destiny or accept their fate. Thus, economic activities are encouraged. He does not give an exhaustive examination of the many opposing statements brought forward in the extensive literature on this issue.

In accordance with Max Weber and subsequent writers in Law, Economics, and the Social Sciences, Hansen addresses the question of why the industrial revolution and its economic and social consequences happened in Europe, the so called Western world, and not elsewhere. Although Weber criticized the Older and the Younger German Historical School (Peukert 1999, 515), Weber's as well as Hansen's analyses of regularity, recurrent patterns, and causality (but not mono-causality) in the economic history clearly stand in the tradition of Gustav Schmoller and the German Historical School. In his earlier publications, especially in his extensive dissertation thesis on the methodological dispute between Gustav Schmoller and Carl Menger and the consequences with regard to the German income taxation, which was introduced at the time (Hansen 1996), Hansen also contributes to the history of economic methodology, and to the Schmoller renaissance (Peukert 2001) in particular.

By referring to legal foundations, religious values, and the sciences, Hansen discusses in the essay under consideration the philosophical and sociological writings by Ernst Topitsch and Hans Albert on the issue of religion and political systems. In his point of view, religious conviction is the major determinant of an individual's economic behaviour. He does not discuss a substitution of values from one context to another, for example religious values might have been retained unchanged in the context of a family. This might hint at a continuation of existing values in a society, whereas Hansen comes to a rather sceptical assessment.

In his study of beliefs and values, Hansen contrasts the six world religions: Judaism, Christianity, Hinduism, Buddhism, Islam, and Taoism. Additional religions, religious groups, and ancient religions remain unconsidered. He refers to the works by Albert

Schweitzer, who in his study of Christianity and the world religions (published in 1924) analyses Hinduism, Buddhism, Taoism, and economic behaviour. Hansen misses current literature in the field of the Far Eastern religions and economic behaviour. His study of Islamic, Jewish, and Christian convictions and economic behaviour is based on recent literature. State, religion and particular legal institutions, such as Islamic Banking, are discussed with regard to economic outcomes.

Religious and Legal Foundations of the Economy: The Corpus Juris Canonici

Hansen indicates religious foundations of the law. Undoubtedly, the ancient Corpus Juris Canonici is originated in Christianity and in the tradition of the ancient Roman Corpus Juris Civilis. After a revision of the Corpus Juris Canonici in 1075 the pope was not only the head of the Catholic Church but also legislator, government, and judge in one person. Sections of contemporary European national law are traced back to the Corpus Juris Canonici. The search for legal foundation of capitalism is a substantial issue in Political Economy, Institutional Economics, and Law & Economics. The search for religious foundations of economic development is very close to that research question.

Hansen states that the ancient Corpus Juris Canonici conforms to individuals' religious requirements at the time. He mentions particular religious institutions, such as taking confession and grace of charity, which all pursued civil acceptance of the law. Consequently, he does conclude that Luther's Reformation and the Protestant Ethic were not the only possible responses to the economic development and individuals' religious requirements at the time. However, some authors, who oppose Max Weber's thesis, corroborate such a conclusion that cannot be rejected in general, but also does not refute the Weber-thesis altogether (Pollack 2007, 376 f.).

In fact, Hansen emphasizes that Weber himself rejects a monocausal interpretation of history.

Unlike other recent writings (Peukert 2010; Fischer 2010, 153), Hansen does not speak of Luther as being a modern economist. Luther addresses social and economic problems of his time. Nevertheless, his work is of current interest due to the ambivalence of work as a calling and work as an occupation. However, he is not a modern economist in terms of modern microeconomic or macroeconomic thinking.

Luther's Reformation, Calvin's Late Protestantism, and their Ideas of Professions as a Calling

Hansen marks similarities and also contrasts between Catholic conviction and Luther's Protestant Ethic. He demonstrates that Luther's Reformation was not only a reformation of religion, but a reformation of the whole intellectual life, law, and individuals' mentality. Luther's Reformation encouraged a secularization of the law. Individual consciousness became gradually more important. The flow of ideas during the Reformation put forth a new religious disposition, by which Hansen means the Protestants' reformed Christian conviction.

While he discusses economic behaviour, Hansen mentions the principle of prohibition of usury, which was supported by Martin Luther, although prohibition of usury could weaken economic development. In fact, it was ingeniously avoided more and more often. Besides, Hansen mentions Luther's and later Veit Ludwig von Seckendorff's idea of profession as a calling (see also: Schöbel 2005). Luther and von Seckendorff (Frambach 2010) perceive any kind of economic activity as a calling. Career entry is perceived as an "ordination" to the profession.

When profession is perceived as a calling, the regulation of professions is an issue of current interest. For example, in Germany some professional groups such as notaries public, tax intermediaries, attorneys, land surveyors, etc., have self-regulated the market for their services, while in other countries these services are unregulated. For these reasons, the OECD has taken an initiative for an OECD-wide regulation, which would unhinge the existing self-regulations, a step back for those countries, where the self-regulation with its policing institutions has a functioning tradition. In case of tax advice and tax return preparation, the degrees of liability are the defining characteristics between the different arrangements (Schöbel 2010, 502 f.).

When Hansen compares Martin Luther's and Johannes Calvin's ideas of Protestantism, he finds broad agreement in general, but differences in detail. Luther's and Calvin's ideas differ with respect to the economic consequences of their lasting impact. Calvin from Geneva argues for a right of succession. He advocates capital accumulation and income from investment of capital, and he disapproves of non-productive use of capital. Capital accumulation and investment are seen to be agreeable to God. In Geneva, the legal rule of prohibition of interest was repealed, but usury was, of course, outlawed. Sumptuary law was established, e.g. regulations of dresses and embellishments.

Calvin also argues in favor of Luther's idea of profession as a calling, and in addition, supports professional success. In this context *ora et labora* have become religious values. Individuals are asked to work and to pray to God. Thus, working, i.e. diligent work, has become a social value of its own. As Hansen points out, the piety postulates require industrial efficiency and diligence, which are both relevant for the subsequent economic development in general, and not only for the future success of the Geneva watch industry.

Catholic Social Values and the German Social Market Economy

Finally, Hansen takes a look at the ideas of the so called Katholische Soziallehre. He finds the German Social Market Economy to be anchored in generally accepted Catholic values of social justice, explicitly put down in the two encyclicals Rerum Novarum (published in 1891) and Quadragesimo Anno (published in 1931).

Hansen mentions the four general principles: personality, solidarity, subsidiarity, and private property. Both encyclicals address the Social Question, which was asked in view of the consequences of the industrialization and having the emergence of different individual religious consciousness in mind. Hansen finds the individualisation to be rooted in Luther's Reformation. The Social Question was raised by social economists such as Adolf Wagner and Gustav Schmoller, and discussed in the Verein für Socialpolitik, which was founded in 1872. In response to the social problems of the middle of the 19th century, members of the Verein für Socialpolitik suggested specific institutional settings instead of a mono-causal interpretation of history as Karl Marx did, for example. Their normative principles and institutional economic proposals and suggestions were gradually adopted by the Catholic Church. The medieval Christian societal construct of the Corpus Christianum was replaced step by step by the concept of the Katholische Soziallehre and its Catholic values of social justice.

After 1948, the normative principles of the Katholische Soziallehre provided the basis for the German Social Market Economy. Hansen describes the religious foundation as to be rooted in the institutional economic writings of the members of the Verein für Socialpolitik. The religious foundation ensured general civil acceptance of the Social Market Economy, a market based economy, which is corrected by the implementation of social institutions designed in accordance to Catholic values of social justice. In view of the religious conditioning of economic development, Hansen has doubts about the sustainability of the Social Market Economy. He misses the mental disposition, which is necessary according to his point of view. Therefore, he suggests a revitalisation of the normative principles of the Katholische Soziallehre, in particular of the general principles of personality, solidarity, and subsidiarity.

Frambach on Protestant Work Ethic and Luther's Idea of Profession as a Calling

In his chapter "Work and Ethics in the Economic Thought during the Reformation", Hans Frambach describes the fundamental changes of work ethic during the Reformation. He states in his thorough re-examination of the protestant work ethic that Luther's writings and the Reformation have brought forth an economic view which is different from the former prevailing Christian conviction.

Frambach refers to the Old Testament, when he outlines that God allowed individuals to work. Luther's interpretation of work was different. In Luther's Protestant ethic, work is not only a kind of divine command but rather a calling. Luther denotes work a duty to God and, thereby, declines the prevailing Christian doctrine of work as being a punishment. There is another peculiarity: Luther does not separate between religious work and physical work. As already mentioned above, he perceives any kind of economic activity as a profession. He criticizes the dominance of ascetic exercises, selling indulgences, and other religious institutions as parasitizing the society.

When Frambach sketches Luther's religious idea of profession, he refers to Max Weber's writings on the issue of profession, where work is associated not with an accidental job, but with a calling. Hansen mentioned the term "ordination", which as a consequence of the Reformation has become relevant for any kind of work. Like Hansen and others, Frambach points out that work has become a value of its own. He also re-examines Weber's and Troeltsch's writings, but does not thoroughly review the long essay by Schmoller (1860) on the history of economic thought in Germany during the period of the Reformation.

Frambach concludes that the Protestant work ethic has influenced economic development because its normative principles became socially accepted, and furthermore, Protestantism allowed for capital accumulation beyond the fulfilment of basic needs.

Martin Luther and Protestant Ethic: a Challenge to Modern Economists?

The theologian Martin Luther (1483-1546) was driven by the political, social and economic circumstances at the time, for example, the shortage of money due to the nobility's demand for expensive spices imported from foreign countries. As mentioned above, Luther was not a "modern economist" as has been suggested by, e.g., Peukert (2010) and Fischer (2010). Neither does he apply modern economic theorising, such as foreign trade theories, nor does he anticipate technical progress and technological change, which shape the later economic development of industrialisation, but nevertheless does he draw attention to economic problems of current interest such as the regulation of professions.

Accidentially, he was much more recognized than other critical writers, such as for instance Johann Rucherath von Wesel (1425-1481), who has criticized indulgences and other religious institutions in his "Disputatio Adversus Indulgentias" and subsequent critical writings half a century before Luther.

Luther's concept of work is very different from the definition of work in modern labour economics. He means farming, hunting, mining (his father was a miner), and trade. The latter distinguishes his concept from a physiocratic perspective. Nevertheless, Schmoller (1860, 471) states that Luther's definition of "work" is very close to that of the Physiocrats.

From Luther's point of view, work not only means an occupation, but also profession as a calling. Occupation stands for the opposite of idleness and is a duty to God. Diligent work is honoured by God. He does not mean effort in terms of modern microeconomic labour market theories. Individuals do not work for economic reasons but due to God's mercy (Schmoller 1860, 478). Because of diligence in his work, a person is given God's blessing.

Luther does not mean labour as a production factor in a production function. Different from economic production theories, he does not describe an input-output-relation. In Luther's opinion, work is in the interest of keeping individuals healthy. He does not think of profits which might result from labour. From his organic view of the economy, economic profits could only come from a division of labour. Also, there are no opportunity costs, and he does not discuss economic problems that stem from a separation between labour supply and labour demand, which happened later as a result of the industrialization.

According to Luther's Protestantism, individual and family economic activities are based on the duty to God. The quality of land, house-building, and farm products are due to God's mercy. Individual work is based on the ethical conviction, to be more precise, the reformed Christian conviction. However, in Luther's writings, work is not only an occupation but also a profession like a calling. Max Weber's writings on professions are influenced by Luther's Protestant work ethic. He distinguishes ethical thinking that considers responsibility with regard to the consequences (Verantwortungsethik) from an ethical thinking as a matter of course, and not in terms of a result (Gesinnungsethik) (Weber 1919, 237 ff.; Schöbel 2003, 52 f.; 2008, 126 ff.).

Especially the ambivalence of the term "work" in Luther's Protestant work ethic as both, an occupation and profession as a calling, encourages modern economists to deal with the classical topic of the so called Weber (but also Sombart) Hypothesis.

References

Barbalet, Jack M. (1998), Weber, Passion and Profits: "The Protestant Ethic and the Sprit of Capitalism" in Context, New York: Cambridge University Press.

Becker, Sascha O.; Woessmann, Ludger (2009), Was Weber Wrong? A Human Capital Theory of Protestant Economic History, in: Quarterly Journal of Economics 124, 531-596.

Becker, Sascha O.; Woessmann, Ludger (2010), The Effect of Protestantism on Education before the Industrialization: Evidence from 1816 Prussia, in: Economics Letters 107, 224–228.

Blum, Ulrich; Dudley, Leonard (2001), Religion and Economic Growth: Was Weber Right?, in: Journal of Evolutionary Economics 11, 207-230.

Fischer, Joachim (2010), Luther in der Wirtschaftswissenschaft des 19. Jahrhunderts: Auswirkungen auf moderne Wirtschaftsethik, Berlin, Münster: LIT-Verlag.

Frambach, Hans (2010), Work and Ethics in Economic Thought during the Reformation, in: Backhaus Jürgen G. (ed.), The Reformation as a Pre-Condition of Reformation, Berlin, Münster: LIT-Verlag.

Hansen, Reginald (1996), Die praktischen Konsequenzen des Methodenstreits: Eine Aufarbeitung der Einkommensbesteuerung, Berlin: Duncker & Humblot.

Hansen, Reginald (2010), Religiöse mentale Disposition und wirtschaftliches Verhalten in der geschichtlichen Entwicklung, in: Backhaus, Jürgen G. (ed.), Religion und Wirtschaft: Die Bedeutung der Reformation, Berlin, Münster: LIT-Verlag.

Iannaccone, Laurence R. (1998), Introduction to the Economics of Religion, in: Journal of Economic Literature 36, 1465-1495.

Jong, Eelke de (2008), Religious Values and Economic Growth: A Review and Assessment of Recent Studies, Nijmegen Center for Economics (NiCE) Working Paper 08-111, Nijmegen, November 2008.

Jong, Eelke de (2009), Culture and Economics: On Values, Economics and International Business, London: Routledge.

Lehmann, Hartmut (1996), Max Webers „Protestantische Ethik“: Beiträge aus der Sicht eines Historikers, Göttingen: Vandenhoeck & Ruprecht.

Long, James Bradford de; Shleifer, Andrei (1993), Princes and Merchants: European City Growth before the Industrial Revolution, in: Journal of Law and Economics 36, 671-702.

Marshall, Gordon (1982), In Search of the Spirit of Capitalism: An Essay on Max Weber's Protestant Ethic Thesis, New York: Columbia University Press.

McCleary, Rachel M.; Barro, Robert J. (2006), Religion and Economy, in: Journal of Economic Perspectives 20, 49-72.

Peukert, Helge (1999), Max Weber (1864-1920), in: Backhaus, Jürgen G. (ed.), The Elgar Companion to Law and Economics, Cheltenham, Northampton: Edward Elgar, 515-526.

Peukert, Helge (2001), The Schmoller Renaissance, in: History of Political Economy 33, 71-116.

Peukert, Helge (2010), Martin Luther: A Modern Economist, in: Backhaus, Jürgen G. (ed.), The Reformation as a Pre-Condition of Reformation, Berlin, Münster: LIT-Verlag.

Pollack, Detlef (2007), Religion, in: Joas, Hans (ed.), Lehrbuch der Soziologie, 3rd ed., Frankfurt am Main, New York: Campus Verlag, 363-393.

Samuelson, Kurt (1993), Religion and Economic Action: The Protestant Ethic, the Rise of Capitalism, and the Abuses of Scholarship, Toronto: University of Toronto Press.

Schmoller, Gustav (1860), Zur Geschichte der national-ökonomischen Ansichten in Deutschland während der Reformations-Periode, in: Zeitschrift für die gesamte Staatswissenschaft 16, 461-716.

Schöbel, Enrico (2003), Otto Veit (1898-1984) as a Fiscal Sociologist and his Fiscal Sociological Approach of Studying Tax Morality, in: European Journal of Management and Public Policy 2, 43-66.

Schöbel, Enrico (2005), Benevolent Governance and Fiscal Federalism in Veit Ludwig von Seckendorff's Teutscher Fürsten Stat (1656): Comment on Erik S. Reinert, in: European Journal of Law and Economics 19, 231-233.

Schöbel, Enrico (2008), Steuerehrlichkeit: Eine politisch-ökonomische und zugleich finanzsoziologische Analyse der Einkommensteuerrechtsanwendung und -befolgung in Deutschland, Frankfurter Abhandlungen zu den gesamten Staatswissenschaften 8, Frankfurt am Main: Haag + Herchen.

Schöbel, Enrico (2010), Self-Regulated Markets for Professional Legal Services: The Case of Tax Intermediaries, in: Journal of Economic Issues 44, 497-504.

Schwaabe, Christian (2006), Die Protestantische Ethik und der „Geist" des Kapitalismus, in: Herz, Dietmar; Weinberger, Veronika (eds.), Lexikon ökonomischer Werke, Stuttgart: Schäffer-Poeschel, 552.

Troeltsch, Ernst (1906), Die Bedeutung des Protestantismus für die Entstehung der modernen Welt, Vortrag gehalten auf der IX. Versammlung deutscher Historiker zu Stuttgart am 21. April 1906, Sonderabdruck aus der Historischen Zeitschrift, München: Oldenbourg.

Troeltsch, Ernst (1911), Die Bedeutung des Protestantismus für die Entstehung der modernen Welt, Historische Bibliothek 24, München: Oldenbourg.

Weber, Max (1904/1905), Die Protestantische Ethik und der Geist des Kapitalismus, in: Archiv für Sozialwissenschaft und Sozialpolitik 20/21, Tübingen: Mohr (First English Translation: Weber, Max (1930), The Protestant Ethic and the Spirit of Capitalism, translated by Talcott Parsons, London: Allen & Unwin).

Weber, Max (1919), Politik als Beruf, in: Baier, Horst et al. (eds.) (1992), Max Weber Gesamtausgabe, Abt. 1, Reden und Schriften, Vol. 17, Wissenschaft als Beruf: 1917/1919[u.a.], ed. by Mommsen, Wolfgang J.; Schluchter, Wolfgang, Tübingen: J.C.B. Mohr (Paul Siebeck), 157-252.

The Reformation in Eugen Dühring's Perspectives

E. James Gay

Abstract

This paper deals with the thought of the today little known German philosopher and political economist Eugen Dühring as it relates to the Reformation. Following a summary of Dühring's biography and philosophy it analyses Dühring's philosophy of history to provide a background for his view of the Reformation. It is argued that Dühring's position on natural law has a certain correspondence to the individualistic tenets of Luther's theology; both men advocate the autonomy of the individual and have a common opposition to theocracy. A closer examination reveals that Dühring's faith in the faculty of reason and his general advocacy of rationalism are in conflict with Luther's faith in God and belief in revelation. Moreover, Dühring's opposition to the strong German state of his day would seem to put him in opposition to what was at least in part as legacy of the Reformation. It is concluded that Dühring's advocacy of natural law put him at odds with the historically orientated German thought of his day making him essentially "an outsider from within". Finally it is stated that research on Dühring's life and thought is likely to provide understanding of what has separated Germany from Western Europe.

I Introduction

The relevance of ancient thought for the development of Christianity has long been the subject of scholarly inquiry. Since the Enlightenment there has been a tendency, most strongly emphasized by Lessing, to place the bible in a series alongside other works in the development of western thought. Even scholars who have rightfully rejected such a historically relativistic approach to understanding religion have emphasized non-Christian elements in Christian ideas. At the beginning of the 20th century Ernst Troeltsch showed how the Stoics' teachings on inherent moral principles influenced the Christian concept of natural law.[1]

If we draw a connection between pre-Christian thought and Christianity, then it should be permitted to move a step forward as it were and ask about Christianity's influence on modern atheistic thought. The philosophers of the Enlightenment were highly critical of religion, but never fully lost their religious views.[2] As Fritz Mauthner has pointed out in his history of atheism, the first passionately atheist philosopher in Germany was Arthur Schopenhauer.[3] A generation later the author of the "Die Welt als Wille und Vorstellung" was followed by a more radical disciple, Friedrich Nietzsche, who made the provocative statement "God is dead". Located in between Schopenhauer and Nietzsche – and in a way a serving as a direct bridge between the two – is the subject of my lecture today Eugen Karl Dühring (1833-1921).[4]

Dühring's philosophy was not only atheistic; it was radically opposed to religion in general. Influenced by August Comte's positivistic philosophy of history, Dühring saw religious tradition as belonging to an immature phase of human history which was soon to be rendered irrelevant by the development of reason and the progress of science. The Reformation is not dealt with in any of his philosophical or political economic works, but the question can be asked as to whether there is a connection between Dühring's

---

1 Troeltsch in: Gierke (1934, p.206) and Köhler (1941, p.11).

2 Cf. Becker (1932).

3 Mauthner (1923).

4 The Nietzsche papers have shown just how strong Dühring's influence on him was. Cf. Venturelli (1986, p.110).

thought and the cultural, religious, political and economical movement begun by Martin Luther in 1517. Dühring's later polemics against Jewry, Christianity and religion in general interest us far less than the question of whether there is an "ideal correspondence" between the core of his philosophy and the historical movement known as the Protestant Reformation.[5]

First I will speak briefly about Dühring's academic career and his philosophy. Then, I will deal with his philosophy of history to provide a background for his perspective on the Reformation. Finally, I will deal with attempt to draw parallels between Dühring's thought and the Reformation while trying to determine its relationship to the main current of modern German thought at the time.

Before I begin allow me to say a few words with regard to the methodology of using a seemingly obscure intellectual figure such as Dühring to gain insight into German history. A scholarly understanding of German history and of the country's position in the modern world should not be attained exclusively with reference to "conventional history" (whose value is of course great), but also through the phenomenology of significant German thinkers of the past in terms of their ideas and their self-understanding. The Heilbronn Symposium, whose mission involves the unearthing of writings of German social scientists for the non-German speaking international scientific community, is an important international forum to discuss and critically analyze German thinkers such as Dühring.

---

[5] In the second half of his career after he had lost his position at the Berlin University, Dühring turned away from objective scientific research and moved more towards polemical freelance activism. In 1880 he published the virulently anti-Semitic work Die Judenfrage als Racen- Sitten- und Culturfrage and one year later *Der Ersatz der Religion durch Vollkommeneres.*

II Life and Philosophy

Eugen Dühring was born in Berlin in 1833. His ancestors came from Sweden a fact of which he was proud.[6] His father had read Rousseau and brought his son up in an atmosphere of free religious thought. This education fostered independence and steadfastness of thought in the young Dühring. He became interested in astronomy and mathematics at an early age and following the death of his father entered one of Prussia's leading gymnasiums as a boarding student. Afterwards he studied law and practiced for some time before an eye ailment, which would later end in complete blindness, would end his legal career. Dühring opted for a career as an academic and writer on scientific subjects. First his wife and later his son acted as his secretary. Dühring attained great notoriety as a lecturer at the Friedrich-Wilhelms Universität in Berlin, his lectures being among the best attended in the 1870s. After being overlooked to become a tenured professor he became disgruntled and his strong polemics against his colleagues lead to his dismissal in 1877. After this time Dühring continued to publish books and became the editor of the magazines *Moderne Völkergeist* and later *Personalist und Emanzipator*.

Dühring's thought incorporates two of the strongest currents of the 19th century: positivism and criticism, but can perhaps best be summed up as a form of idealistic materialism. Philosophy is defined by him as the evolution of the highest form of consciousness of life and the world and is inherently connected with scientific progress. More pointedly than Kant and Schopenhauer he asserts that the *law of sufficient reason* is a law of human thought and not a law of reality. Dühring postulated a *principle of insufficient ground* which placed the burden of proof with anyone bringing forth a new statement; that which is given must be considered as

---

[6] For his own account of his youth cf. Dühring (1882, p.1).

established.[7] Philosophy according to Dühring should aim at a comprehensive account of reality, an account that is consonant with the theories of natural science. A complete knowledge of reality is possible if we restrict ourselves to what is given, utilizing "rational imagination", which he sees as the human organ for philosophizing. The outcome of this activity guided by knowledge (Wissen) and will power (Wollen) is a comprehensive view of the world.

The fundamental law that we are to use in apprehending reality is the law of the determinate number. This law provides an easy solution to the autonomies in which reason finds itself when seeking information not taken from experience. It states that all thinkable numbers are determined or complete and that the notion of an infinite or undetermined number is therefore impossible. The history of the universe has an absolute beginning. A primordial being lies beyond the first event in time, though this can only be defined by negating the events in time. [8] This "being" contains the roots of every event and every object although it – paradoxically - does not consist of events and is not an object. History develops out of this primordial being through an evolutionary process from the more homogenous to the more diverse.

Dühring was also one of the early German thinkers to follow Schopenhauer and to further develop the question of a philosophy of life (Lebensphilosophie). The terms "pessimism" and "optimism" became catchwords that demonstrated a new need to explain life which had become ever more complicated since the Industrial Revolution. Dühring asked the question: where do our assessments of life come from? In his book *Der Werth des Lebens* he examines emotions such as love, honour, hate and revenge to understand the basis of how we perceive things. Dühring came to take an optimis-

---

[7] Dühring (1865, p.88).

[8] Dühring (1875, p.16f).

tic view of the world and scorned the metaphysical pessimism of Schopenhauer. Pessimism has, however, played a necessary role in history.

III Dühring's View of History

Although Dühring was a product of the German sciences of the state (Staatswissenschaften), according to his biography he was against the strong emphasis, or as he saw it, over-emphasis, of history in German education from his early days at the university onwards. The sympathy for a moral or natural legal perspective which he developed during his study of law in Berlin put him at odds with the majority of German scholars of his day and gave him a stronger orientation towards Western European and American thought.[9] He condemned the German propensity for "false or pseudo-historicism", which he believed to have strong political and theological biases.[10]

True historical science according to Dühring should concentrate on the "forces of nature" from which historical facts are created. Influenced by the natural science of the 17th century he wrote that history should resemble mechanics. Years before Nietzsche's famous work on the "use and abuse of history for life", Dühring warned against a false relativism that gives value to certain events "only for a given time". General considerations that exist above any given conjuncture should be emphasized. Significant events are the result of forces that appear again and again. Dühring also warned against

---

9 Dühring's mentor in the field of social science was the American Henry C. Carey who in appreciation of the work Dühring had done at publisizing his writings left Dühring a sizable inheritance when he died in 1879. Ernst Troeltsch's ideas on how Western European and German though diverged from one another were presented in his lecture "The Idea of Natural Law and Humanity in World Politics". In: Gierke (1950, pp.201-221).

10 On Dühring's views on historicism cf. Wittkau (1994, pp.40).

scholasticism that becomes alienated from the world and has no practical value for life. True historicism should not shy away from making judgments.

History consists for Dühring of laws of change which shape the state, society and peoples. Every political construction is finite and will be replaced by others. There is a certain "antagonism of forces" that guarantee change and diversity. Death is a necessary component of history and destruction is one of its essential elements.

The two thinkers who shaped Dühring's view of history most were August Comte and Henry Thomas Buckle. Comte's well-know three stage development of history (from the theological to the metaphysical to the positive or scientific stage) was condensed by Dühring into two phases one before and one after the French Revolution.[11] Henry Thomas Buckle attempted to apply the natural sciences to history in order to show the laws of cultural progress their role in the development of civilization. Instead of concentrating on princes, kings, battles and wars, Buckle emphasized less noticeable developments such as climate, nutrition and soil as decisive elements in history.[12]

Dühring's historical thought also contained a strong element of individualism. The history of ideas is shaped by great men who paved the way for intellectual progress and freedom. Such men were however to be seen as products of their times and a "cult of heroes" as Thomas Carlyle had espoused should be avoided. Dühring had a strong liking for the intellectual outsiders who fought for unpopular ideals; in fact he went as far as to say that the great minds of noble character who stood for righteousness were inevitably at odds with their contemporaries (as Dühring was him-

---

[11] Dühring (1875, p.301).

[12] Cf. Fuchs (1992).

self of course) and often persecuted. A natural feeling for justice, a heroic spirit (Gesinnung) is passed down through history pitting those who possessed it against the powerful suppressors who exist in the present. As will be shown, from a purely political perspective it seems plausible that Dühring could have had an affinity for the movement of the Reformation which originally developed from the principle of individual belief as opposed to traditional rules lay down by a centralized church.

IV Dühring and Protestantism

As mentioned in the introduction, the fact that Dühring was an avowed atheist and opponent of religion will not hinder us from searching for traces of religious thought in his thinking. As just mentioned, Dühring's world view is rooted in the general principles of scientific progress, freedom and justice. These values were not glib slogans – as they are for so many politicians today - but rather elements belonging to the core of a Weltanschauung which was based on the belief in the steadfast power of the intellect. Unlike Schopenhauer and later Sigmund Freud who both championed irrational factors of the mind, Dühring had an unwavering belief in the rational faculties of the human intellect to better society and mankind in general. As Hani Binder pointed out, this inclination of Dühring's was inevitably to lead him to the concept of natural law (Naturrecht), which was in the process of being swept away in by the current of German historicism.[13]

Natural law is an extremely broad field and it would go well beyond the framework of this lecture to discuss the phenomenon in detail. However, a common denominator in the various theories which apply to Dühring can be given: the belief that every person

---

[13] Binder (1933, p.42). On the opposition to natural law in Germany cf. Troeltsch, in: Gierke (1934, p.202).

has certain inherent rights that are given to all men and women as a human beings. Nature or universal reason has granted humanity a law from which the norms of all human law must be derived. As John Locke formulated it, man as a rational being with a certain rational propensity to enter society has duties towards all other men, the law of nature not permitting that men are divided into hostile societies; as driven by inner instinct to preserve himself, he has duties towards himself.[14] For proponents of natural law individual freedom must be unrestrictedly supported as justice requires so. Truth that is brought forth by reason is not allowed to be valid for only some people but must be realized for all human beings according to the principle of nature. If the individual is granted these inalienable rights by nature then he or she is not allowed to be put under the force of a community or a state should if human rights violations are to be avoided.

Binder correctly pointed out that Dühring's Weltanschauung is based in natural law. His thoughts on individual sovereignty and his emphasis on the individual's rights as related to the community resonated with the natural philosophers of the 17th and 18th centuries.[15] The postulate of freedom which stems from a rule of justice which is the same for all human beings was seen as the basic principle for all thought and action, for all institutions and measures and was rooted in the philosophy of natural law.[16]

From the premise of natural law Dühring developed a moral and political philosophy which aimed at reforming society by abolishing forced rule. His system of philosophy was laid down in his

---

[14] Locke (1954,pp.110).

[15] Cf. Binder(1933, p.44).

[16] Dühring was critical of some natural law theories of his day, but remained anchored in an individualistic perspective of natural law himself. For him the principle of revenge became the basis of all penal law. Cf. Dühring (1882, p.282).

textbook on philosophy from 1875 (Cursus der Philosophie). Here he advocated the creation of a free society (Freie Gesellschaft) which was to be implemented through a type of socialism which he termed societarianism. As the sovereignty of the individual is supreme any violation against it must be revoked. With the authority of natural right in mind Dühring wished to abolish the dichotomy of domination and servitude by creating a society where people were not forced into actions against their will. The idea of emancipation became a pillar of his philosophy.

The most salient historical event which influenced Dühring's brand of thinking was the French Revolution which Dühring glorified to the point of making it the turning point of human history as mentioned earlier. However, from a political perspective there are parallels to the Reformation as well. Luther's justification of salvation through faith did not merely advocate passivity, but rather was a calling for the subjective activism of the personality. In the *Babylonian Captivity of the Church* he wrote: "Every individual is by himself, his faith is required."[17] This emphasis on the spontaneous personality and its freedom, as proclaimed by Luther, was a main attribute of the Reformation and was mirrored in Dühring's "societarian" views. Whereas the pious Luther wished to free Christianity from the theocratic rule of the church in Rome, the atheist Dühring wished to emancipate man from any and all forceful subjugation found in society. For Dühring the suppressive powers included not only the tyrannical power of the force state (Gewaltstaat), but also religion itself.

With regard to the Dühring's views on religion we must again make reference to Dühring's philosophy of history and the influence of the Englishman Henry Thomas Buckle. As mentioned earlier, Buckle believed that the forces of nature shaped history; he

---

[17] „Da steht jeder Einzelne für sich allein, sein Glaube wird verlangt." Luther (1933, p.414).

was of the opinion that religion was the result of environmental conditions, i.e. that the differing natural conditions of the earth brought forth the various religions. Buckle believed that the non-European peoples had in their development been exposed to harsh natural conditions which gave them a propensity imagination at the expense of reason and understanding. The great religions therefore originated in and evolved from Asia and not from Europe.[18] Influenced by Buckle, Dühring was convinced that superstitious and harmful religious ideas came from Asia having been imported by the Jews to Europe; through the influence of Christianity the minds of the Europeans had become as it were enslaved by backward religious doctrine.[19]

Although Dühring is explicitly critical of Protestantism accusing it of directly translating Hebrew documents in a way which clashes with the essence of modernity, there are parallels between his and Luther's views of theocracy. Dühring warned of a theocracy - in its purest form as embodied in the Jewish religion of the Old Testament – which perpetuated superstition and threatened individual freedom and cultural progress. The main thrust of Luther's teachings was towards attaining moral independence and a faith which was not based solely on written law. Where the pious Christian Luther wished to preserve the purity of, as he saw it, true Christianity, the atheist Dühring wished to preserve the purity of science (which he believed also contained a moral calling) and society as a whole. Both men were weary of forces which would hinder the sovereign individual from acting freely. For Dühring this danger was rooted primarily in Judaism and for him Jews epitomized mentality of servitude (Knechtsinn), originally through their servility to their vengeful god, later to the strict regulation of the rabbis and finally

---

[18] Cf. Fuchs (1994, pp.128).

[19] Dühring (1875, pp.316).

through their blind service to the ruling politics of the modern world.[20]

Despite the apparent similarity between Luther and Dühring with regard to individual sovereignty it would be a mistake to assume a deeper affinity between the two. In fact it should be emphasized that their views of the world appear almost diametrically opposed. Luther's belief in revelation caused him to become in many ways anti-rational and for the Protestant theologian Ernst Troeltsch Luther signified a step back into the Middle Ages.[21] As already shown, Dühring looked primarily to the future and was opposed to any form of mysticism valuing the sober intellect above all else.

Although Luther had professed the value of salvation by faith alone (sola fide), the Reformation held steadfast to the institution of the church and in Germany became incorporated into the state.[22] This tended to create a culture of compulsion the idea of which was strongly combated by the emancipating tenets of Dühring's philosophy. According to Troeltsch, the Reformation in Germany which resulted in an institutionalization of the church within the state resulted in a separation of state and Christian morals. Politics and morality were thus divided with the development of administrative ethics and personal ethics. The war policies of Bismarck were, according to Troeltsch, made possible by the historical principles of Lutheranism.[23]

---

[20] Ebenda (1875, p.392) Dühring along with Wilhelm Marr was one of the first Germans to oppose not only religious Jews, but also to secular Jews. It is well known that Martin Luther became strongly opposed to the Jews later in his life as well.

[21] Köhler(1941, p.241).

[22] Ibid,, pp.277).

[23] Ibid.

Although Dühring was a graduate of the German institution of the sciences of the state (Staatswissenschaften) and had even written a tract on social policy for Bismarck, he condemned the German state as being tyrannical and disliked Bismarck's war policies. As touched upon earlier, Dühring was also in opposition to the intellectual climate of the German elite which was based more on the ideas of the romantic Counter-Revolution than the French Revolution which Dühring revered.[24] Insofar as the German thought of his day was the result of the Reformation, we would have to see Dühring world view as being opposed to the Reformation.

V Conclusion

We have dealt with the life and philosophy of the German philosopher and political economist Eugen Karl Dühring as it relates to the Reformation. The result of our analysis is the thesis that despite his individualism, his theories for emancipation and his advocacy of a society free from compulsion - which would seem to put him in line with the Reformation at least politically - the Reformation would have to be viewed primarily negatively from the perspective of Dühring's thought and philosophy. As a positivist and atheist Dühring placed little value on the the Reformation as a historical event. However, his views on natural law put him in line with the Christian tradition of social philosophy which the Reformation had been influenced by. Dühring was very much at odds with the dominant intellectual climate in his country which had been shaped substantially by the Reformation. His ultra-rationalistic convictions as well as his optimistic belief in humanity and progress divided him from the general German intellectual tradition of his time and place him closer to the Western European of thought than to the German thought of his day.

[24] Gierke, (1951, p.203).

Finally, as we hold the belief that it is not merely economics but primarily thought and ideas which should mould and shape the structure of society, it should be emphasized that focusing on the intellectual phenomena of significant thinkers of the past is methodologically sound. As a social scientist at odds with his own national heritage, as an "outsider from within" as it were, we believe the research of a German like Dühring can provide valuable insight into the "dilemma of German history" which seems no closer to being resolved than it was at the time of historians' dispute (Historikerstreit) in 1986. The separation of Germany and from Western Europe first seen following the French Revolution and then dramatized through two world wars in the 20th century coincided with Europe losing its world hegemony and for this reason alone it is important to ask what divides Germany from Europe.

References

Becker, C. (1935), The Heavenly City of the Eighteenth Century Philosophers, Yale University Press, New Haven.

Binder, H. (1933), Das sozialitäre System Eugen Dührings, Gustav Fischer, Jena.

Dühring, E. (1865), Cursus der Philosophie als streng wissenschaftlicher Weltanschauung und Lebensgestaltung. Erich Koschny, Leipzig.

Dühring, E. (1882), Sache, Leben und Feinde. Als Hauptwerk und Schlüssel zu seinen sämtlichen Schriften, H. Reuter, Karlsruhe und Leipzig.

Fuchs, E. (1994), Henry Thomas Buckle, Geschichtsschreibung und Positivismus in England und Deutschland, Leipziger Universitätsverlag.

Köhler, W. (1941), Ernst Troeltsch, J.C.B. Mohr (Paul Siebeck), Tübingen.

Locke, J. (1954), Essays on the Law of Nature, Clarendon Press, Oxford (1676).

Luther, M. (1933), Von der babylonischen Gefangenschaft der Kirche, Kaiser, München.

Mauthner, F. (1923), Der Atheismus und seine Geschichte im Abendlande, Bd.4, Stuttgart und Berlin.

Troeltsch, E., The Ideas of Natural Law and Humanity in World Politics, in: Gierke, O. (1934), Cambrigde University Press.

Venturelli, A., (1986),"Asketismus und Wille zur Macht. Nietzsche's Auseinandersetzung mit Eugen Dühring, in: Nietzsche Studien, Bd. 15.

Wittkau, A.(1994), Historismus, Zur Geschichte des Begriffs und des Problems, Vandenhoeck & Ruprecht, Göttingen.

Division of Labour and Rent Seeking in Moral Enforcement: The Case of Confession**

*Benito Arruñada**

Abstract

Moral codes are produced and enforced by more or less specialized means and are subject to standard economic forces. This paper argues that the intermediary role played by the Catholic Church between God and Christians, a key difference from Protestantism, faces the standard trade-off of specialization benefits and agency costs. It applies this trade-off hypothesis to confession of sins to priests, an institution that epitomizes such intermediation, showing that this hypothesis fits cognitive, historical and econometric evidence better than a simpler rent-seeking story. In particular, Catho-

---

** The author acknowledges the help of Manuel F. Bagüés and the comments received from Douglas W. Allen, Robert J. Barro, Lee Benham, Daniel Beunza, William Cooper, Fernando Díez, Rui de Figueiredo, Nuno Garoupa, Edward L. Glaeser, Jesús Huerta de Soto, Dean Lueck, Rachel M. McCleary, Eduardo Melero, Lewis S. Mudge, Celestino Pardo Núñez, Danilla Raskov, Steven Shavell, Armando Rodríguez Valledor, Pablo Spiller, Raúl Viedma, Fredrik Wallenberg, David S. Wilson, three reviewers and seminar and conference participants at Berkeley, Harvard, Instituto de Empresa, Pompeu Fabra, Oviedo, UAM and Washington University, and ALEA, EALE, FAES, ISNIE, SSSR, as well as the research assistance of Petar Balachev and Andrés Jariod. The usual disclaimers apply. This study received financial support from the Spanish Ministry of Education and Science, through grant SEJ2005-03871/ECON and the European Commission through the Integrated Project CIT3-513420.

* Department of Economics and Business. Universitat Pompeu Fabra, and Barcelona GSE. Trias Fargas, 25. 08005-Barcelona (Spain). E-mail: benito.arrunada@upf.edu.

lics who confess more often are observed to comply more with the moral code; however, no relationship is observed between mass attendance and moral compliance.[1]

Keywords: religion, institutions, confession, morals, law enforcement.

1. Motivation

Oral confession of sins to priests is an interesting institution for three reasons. First, it is a highly complex, organized and sophisticated (though not necessarily superior) form of producing moral enforcement. Moral codes often emerge from spontaneous processes which use non-specialized resources, while Christian confession is highly managed and relies on specialized resources. It therefore epitomizes religious intermediation in which priests or, more generally, a church organization acts as an agent between God and the faithful. Second, this moral intermediation was a central issue in the development of Western civilization, as shown most explicitly when the Protestant Reformation drastically reduced the intermediary role played by the Church. Third, understanding how confession works will help us understand how we now produce and enforce moral codes through more spontaneous, less specialized means, and the problems these may entail.

Most authors see confession as oppressive or ineffective. Among them, Adam Smith, for whom confession gave the clergy too many opportunities for improving their revenues,[2] and Max Weber (1920a), for whom easy forgiveness through confession motivates

---

[1] Appendix with Figures online available at: http://www.uni-erfurt.de/finanzwissenschaft/

[2] Smith's critique occupies most of the last chapter of *The Theory of Moral Sentiments* (1759), focusing it on the agency costs of confession in *The Wealth of Nations* (1776:789-90).

individuals' productivity less than Protestant salvation by grace alone. The Weber thesis has prompted many works at the macroeconomic level, trying to explain growth differentials as a consequence of the dominance of different religions. Previous analyses have also emphasized the negative elements of confession. For instance, the theology of purgatory, seen by Ekelund, Hébert and Tollison (1992) as an invention designed to facilitate price discrimination. Likewise, the establishment of Mendicant Orders is conceived by Schmidtchen and Mayer (1997) as a device to extract parishes' rents. Because these works assume perfect rationality, they see penance as the price paid for eternal salvation, this being a mere consumption good of constant quality, whatever its production process. This perspective is useful, as discussed in section 0, but does not explain the function and persistence of confession. In particular, the argument by Ekelund, Hébert and Tollison (hereafter EHT, who see Catholic confession purely as a rent extraction device, is incomplete. Rent seeking, and agency costs more generally, are inherent in all kinds of trade and specialization between self-interested individuals transacting in a world of imperfect information (Barzel 1997:14). Therefore, the presence of even systematic rent seeking does not fully explain the role of such a complex institution.

Some other thinkers considered confession of sins useful for psychological and social welfare. The development of its supporting theology during the late Middle Ages, grounded on free will and salvation by works, is even seen as a stepping stone of Western civilization (White 1978, Delumeau 1992, Hopkins 1999). The doctrine of penance, in particular, is often viewed as a main source of Western criminal law (Berman 1983).

This article draws a more balanced picture. Section 0 presents the analytical framework, which sees confession as a form of specialization burdened with agency costs. It focuses on the superior incentives that this specialization makes possible and the presence of agency costs. The remaining sections test this argument relying on behavioral, historical and quantitative evidence. Section 0 explains the cognitive roots of the costs-and-benefits trade-off. Section 0 interprets the historical evolution of Christian confession of sins in terms of exogenous changes and innovations affecting the balance of costs and benefits. Section 0 does the same with the modern situation. Section 0 provides supportive econometric evidence. Section 0 concludes.

2. Analytical framework: specialization advantages versus agency costs

In most social exchange, different agents may act as enforcers: impartial *third parties* such as judges; *second parties* when they are in a position to retaliate; and *first parties*, who evaluate their own conduct relative to their moral codes and then reward or punish themselves psychologically.

We often envision first-party enforcement as a purely individual matter but we also often consult others about the moral worth of our actions. When doing this, we are allowing a third party to help in our first-party enforcement. Catholic confession also introduces a third party, the confessor priest, into first-party enforcement. Confessors hear repentant believers orally confessing their sins (their breaches of the moral code) and then counsel, examine, judge, set penance and eventually forgive them. Compared to other types of moral enforcement, confession therefore uses more specialized resources — priests — to provide quality confession services and theologists to refine the moral code. In contrast, other types of religious enforcement are less specialized, relying instead on believers self-examining themselves without external help, or mutually controlling each other through informal monitoring or public confessions.

As with any other type of economic specialization, specialized confession can be expected to produce better outcomes—mainly more effective self- and social control — at lower costs. Greater specialization, however, should also cause additional agency costs, as priests can exploit confessions for the Church's and their own benefit.

The sustained hypothesis in this paper is that confession presents this trade-off of costs and benefits and is not, as often claimed, a mere rent-seeking device. In particular, considering specialization advantages, confession should be (a) more effective than other religious practices, such as prayer or mass attendance, in enforcing the moral code (*enforcement proposition*). However, confession should also (b) provide greater scope for priests to condition penitents' behavior to the benefit of themselves or the Church (*rent-extraction proposition*).

The greater explanatory power of this costs-and-benefits hypothesis will be verified by showing that it fits in better with human nature, history and quantitative data than the rent-seeking hypothesis. Cognitive sciences show that it suits the design of the human mind. The history of confession amounts to a parallel increase of specialization and safeguards against opportunism. Lastly, Catholics who confess more often also help the poor more and give more money to the church, after controlling for demographic variables and discarding possible hidden effects. Furthermore, confession is also more effective in inducing moral compliance than attending mass, as those attending masses more often do not significantly help the poor more.

3. Cognitive evidence

From a conventional perspective based on rational choice and utility maximization, religion and even the existence of morality are hard to explain. Findings in cognitive sciences, however, suggest that having a moral sense and, in particular, religious beliefs and practice can improve fitness. Functional explanations of religion emerge naturally from this view, complementing the rationality assumption and clarifying the potentially adaptive role of beliefs, irrespective of whether they are true or false. We are evolved for fitness, not for truth, and beliefs can be adaptive yet contrary to truth.

Just like any other product of evolution, the human mind is adaptive to a certain environment. However, many of its structures have become non-adaptive since human beings modify their environments faster than the pace of adaptation attainable by natural selection.[3] For instance, our food preferences are better adapted to the scarcity and life style of hunter-gatherers living in the Pleistocene than to modern humans. We therefore need non-genetic control devices for all sorts of instincts, both in the individual and social spheres. From this perspective, religions are cultural adaptations that help modern humans to exert self- and social control over ancient instincts. A classic example comes from Adam Smith's remark that "[i]n the Decalogue we are commanded to honour our fathers and mothers. No mention is made of the love of our children" (Smith 1759:266): we need a cultural complement to induce help to our parents but not to our children. The same can be argued about the need to postpone gratification (our subjective discount rate being too high for today's world), to avoid revenge (as we now live in a legal environment) or to reduce xenophobia (in order to facilitate trade with strangers), to mention just three examples. Even Communists have come to appreciate the pro-social role of religion.[4]

Catholic confession, and Catholic theology more generally, fits well in this analysis by providing an institutionalized structure that strives to improve on purely emotional morality. Not only Adam

[3] See Tooby and Cosmides (1992), Cosmides and Tooby (1992).

[4] "Religion in China: When Opium Can Be Benign," *The Economist*, February 1, 2007.

Smith (1759), with his emphasis on sympathy and compassion, but also modern cognitive accounts, such as those by Boyer (1994, 2001) and Haidt (2003), are grounded on emotions and instincts. Catholicism built a rationalistic moral code and encouraged individuals to account for their actions rationally, balancing good and bad, instead of merely responding to moral emotions which might be maladapted to the environments built by humans since the Pleistocene. Confession was the main instrument used by the Church for consistently applying this ideal of rational control of emotions. Such an ideal of emotional control is as necessary now as in the past, to judge from the constant flow of new solutions, including the "self-help" industry and its "emotional intelligence" branch (Goleman 1995).

Cognitive sciences also provide a basis for the cost side of this paper's argument, because some scholars interpret religion in terms of exploitative use of mental tools previously designed by natural selection to solve other problems and therefore consider it to be a cultural parasite or by-product. One such is Boyer (2001) who emphasizes parasitism and asserts that humans have a "moral sense" that does not need religion to function. They suggest that this weakness in the deep design of the human mind could be used by "experts" (that is, priests in Catholicism) to exert control over others for their own benefit. Similarly, Dawkins has argued vigorously about the costs of religious beliefs (2001).

The potential for agency costs is also clear in confession, as confessors gain information advantages and opportunities to influence others. But confession may also lead to clear benefits related to self- and social control. It improves individual rationality and fitness, by helping to control ill-adapted mental modules in a rapidly-changing environment. In addition, it provides incentives and articulates enforcement mechanisms that inhibit free-riding, an essential ingredient for intra-group cooperation, by detecting and punishing cheaters and by promoting conformity.

Confession also fits this cognitive argument because the functioning of confession relies on basic instincts, with emotions such as shame and guilt playing fundamental roles, as in other moral constructs (Haidt 2003). However, it is not raw but channeled emotions that play a role in confession, thus providing the potential for greater adaptation. Shame *management* was an important aspect of the education of confessors, who had to draw a fine line by using shame to motivate sinners without alienating them. Similarly, guilt is also managed to avoid both the lax rationalization of wrongs and excessive scrupulousness (Tentler 1977). Many other emotions moonlight as code enforcers. For instance, disgust at the sight of blood and body fluids plays a prominent role in many sex-related taboos and this was used until recently for controlling sexual behavior.

Finally, a substantial body of empirical evidence shows that repentance and forgiveness produce cooperative and psychological benefits in both humans and animals. Some forgiveness has been shown to achieve better results than tit-for-tat strategies in the iterated prisoner's dilemma, especially when cooperation and defection are hard to distinguish, as first argued by Axelrod (1984). Forgiveness also enhances psychological well-being (Krause and Ellison 2003) and has positive consequences in terms of health (McCullough, Pargament and Thoresen 2000) and pro-social behavior (Wuthnow 2000). Confession should have similar cathartic effects. It is well established that reconciliation also happens among primates, supporting the view that it helps social animals to cope with conflict.[5] Substantial demand for the relief given by confession is also appar-

[5] Post-conflict interaction seems to work as a form of reconciliation, with positive effects for maintaining relationships (Waal 1997). See also Flack and de Waal (2000:10-12) and the accompanying discussion.

ent from the creation of substitutes and the proliferation of fee-based confession services, which focus on overcoming guilt.[6]

Considering these behavioral foundations, it comes as no surprise that "confession is one of the most widespread practices in the world, represented on every continent in every known period of history" (Sullivan 1987:233). The common element in different cultures is the verbalization of wrongs committed in order to repair a breach in the relation of the individual or the group with God. In primitive cultures, it was often a restorative and purifying requirement in rites of passage (circumcision, marriage, childbirth, new year), in the preparation of crucial stages of the production cycle (the hunting season) and in the treatment of sickness.[7] This prevalence should help to dispel the misconception that sees confession as a Catholic invention. More to our point, this nature of confession as a "cultural universal" confirms that it is deeply rooted in our minds.

In line with these cognitive perspectives, this article sees institutions — including the Church and, in particular, Catholic confession — as artificial constructs that serve to improve adaptation to a relatively "unnatural" environment, with human reason being one of many decisional mechanisms (Arruñada 2008a). In this conceptual framework, first, institutions — including confession — constrain individuals; second, individuals decide within their biological and institutional constraints; third, individuals, their offspring and

[6] Two examples: the fee-based "Confession line" telephone service advises callers to "let go guilt and shame" (http://confession900line.com/2395827/, accessed September 8, 2002); and another service claims to be "designed to help you ease the burden of guilt…. Only $15 a month" (http://www.myselfhelp-.com/Programs/OG.html, accessed July 23, 2005). Substitutes range from psychological therapy to many vicarious forms, such as talk shows and agony columns.

[7] For descriptions in different religions see Aune (1987) and Bianchi (1987).

their groups enjoy the consequences of such decisions; and, finally, institutions are modified by different means — from imitation to group disappearance —, but mainly as a consequence of relative group performance in a changing technological environment. Therefore, the logic behind institutional arrangements is mainly driven by evolution, adaptation and survival. This view is consistent with findings in behavioral economics showing that utility maximization — whatever its merits as a working assumption in many scientific endeavors — is often a poor predictor of actual behavior (see, e.g., Rabin 1998 and Mullainathan 2005). More importantly, it indirectly calls attention to the rationalizing function of institutions, such as, in our case, confession of sins,[8] showing again that institutions serve not only to solve problems between individuals but also within individuals, as argued, for instance, by Mullainathan (2005).

4. Historical evidence

The history of confession also supports the main claim in this paper in that it consists of a series of innovations boosting specialization and, consequently, both its enforcement benefits and its agency costs. In primitive Christianity, reconciliation of sinners follows the patterns found in many sectarian movements, including Communism (Riegel 2005: mainly 113-118): wrongdoers were expelled unless they made more or less voluntary public confession, which was to be followed by harsh penances with not fully reconciliatory effects. This prominence of non-specialized social enforcement is consistent with our argument if we consider that the first Christians

---

[8] In particular, demand for confession ties in well with works in behavioral economics that model and test how human beings find it difficult to self-control their behavior and therefore need commitment devices to overcome their bounded rationality in this field. See, for example, the references in Rabin (1998:38-41) and Mullainathan (2005).

were relatively well-off and, therefore, well-educated (Stark 1996:29-33).

During the early Middle Ages, confession became reiterable, instead of once in a lifetime; and penance gradually became less harsh and was increasingly performed after absolution instead of before. Confession also became more private, with public confession first reserved for public sins (since the 4th century) and later abandoned; and increasingly addressed to specialists (first to bishops, then to priests). As from the 12th century, instead of priests imposing penances on sinners, they were advised to bargain with them (Tentler 1977:17). Penances had to be accepted and set in proportion to the individual's strength. At the same time, a more prominent role was given to purgatory, this being a situation of temporal punishment for sinners who were absolved but were not completely free from venial sins, or had not fully paid "satisfaction" for their sins. Finally, annual confession was eventually made obligatory at the 4th Lateran Council in 1215, completing a model that is still in place in the Catholic church.

4.1 How these changes increased benefits

This transformation radically altered the relative importance of the different types of enforcement and provided substantial specialization advantages, mainly of two types. First, private confession to a priest made secrecy possible, and secrecy is more conducive than public knowledge to truly moral, first-party enforcement. Second, priests could accumulate expertise and manage confessions in a professional manner.

Primitive confession can hardly be considered "moral" because of its emphasis on external enforcement. As can be seen today in some religious movements, public confession is often part of sectarian systems that merge moral and social enforcement, minimizing individual freedom (section 0). Compared to previous public confession and penance, private confession fosters the development of first-party enforcement, a genuine moral system which can then work in parallel with an increasingly separated and specialized legal system. Spiritual penalties were introduced once secular ones were in place while, previously, both were merged together (Lea 1896[1]:45). Specialization also took place within the religious sphere, as the *internal forum* of conscience for the relation between sinner and God was separated from the *external forum* for the relation between the sinner and the congregation or church. Moral enforcement is therefore separated from social enforcement. The two systems can thus rely on different information and can specialize in different areas of conduct.

Second, having priests hearing confessions made it possible to develop more sophisticated incentives, based on subjective evaluation of performance and face-to-face interaction. On the one hand, priests can set standards of behavior adjusted to individual circumstances, thus increasing motivation for recurring sinners and making Church membership appeal to a wider range of people.[9] This also reduced the problems posed by the categorical and contradictory structure of moral rules that have to be applied to a wide variety of situations in which compliance is not always socially optimal.[10] On the other hand, confessing to specialists involves face-to-face interaction, allowing the oral expression of guilt and the verbalization of emotional experiences, which have been shown to improve physical and mental health (Pennebaker 1989, 1997), with probably greater effects than the more abstract confession to God (Krause and Ellison 2003), and may help improve internalization of skills and develop a richer mental life (Toulmin 1979). Confession can thus be effective even when the priest is poorly qualified. Similarly, oral confession reduces the risk of self-deception, by utilizing in-

---

[9] See, for instance, Delumeau (1992:293-295) and Tentler (1977:318-340).

[10] Emphasized by Kaplow and Shavell (2002 and 2007) and Shavell (2002), for whom "moral rules cannot be too detailed and nuanced."

nate psychological structures, therefore requiring less investment in indoctrination.[11] It also lessens the symmetric risk that strong-willed individuals will set themselves excessively rigorous rules, a risk pointed out by Bénabou and Tirole (2004).

4.2 Innovation in safeguards

These advantages come, however, at the cost of developing specialized human capital and increasing the scope for priests' opportunism. In terms of effort, opportunism goes from providing insufficient access to confession services to performing the function inadequately and taking penance and absolution decisions that are too lenient or too strict. Confessors may also misuse their position to obtain personal benefits, from sexual access or inheritance rights to promoting their own ideology. Furthermore, it also opens new avenues for opportunism at higher levels in the hierarchy. Some Popes, for instance, sold indulgences conferring salvation, not only remission of temporal punishment.

Growing specialization therefore made it necessary to contain opportunism by devising additional safeguards, most of which were set up around two critical moments (1215, Fourth Lateran Council, and 1545-63, Council of Trent) when the Church faced strong heretical competition in the form of Albigensianism and Protestantism) and reacted to them, with strikingly similar measures.

First, the church invested heavily in reputation and capital, both physical and human: cathedrals were built, the new Gothic and Baroque styles appeared, teaching by example and training were es-

[11] Human brains have evolved innate difficulties for lying (Damasio 1994), often fall prey of self-deception (Trivers 1985, 2000), reach self-serving judgments about fairness (Kahneman and Tversky 1995) and are well-equipped to detect cheaters (Trivers 1971, 1985; Cosmides 1985, 1989; Cosmides and Tooby 1992), all of these being traits that are significantly affected by direct personal contact.

sential in both the Mendicant and Jesuit Orders,[12] and the Council of Trent founded the network of diocesan seminars.

Second, new "product divisions" were set up with an emphasis on confession: in the 13th century, the Mendicant Orders and, in the 16th, the Jesuits. These provided product specialization: Mendicants in preaching and giving example, Jesuits in teaching and both also in confessing and refining the moral code. These orders also brought competition within the church, helping to overcome the laxity and ignorance of the secular clergy, which was organized not on a product basis but on a geographical basis.

Third, rules were developed, including those on jurisdiction and reserved cases (defining who had the right to confess whom about what, with special attention on how priests were also hierarchically controlled by confession), on how to extract confessions (from a system in which priests merely imposed penalties to one in which they negotiated them with penitents), on how to conduct confessions (from regulating postures to mandating the use of confessional boxes in the second half of the 16th century), and on secrecy (seal of confession). Mandatory annual confession has often been seen as exploitative but it was also a safeguard for both penitents and priests — for penitents, because it forced them to self-examine themselves and confess at least once a year, helping them to make more consistent choices over time;[13] for priests, because it estab-

---

[12] Compare with Schmidtchen and Mayer (1997), who model the licensing of the Mendicants as a way of appropriating rents by the Pope, an argument inconsistent with the greater discretion given to confessors compared to the earlier penitential system.

[13] In the Catholic faith, good deeds increase the chances of reaching eternal salvation. Believers therefore face the typical intertemporal tradeoff of short term effort versus long term benefits, about which findings in Behavioral Economics show that we tend to make inconsistent choices and procrastinate (see, for a summary and references, Rabin [1998:38-41]). Applying the argument suggested by Mullainathan (2005) in the context of economic development, by

lished a regular pattern that made it harder for them to collude with penitents. Furthermore, annual confession added little in terms of rent seeking, because rents can be more easily captured from penitents close to death and, before annual confession was mandatory, people already confessed before death, which provided plenty of scope for rent seeking.

Fourth, developing and updating of the moral code was dealt with by specialists within the church, instead of being left to informal social interaction or to the confessor priests, leading to the development of Casuistry, a detailed analysis of how good Christians should behave in specific situations. This centralization on moral rulemaking was necessary for guiding and safeguarding priests' decisions, playing a role similar to that of sentencing guidelines in civil judicial systems. It also produced crucial innovations, mainly the key elements in criminal law, such as consideration of aggravating and extenuating circumstances (Berman 1983: Ch. 4). More generally, it promoted and put into practice a rationalistic, calculating morality, full of trade-offs in its detailed analyses of causes, motives and circumstances.[14] Furthermore, far from freezing the

---

subjecting believers to an annual judgment, annual confession spread pressure over time and this probably helped believers to make more consistent choices about how well to behave in their worldly lives. (The same argument could help explain the signaling role given to good deeds within Calvinism).

[14] Casuistry has often been criticized since the Reformation because of its rationalistic ambitions (for instance, by Adam Smith 1759 and Henry Lea 1896). This criticism might be misguided, however. All societies have to produce a moral code, and the question is between more formal, centralized and rationalistic production by specialists (be they priests or, more often now in the West, intellectuals) versus informal, decentralized and emotional production by lay persons. Thus, the rationalism of Casuistry was to be missed later in Protestant theology (Santayana 1916). See also Jonsen and Toulmin (1988).

Christian moral code, Casuistry adapted it in parallel with new market relations and urban life.[15]

Lastly, theological innovations also provided additional safeguards, mainly through the renewed emphasis on purgatory and ambiguity about the need of contrition for forgiveness. In particular, belief in purgatory kept incentives alive even after absolution, as it motivated penitents to produce additional satisfaction during their lives and after death. Understandably, belief in purgatory grew in importance once penances became less harsh and confession reiterable. Similarly, ambiguities in the theology of confession, which have been criticized as confused (Lea 1896) and paradoxical (Tentler 1977:365), can be explained in terms of optimal deterrence: ambiguous rewards (making salvation depend on a vague degree of contrition and the resolve not to sin anymore) seem reasonable when considered as a subjective evaluation of performance, because they contain the dysfunctional "gaming" behavior induced by a more explicit and objective evaluation, as modeled by Baker, Gibbons and Murphy (1994).

---

[15] Confession manuals, for instance, soon focused on sins committed by professionals in the exercise of their trade, arguably in response to the economic growth and greater specialization achieved during the 13th century (Le Goff 1980). A similar adaptation in the discussion of sins related to birth control is reported by Biller (1998b). More importantly, the whole idea of purgatory has been linked to economic changes during the first two centuries of the millennium (Le Goff 1984). The new theology was also contemporary with the reappropriation of ancient Greek science, with changes in Christian ethics in favor of technological change (Benz 1968, White 1978), and with other theological ideas that have been considered essential for human dignity and liberty (Novak 1998). A few centuries later, the liberal reversal of the scholastic treatment of usury and many other commercial issues led by the theologians of the Salamanca school was also in step with the problems posed by inflation during the 16th century (Grice-Hutchinson 1952, Rothbard 1995:97-133).

4.3 Alternative interpretations

This costs-and-benefits interpretation of confession acknowledges that its evolution must have created new agency costs, but these might have been only the price of additional specialization advantages over and above agency costs. This view affects, in particular, changes introduced in the 13th and 16th centuries, and departs drastically from the view held in several works by Ekelund, Hébert and Tollison (EHT 1992, 2002, 2004, 2006) who see purgatory, the sale of indulgences, confession and, apparently, the whole functioning of the Church purely as rent extraction devices.

In their 1992 work, EHT explain the greater role given to purgatory and the restructuring of confession in the 13th century as price discrimination. However, these innovations were introduced at a time of substantial heretical competition, which would make price discrimination less viable. A simple, lower-price interpretation does not fit the facts either, both because the reform upgraded a more lenient practice and because contemporaneous heresies held both higher and even lower standards (Biller 1998a:18-23). Again, this does not preclude an evolution in the direction of leniency in later centuries.

Similarly, EHT (2002) argue that rent seeking through price discrimination was the main feature of the system in the 16th century, causing the Reformation.[16] However, EHT disregard an alternative

---

[16] Ekelund, Hébert and Tollison (2002) recognize, however, that rent seeking in itself does not account for the failure of the Reformation to take root in much of Europe. They therefore assume that rent seeking was more prevalent in countries where the Reformation failed and then test this assumption indirectly, through laws on primogeniture. This poses two problems. In addition to the debatable link between primogeniture and rent seeking, their source of data (Swanson 1967) describes a map of European inheritance customs that runs counter to most published work on the subject (see Le Roy Ladurie [1976:27], Thirsk [1976:179, citing Abel 1958:154] and Todd [1990:35]), leading them, for instance, to wrongly classify Sweden and Denmark as areas of partible-

explanation of the Church's price structure, which used higher "prices" for the same sin when committed by wealthier penitents. (Evidence on this pricing structure is clear from penances with a time and, therefore, opportunity-cost dimension and from indulgences, which were usually prized as a proportion of personal income and wealth).[17] This alternative explanation is grounded on the well-established theoretical result that, when wealth varies among individuals, optimal-deterrence sanctions increase with wealth (Polinsky and Shavell 1991). This makes it difficult to distinguish optimal sanctions from a price discriminating schedule for those sanctions that took the form of monetary compensation going to the Church (and also, usually, to the Crown). Furthermore, in many such instances, when using monetary prices in the remission of time in purgatory, the Church was following a practice that has become a standard recommendation in the economic analysis of criminal law at least since Becker (1968), namely, that fines — being socially cost-free — are more efficient and should be exhausted before resorting to socially costly forms of punishment (for example, Posner 1998:246, Polinsky and Shavell 2000:70). Overall, explaining the Reformation as a reaction against the Church's rent-seeking is as partial as seeing it as a way of expropriating the Church's wealth, a rent-seeking argument in the opposite direction, which also offers plenty of supporting evidence (Cameron 1991:294-96).

Finally, EHT (2004) interpret the Counter Reformation and, in particular, the reforms decided at the Council of Trent as a mere reduction of the "price" (or an increase in quality) charged by the Church, forced on it by the competition of Reformers and "financed" by lower rent seeking. However, the measures that they

---

inheritance and France and Spain as jurisdictions under primogeniture, which was not the case for most of their regions.

[17] See Lea (1896 [vol. 3]:155-162, 179-180, 192, 390, 427, 435, 437).

summarize (for instance in their Table 1[18]) either change the technology or were designed to reduce agency costs within the Church, an aspect that EHT inevitably overlook as a consequence of seeing the Church as a purely Neoclassical firm. To the extent that the measures succeeded in reducing inefficiencies, such increases in quality do not merely reduce the effective price but also increase the value of services and, more to the point, were financed not from rents previously enjoyed by the Church but from efficiency gains obtained through organizational innovation.

5. Modern confession

The costs-and-benefits explanation also fits in with the modern evolution of the practice of confession in Christianity. Within the main branches of both Catholicism and Protestantism, confession to priests has experienced a protracted decline, leading to greater introspection and general absolution without personal oral confession. The maintenance of confession in many Protestant churches centuries after the Reformation indicates that there was a demand for it on the part of believers and that it may afford benefits. In the mainstream of both Catholicism and Protestantism, the increase in introspection and the decline in oral confession parallel greater education of the laity and economic development. In the fringes of both, many religious movements have also relied on primitive forms of public confession and external enforcement by priests and lay leaders.

[18] For example, EHT consider the establishment of seminars and the strengthening of preaching as advertising (2004:696).

5.1 Mainstream Christianity

Most Protestant churches retained voluntary confession well after the Reformation.[19] Initially, Lutheran churches kept the duty of confessing to a minister before communion, even though they revoked the annual obligation to confess, suppressed penance, and required the liturgy to emphasize that forgiveness came from God and not from the priest or the Church. There was, therefore, lesser but still substantial specialization. Personal confession was important as late as the end of the 19th century and triggered fierce competition among priests for the fees paid by penitents. Calvin even prescribed annual private confession, though the Helvetic churches soon moved to direct confession to God. The Huguenots also encouraged private confession. The Anglicans retained voluntary confession with priestly absolution, and some sections have practiced it until recently.[20]

In most churches, however, different versions of general confession and absolution became dominant in the centuries following the Reformation. Today, mainstream Protestants confess in silence and directly to God, most often through the general statements of confession and absolution of the Communion service.

The Reformation also triggered substantial changes in the organization and practice of Catholic confession, which are also consistent with the argument in the paper, as they increase introspection and first-party enforcement in addition to agency costs. First, preliminary self- examination was prescribed at the Council of Trent (Lea

[19] "The abolition of the confessional (as opposed, say, to the abolition of the mass or the removal of images) does not seem to have been a very high priority in the popular reformation. The reformers blew hot and cold over it, intending still to retain some sort of private confession of sins before communion as a means of reassurance" (Cameron 1991:308).

[20] In addition to Lea (1896[1]:515-523), see Caspari (1950:222-223) and Tentler (1977:349-351).

1896[2]:413, n. 1). Second, the Jesuits, often seen as the army of the Counter-Reformation, emphasized self-examination of conscience and, from their very beginning, were dedicated to educating the laity, developing character and self-control. Third, moral doctrine evolved to increasingly flexible positions, with the exception of a brief period of rigor from around 1640 to 1750 which caused a sharp drop in the practice of confession. This flexibility tried to maximize moral improvement by re-emphasizing individual circumstances and introspection, reducing the postponement of absolution, giving more weight to preserving personal reputation and requiring full conscience for a sin to be mortal (Delumeau 1992:101-148).

More recent evolution confirms these tendencies. Since the last third of the 20th century, confession has been in crisis, as many Catholics do not comply with the annual duty to confess and most of those who do confess have moved away from detailed confession.[21] Furthermore, many parishes practice general group absolution instead of individual confession, using a loophole in Canon law.[22] More importantly, general absolution seems to be preferred by both the laity and the clergy, at least in developed countries.[23] The official position of the Church has yet not changed, however, but it is allowing Catholics who do not confess to remain in the

---

[21] Estimates of compliance with the annual duty to confess were around 50% for American Catholics in the 1990s (Davidson *et al.* 1997, Lee *et al.* 2000).

[22] General absolution has been widespread, as evidenced by the numerous controversies and confirmation of the formal rules. See, for example, McClory (2001) and Congregation for Divine Worship (2000), Pope John Paul II (1984) and Ratzinger (2002).

[23] These tendencies seem to be universal. Apparently, the demand of many poor Christians (both Catholics and Protestants) living in less-developed countries for a traditional and soundly institutionalized religion, analyzed by Jenkins (2002), seems to be better satisfied by sectarian movements, both Protestant and Catholic, than by traditional Catholic solutions.

Church, and rules against general confession are being enforced leniently.[24]

This evolution towards greater introspection and less oral confession in mainstream Christianity is consistent with an education argument, according to which the comparative advantage of confession decreases with the level of education of the laity,[25] as educational improvements took place later in Catholicism in parallel with the decline of confession. It is also consistent with the fact that many Protestant churches maintained confession for several centuries after the Reformation, at a time when Protestant regions were not more literate than Catholic regions. Later on, when confession was abandoned in Protestant regions earlier than in Catholic regions, this took place at a time when literacy rates had switched, becoming higher in Protestant than in Catholic regions.[26] To the extent that education and economic development have evolved in parallel, the same argument applies in terms of a potential cost decrease of confession services.[27]

---

[24] Evolution in the Orthodox churches has followed a pattern that also fits the argument. For example, confession is still obligatory in the Russian church (Volkova 2001) but the American church introduced general absolution in 1972 (Schmemann 1972).

[25] A higher level of education could make self- and social enforcement easier and/or confession more costly for the laity.

[26] See Graff (1987). For a recent analysis of Protestantism as a source of greater literacy, see Becker and Woessmann (2009).

[27] The working paper version of this article (Arruñada 2008b) develops and tests these additional arguments, explaining the current decline in confession as a consequence of the rise in education, which makes moral self-enforcement less costly; and the productivity gap suffered by confession services, given their necessarily interpersonal nature.

5.2 Alternative movements

The decline in private confession to priests is also visible in the reliance of both Protestant and Catholic new religious movements on more primitive and less specialized forms of confession and social enforcement: their confessions are often public, and penalties are harsh and may include separation from the group. Within Protestantism, the Geneva of Calvin provided an early paradigm with its intrusive social controls, such as "family visitation," a practice adapted by Calvin from monastic orders and followed to this day by some reformed churches, by which two elders, or an elder and a minister, regularly visit each home to discuss the spiritual health of the family (see, for instance, Jong 1992-1994). A classic account of these practices was given by Weber in his description of American sects (1920b). More recently, young Protestant churches, like the Church of the Nazarene, still recommend oral confession (Isbell 2005).

Similarly, Catholic movements, like Opus Dei, Legion of Christ, Focolare, Communion and Liberation and the Neo-Catechumenate rely more on hierarchical and mutual control than on the more subtle mix of first- and third-party enforcement characteristic of sacramental confession. They use frequent and detailed "manifestations of conscience" to lay superiors and denunciation and public confession ("confidence", "fraternal correction" and "brief circle" in Opus Dei), which often overlap and are more important than sacramental confession. The nature of these forms of hierarchical and social enforcement is revealed by their recurrent collision with sacramental confession, going back to the 13th century, when the Templars were accused of receiving absolution from their lay masters (de la Croix 2005). Much later, the use of manifestation of conscience in monastic orders often led to abusive control of members, until a Papal decree drastically limited it in 1890. The decree, however, did not prevent the founder of Opus Dei from considering this practice more important than sacramental confession.[28] The fact that confession was not deemed sufficient in these movements and that it often even collided with these other forms of spiritual direction points to the relatively restrained nature of confession and the greater protection it provides to the individual.

6. Quantitative evidence

The sustained hypothesis of this paper, according to which confession produces both enforcement benefits and agency costs, will now be tested and compared to the alternative rent-seeking hypothesis by examining how the frequency of confession and two other religious practices — praying and attending mass — interact with two stated actions — helping the poor and giving money to the Church. The three religious practices proxy for three types of moral enforcement: prayer, which mostly involves an individual dialogue with God and is unobserved by third parties, represents first-party moral enforcement; confession, which consists of both self-examination and a more or less judicial dialogue with a priest, represents a mix of first and specialized third-party enforcement; and mass attendance, which is communal and is publicly observed by other members of the community, a version of social, non-specialized third-party enforcement. The degree of help directly provided to the poor proxies for the effectiveness of moral enforcement, while the amount of money given to the Church — which poses much more serious agency problems — proxies for agency costs. These two dependent variables are further discussed at the end of the section.

---

[28] See Walsh for a general description of Opus Dei that emphasizes the conflict between manifestation of conscience and sacramental confession (1989:112-119); and, for also critical descriptions by former members, Tapia (1994), on Opus Dei; Lenon (2003), on the Legion, and Urquhart (1999) on the rest.

The costs and benefits hypothesis predicts a positive relation between frequency of confession and both action variables. On the contrary, the rent-seeking hypothesis predicts a positive effect on church giving but either a nil or negative effect on helping the poor. That is, rent seeking arguments seeing confession as ineffective predict a nil effect, but those which see it as a price for committing sins (for instance, Weber) predict a negative effect.

To explore the relationship between religious practices and actions, I will regress actions on religious practice variables, controlling for demographic features (education, income, sex, marital status, age, race, the fact that the respondent and ancestors were born in the USA, the level of education of the respondent's parents, and the respondent's intensity of belief in hell, heaven and salvation), using both ordered probits and ordinary least squares (OLS).[29]

The data come from a survey conducted in 1994 on 4,554 Indiana Catholics, and the variables are summarized in Table 1.[30] All variables, except sex and marital status, have been standardized to have mean zero and standard deviation one.

The econometric results presented in Table 2 are more consistent with the costs-and-benefits hypothesis than with the rent-seeking hypothesis. In particular, results show that the coefficient of the frequency of confession is significantly and positively related to the propensity of Catholics to help the poor. This interaction seems to be even greater than the also positive relationship observed in the amount of money given to the church. Furthermore, the coefficients of confession are in line — both in sign and significance — to

---

[29] Simple OLS models may be affected by omitted variables that might be influencing both the outcome and explanatory variables of interest, and producing inconsistent estimates. See, however, Arruñada (2008b) for an analysis using instrumental variables that produces similar results.

[30] Appendix with Figures online available at: http://www.uni-erfurt.de/finanzwissenschaft/

those of praying to God, a practice close to first-party enforcement. Comparing the confession coefficients with those obtained for mass attendance is also revealing, because attending mass more often (which might be taken as a proxy of non-specialized social enforcement) is not only associated with giving substantially more money to the church but seems to be ineffective in terms of good actions, as shown by the insignificant effect on helping the poor. Furthermore, all these results are robust to different specifications, as well as to other outcome variables, such as volunteering in church activities.

For this sample of Catholics, confession of sins therefore appears to be effective in improving enforcement of the moral code. In addition, when compared to other religious practices, confession seems to be more effective than attending mass (our proxy of social non-specialized enforcement) and not more "exploitative" than both praying to God and attending mass. Because the metric scale for the variables is not clearly established, comparing the effects of the explanatory variables is not fully appropriate when they have significant coefficients of the same sign,[31] as happens in some of the *Give Money to Church* equations. However, considering that standardized variables are been used, it is unlikely that distortions introduced by treating ordinal variables as metric variables will overcome the substantial differences in the estimated coefficients (the coefficient of attending mass might be as high as ten times that of confessing sins).

Some reinterpretations of the variables would reinforce the view of confession as a technology of moral enforcement, because the *Help the Poor* variable is less ambiguous than the *Give Money to Church* variable. Helping the poor is clearly linked to compliance with the

---

[31] See, however, Labovitz (1967, 1970) and Kim (1975), who show how correlation coefficients are quite robust with respect to ordinal distortions in the measurement.

Catholic moral code while giving money to the Church might measure the Church's rents but also compensation for greater use of the Church's services or — especially for money given secretly — moral compliance. In other words, understanding money contributions as exploitation is doubtful for two reasons. First, most money collected by the Church is not captured as rents but used to finance Church activities and charities. This issue brings us back to the criticism of EHT in section 0 because EHT consider all Church revenue as rents. In terms of the econometric model, this leads us to consider *Give Money to Church* as a proxy of moral enforcement, an interpretation that — considering its positive coefficient in some equations — would further refute the rent-seeking hypothesis, as confession would also be effective in this dimension of moral enforcement. Consequences for the costs-and-benefits hypothesis are less clear because the absence of agency costs may result from active organizational safeguards, as explained in section 0. A second interpretation relies on the private benefits provided by confession, which may lead those Catholics who confess more to compensate the Church more for their greater consumption of Church services. This would tie in with the historical practice of paying a fee to confessors.

A preliminary test of these ideas was implemented by considering *Help the Poor* as a proxy for moral compliance and introducing it as an additional control in different variants of the model in Table 2 (with and without interaction with confession frequency, as well as running individual regressions for the different levels of help provided to the poor). The resulting coefficient estimated for the frequency of confession does not change substantially with respect to Table 2 and remains significantly positive. This provides some additional support for the role of confession in increasing agency costs as well as benefits, as those Catholics that confess more seem to give more money to the Church even after controlling for moral compliance. These results must be handled with extreme caution, however, because of the heroic assumptions behind the analysis. Furthermore, there are no good proxies available for the private benefits of Church services. For instance, education could be controlling for some private benefits but not for others if educated Catholics get less value from confession than from mass attendance.

7. Summary and concluding remarks

Contrary to partial rent-seeking views, this article shows that Catholic confession responds to the common trade-off of specialization advantages and agency costs. Specialization advantages come from having priests acting as first-instance judges of moral conduct, both completing and enforcing a moral code for the purpose of self and social control. As with any specialization, however, confession is also subject to agency costs. This trade-off of specialization advantages and agency costs changes with both external circumstances and the functioning of safeguards controlling agency costs.

The argument was tested on behavioral, historical and econometric data, comparing its explanatory power with respect to the alternative rent-seeking story.

First, cognitive sciences provide solid grounds for both the benefits and the costs sides of the argument. The moral sense, religion and, in particular, confession are shown to both rely on and control ancient instincts that may be maladapted in our current environment. Experimental psychology also shows that repentance and forgiveness produce cooperative and psychological benefits. Work in cognitive sciences also suggests, however, that religiosity could be a parasite in our mental endowment that may be misused by experts (priests in Catholicism) for their own benefit.

Second, the history of confession also supports the costs and benefits argument. Privatization of confession in the Middle Ages made possible the evolution towards truly moral, first-party enforcement, which can thereafter work in parallel with increasingly separated and specialized legal systems. Private confession is also conducive to developing human capital specialized in confession as well as implementing a more sophisticated and allegedly more motivating system of incentives. It also provides greater scope for exploitation, however, and this is shown in the historic struggle to implement more effective safeguards against priests' opportunism. The evolution after the Reformation also fits the argument when considering that confession declines slowly in most Protestant churches after the Reformation and, in both Protestant and Catholic areas, seems to parallel increases in education. Similarly, primitive forms of public confession re-emerge in sectarian movements within both Protestantism and Catholicism, leading to oppressive forms of social, non-specialized enforcement.

Third, econometric results support the view that confession to a priest is effective in moral enforcement, as those Catholics who confess more often also help the poor more. Confession also seems to be more effective than other religious and not exclusively Catholic practice: attending mass. There is also some support for the presence of agency costs, but not for greater agency costs in confession than in praying or attending mass. On the contrary, the estimated impact of attending mass is greater, and this difference is not likely to be due to scaling problems.

The costs-and-benefits tradeoff can be applied to other contexts and other moral enforcement mechanisms. For example, the role of scholars in traditional Islam have been seen as a form of intermediation between God and believers that is increasingly absent in modern political Islam (Feldman 2008). More generally, the growing role of education and the mass media in conforming morality opens up new opportunities for both specialization advantages and agency costs, and poses the more basic question regarding how we are now writing and enforcing the moral code. Specialization advantages are certainly attained by formal education systems while informal education depends more on market forces and occasional herding behavior. Agency costs are also present, however, in both the formal and informal processes, as exemplified by the occasional alleged capture of some formal education systems by teachers and of mass media by elite journalists.

References

Abel, Wilhelm. 1958. *Agrarpolitik*, 2nd ed. Göttingen: Vandenhoeck & Ruprecht.

Arruñada, Benito. 2008a. Human nature and institutions. In *New institutional economics: A guidebook*, eds. Eric Brousseau and Jean-Michel Glachant, pp. 81-99. Cambridge: Cambridge University Press.

Arruñada, Benito. 2008b. Specialization and rent-seeking in moral enforcement: The case of confession. Universitat Pompeu Fabra, *Economics and Business Working Paper Series* 653 (http://ssrn.com/abstract=394642, accessed May 13, 2009).

Aune, David E. 1987. Repentance. In *The encyclopedia of religion*, vol. 12, ed. Mircea Eliade, pp. 337-42. New York: MacMillan.

Axelrod, Robert. 1984. *The evolution of cooperation*. New York: Basic Books.

Baker, George P., Robert S. Gibbons and Kevin J. Murphy. 1994. Subjective performance measures in optimal incentive contracts. *Quarterly Journal of Economics* 59:1125-56.

Barzel, Yoram. 1997. *Economic analysis of property rights*, 2nd ed. Cambridge and New York: Cambridge University Press.

Becker, Gary S. 1968. Crime and punishment: An economic approach. *Journal of Political Economy* 76(2):169-217.

Becker, Sascha O., and Ludger Woessmann. 2009. Was Weber wrong? A human capital theory of protestant economic history. *Quarterly Journal of Economics* 124(2): 531-96.

Bénabou, Roland, and Jean Tirole. 2004. Willpower and personal rules. *Journal of Political Economy* 112(4):848-86.

Benz, Ernst. 1968. *Evolution and Christian hope: Man's concept of the future from the early Fathers to Teilhard de Chardin.* (Translated by Heinz G. Frank). Garden City, New York: Anchor-Doubleday.

Berman, Harold J. 1983. *Law and revolution, the formation of the Western legal tradition.* Cambridge: Harvard University Press.

Bianchi, Ugo. 1987. Confession of sins. In *The encyclopedia of religion*, vol. 4, ed. Mircea Eliade, pp. 1-7. New York: MacMillan.

Biller, Peter. 1998a. Confession in the Middle Ages: Introduction. In *Handling sin: Confession in the Middle Ages*, York Studies in Medieval Theology II, ed. Peter Biller and Alastair J. Minnis, pp. 3-33. Woodbridge and Rochester: The University of York and Boydell & Brewer.

Biller, Peter. 1998b. Confessors' manuals and the avoiding of offspring. In *Handling sin: Confession in the Middle Ages*, York Studies in Medieval Theology II, ed. Peter Biller and Alastair J. Minnis, pp. 165-87. Woodbridge and Rochester: The University of York and Boydell & Brewer.

Boyer, Pascal. 1994. *The naturalness of religious ideas: A cognitive theory of religion.* Berkeley: University of California Press.

Boyer, Pascal. 2001. *Religion explained.* New York: Basic Books.

Cameron, Euan. 1991. *The European reformation.* Oxford: Oxford University Press.

Caspari, Walter A. 1950. Confession of sins. In *The new Schaff-Herzog encyclopedia of religious knowledge*, vol. 3, ed. Samuel Macauley Jackson, pp. 221-23. Grand Rapids, Michigan: Baker Book House.

Congregation for Divine Worship. 2000. Circular letter concerning the integrity of the Sacrament of Penance. March 20. Available at http://www.antigonishdiocese.com/circularletter.html.

Cosmides, Leda. 1985. *Deduction or Darwinian algorithms? An explanation of the 'elusive' content effect of the Wason selection task.* Ph.D.

Dissertation. Harvard University: Department of Psychology.

Cosmides, Leda. 1989. The logic of social exchange: Has natural selection shaped how humans reason? Studies with the Wason selection task. *Cognition* 31:187-276.

Cosmides, Leda. and John Tooby. 1992. Cognitive adaptations for social exchange. In *The adapted mind*, eds. Jerome H. Barkow, Leda Cosmides and John Tooby, pp. 163-228. New York: Oxford University Press.

Damasio, Antonio R. 1994. *Descartes' error: Emotion, reason and the human brain*. New York: Grosset/Putnam.

Davidson, James D., *et al.* 1997. *The search for common ground: what unites and divides Catholic Americans*. Huntington: Our Sunday Visitor Publishing.

Dawkins, Richard. 2001. Time to stand up. Freedom from religion foundation. Wisconsin: Madison, September 2001. Available at http://ffrf.org/timely/dawkins.php.

De La Croix, Arnaud. 2005. *Los templarios: En el corazón de las cruzadas*. Barcelona: Ariel. (Translated by Mari Carmen Doñate, original ed. *Les templiers: Au coeur des croisades*, Paris: du Rocher 2002).

Delumeau, Jean. 1992. *La confesión y el perdón: las dificultades de la confesión, siglos XIII a XVIII*. Madrid: Alianza. (Translated by M. Armiño, original ed.: *L'aveu et le pardon. Les difficultés de la confession XIII-XVIII siècle*. Paris: Arthème Fayard 1990).

Ekelund, Robert B., Jr., Robert F. Hébert and Robert D. Tollison. 1992. The economics of sin and redemption: Purgatory as a market-pull innovation? *Journal of Economic Behavior and Organization* 19(1):1-15.

Ekelund, Robert B., Jr., Robert F. Hébert, and Robert D. Tollison. 2002. An economic analysis of the protestant reformation. *Journal of Political Economy* 110(3):646-71.

Ekelund, Robert B., Jr., Robert F. Hébert, and Robert D. Tollison. 2004. The economics of the counter-reformation: Incumbent-firm reaction to market entry. *Economic Inquiry* 690-705.

Ekelund, Robert B., Jr., Robert F. Hébert, and Robert D. Tollison. 2006. *The market for Christianity*. Cambridge, MA: MIT Press.

Feldman, Noah. 2008. *The fall and rise of the Islamic state*. Princeton: Princeton University Press.

Flack, Jessica C., and Frans B. M. de Waal. 2000. 'Any animal whatever': Darwinian building blocks of morality in monkeys and apes. In *Evolutionary origins of morality: Cross-Disciplinary perspectives*, ed. Leonard D. Katz. Bowling Green: Imprint Academic.

Goleman, Daniel. 1995. *Emotional intelligence: Why it can matter more than IQ*. New York: Bantam.

Graff, Harvey J. 1987. *The legacies of literacy: Continuities and contradictions in Western culture and society*. Bloomington: Indiana University Press.

Grice-Hutchinson, Marjorie. 1952. *The school of Salamanca. Readings in Spanish monetary theory 1544-1605*. Oxford: The Clarendon Press

Haidt, Jonathan. 2003. The moral emotions. In *Handbook of affective sciences*, eds. R. J. Davidson, K. R. Scherer and H. H. Goldsmith, pp. 852-70. Oxford: Oxford University Press.

Hopkins, Keith. 1999. *A world full of gods: The strange triumph of Christianity*. New York: The Free Press.

Isbell, Tim. 2005. Confession, a key to Christian growth. Cupertino: New Life Church. Available at http://www.nlnc.org/stuff/confession.html.

Jenkins, Philip. 2002. *The next Christendom: The coming of global Christianity*. New York: Oxford University Press.

John Paul II. 1984. *Reconciliatio et paenitentia*. December 2. Available at http://www.vatican.va/holy_father/john_paul_ii/apost_exhortations/documents/hf_jp-ii_exh_02121984_reconciliatio-et-paenitentia_en.html.

Jong, Peter Y. de. 1992-1994. Taking heed to the flock: A study of the principles and practice of family visitation. Series of articles published in *Ordained Servant*, 1(2)-3(3), April 1992-July 1994. Available at http://www.opc.org/OS/Ordained_servant.html.

Jonsen, Albert R., and Stephen. Toulmin. 1988. *The abuse of casuistry: A history of moral reasoning*. Berkeley: University of California Press.

Kahneman, Daniel, and Amos Tversky. 1995. Conflict resolution: A cognitive perspective. In *Barriers to conflict resolution*, eds. Kenneth Arrow, Robert Wilson, Lee Ross, Amos Tversky and Robert H. Mnookin, pp. 44-60. New York and London: Norton.

Kaplow, Louis, and Steven Shavell. 2002. Human nature and the best consequentialist moral system. *Harvard Law and Economics Discussion Paper* 349.

Kaplow, Louis, and Steven Shavell. 2007. Moral rules, the moral sentiments and behavior: Toward a theory of an optimal moral system. *Journal of Political Economy* 115:494-514.

Kim, Jae-On. 1975. Multivariate analysis of ordinal variables. *American Journal of Sociology* 81:261-98.

Krause, Neal, and Christopher G. Ellison. 2003. Forgiveness by God, forgiveness of others, and psychological well-being in late life. *Journal for the Scientific Study of Religion* 42(1):77-93.

Labovitz, Sanford. 1967. Some observations on measurement and statistics. *Social Forces* 46:151-160.

Labovitz, Sanford. 1970. The assignment of numbers to rank order categories. *American Sociological Review* 35:515-24.

Le Goff, Jacques. 1980. Trades and professions as represented in medieval confessors' manuals. In *Time, work and culture in the Middle Ages*, Jacques Le Goff, pp. 107-21. Chicago: Chicago University Press.

Le Goff, Jacques. 1984. *The birth of purgatory*. Chicago: University of Chicago Press. (Translated by A. Goldhammer, original ed.: *La naissance du Purgatoire*. Paris: Gallimard 1981).

Le Roy Ladurie, E. 1976. Family and inheritance in sixteenth-century France. In *Family and inheritance: Rural society in Western Europe, 1200-1800*, eds., pp. 37-70. Jack Goody, Joan Thirsk and E. P. Thompson, Cambridge: Cambridge University Press.

Lea, Henry Charles. 1896. *A history of auricular confession and indulgences in the Latin Church*, Greenwood Publishing Group, Inc., 1968. (Reprint of the 1896 ed. London: Swan Sonnensschein & Co).

Lee, Bernard J. Lee, *et al.* 2000. *The Catholic experience of small Christian communities*. Mahwah: Paulist Press.

Lenon, J. Paul. 2003. Aspects of concern regarding the legionaries of Christ. American Family Foundation Conference. Enfield, October 18. Available at http://www.regainnetwork.org/pdf/QuestioningDoubtDissentDiscouragedAug.pdf.

McClory, Robert. 2001. Cardinal, pastors discuss general absolution. *National Catholic Reporter*, July 27. Available at http://www.natcath.org/NCR_Online/archives/072701/072701g.htm.

McCullough, Michael E., Kenneth I. Pargament and Carl E. Thoresen, eds. 2000, *Forgiveness: Theory, research, and practice*, New York: Guilford Press.

Mullainathan, Sendhil. 2005. Development economics through the lens of psychology. In *Proceedings of the annual Bank conference on development economics: Lessons of experience*, eds. Francois Bourguignon and Boris Pleskovic, pp. 45-70. Washington and New York: The World Bank and Oxford University Press.

Novak, Michael. 1998. The Judeo-Christian foundation of human dignity, personal liberty, and the concept of the person. *Journal of Markets and Morality* 1(2):107-21.

Pennebaker, JamesW. 1989. Confession, inhibition, and disease. In *Advances in Experimental Social Psychology* 22, ed., L. Berkowitz, pp. 212-44. New York: Academic Press.

Pennebaker, James.W. 1997. *Opening up: The healing power of expressing emotions*. New York: Guilford Press.

Polinsky, A. Mitchell, and Steven Shavell. 1991. A note on optimal fines when wealth varies among individuals. *The American Economic Review* 81(3):618-21.

Polinsky, A. Mitchell, and Steven Shavell. 2000. The economic theory of public enforcement of law. *Journal of Economic Literature* 38(1):45-76.

Posner, Richard A. 1998. *Economic analysis of law*, 5th ed. Boston: Aspen.

Rabin, Matthew.1998. Psychology and economics. *Journal of Economic Literature* 36(1):11-46.

Ratzinger, Joseph. 2002. Presentation of Misericordia Dei. *L' Osservatore Romano* (English weekly ed.), May 8. Available at http://www.ewtn.com/library/CURIA/cdfpres.htm.

Riegel, Klaus Georg. 2005. Marxism-Leninism as a political religion. *Totalitarian Movements & Political Religions* 6(1):97-126.

Rothbard, Murray N. 1995. *An Austrian perspective on the history of economics (I): Economic thought before Adam Smith.* Cheltenham: Elgar.

Santayana, George. 1916. *Egotism in German philosophy* London: Dent and Sons.

Schmemann, Alexander. 1972. Confession and communion. Report to the Holy Synod of Bishops of the Orthodox Church in America, February 17. Available at http://www.oca.org/DOCencyclical.asp?SID=-12&ID=3.

Schmidtchen, Dieter, and Achim Mayer.1997. Established clergy, friars and the Pope: Some institutional economics of the Medieval Church. *Journal of Institutional and Theoretical Economics*, 153(1):122-49.

Shavell, Steven. 2002. Law versus morality as regulators of conduct. *American Law and Economics Review* 4(2):227-57.

Smith, Adam. 1759. *The theory of moral sentiments*. Indianapolis: Liberty Fund (1982).

Smith, Adam. 1776. *An inquiry into the nature and causes of the wealth of nations*. Indianapolis: Liberty Fund (1981).

Stark, Rodney. 1996. *The rise of Christianity: A sociologist reconsiders history*. Princeton: Princeton University Press.

Sullivan, Lawrence. E. 1987. Healing. In *The encyclopedia of religion* 6, ed. Mircea Eliade, pp. 226-37. New York: MacMillan.

Swanson, Guy E. 1967. *Religion and regime: A sociological account of the reformation*. Ann Arbor: University of Michigan Press.

Tapia, María del Carmen. 1994. *Tras el umbral: Una vida en el Opus Dei (Un viaje al fanatismo)*, (2nd revised ed. Barcelona: Ediciones, 2004). English ed.: *Beyond the threshold: A life in Opus Dei*. New York: Continuum (1997).

Tentler, Thomas N. 1977. *Sin and confession on the Eve of the reformation*. Princeton: Princeton University Press.

Thirsk, Joan. 1976. The European debate on customs of inheritance, 1500-1700. In *Family and inheritance: Rural society in Western Europe, 1200-1800*, eds. Jack Goody, Joan Thirsk and E. P. Thompson, pp. 177-91. Cambridge: Cambridge University Press.

Todd, Emmanuel. 1990. *L'invention de l'Europe*. Paris: Seuil.

Tooby, John, and Leda Cosmides. 1992. The psychological foundations of culture. In *The adapted mind: Evolutionary Psychology and the generation of culture*, eds. Jerome. H. Barkow, Leda Cosmides and John Tooby, pp. 19-136. New York: Oxford University Press.

Toulmin, Stephen. 1979. The inwardness of mental life. *Critical Inquiry* 6(1):1-16.

Trivers, Robert L. 1971. The evolution of reciprocal altruism. *Quarterly Review of Biology* 46:35-57.

Trivers, Robert L. 1985. *Social evolution*. Menlo Park: Benjamin/Cummings.

Trivers, Robert L. 2000. The elements of a scientific theory of self-deception. In *Evolutionary perspectives on human reproductive be-*

havior, eds. Dori LeCroy and Peter Moller, pp.114-31. Annals of the New York Academy of Sciences 907.

Urquhart, Gordon. 1999. *The Pope's armada: Unlocking the secrets of mysterious and powerful new sects in the Church*. Amherst: Prometheus.

Volkova, Elena. 2001. Burning candles and burnt hearts of Russia: Christianity in life and literature. Lecture given in the University of Durham, UK, February. Available at http://www.hello-online.ru/-downloads/burncand.doc.

Waal, Frans B. M. de. 1997. The chimpanzee's service economy: Food for grooming, *Evolution and Human Behavior* 18(6):375-86.

Walsh, Michael. 1989. *The secret world of Opus Dei: An investigation into the powerful, secretive society within the Catholic Church*. London: Grafton Books. (Reprint: San Francisco: Harper Collins, 2004).

Weber, Max. 1920a, *The protestant ethic and the spirit of capitalism*. (Translated by T. Parsons, 1930). London and New York: Routledge (1992).

Weber, Max. 1920b. The protestant sects and the spirit of capitalism. Available at http://www.ne.jp/asahi/moriyuki/abukuma/weber/world-/sect/sect_frame.html.

White, Lynn Jr. 1978. *Medieval religion and technology*. Berkeley: University of California Press.

Wuthnow, Robert. 2000. How religious groups promote forgiving: A national study. *Journal for the Scientific Study of Religion* 39(2):125-39.

The Different Work Ethics of Protestants and Catholics: an Econometric Analysis [1]

Benito Arruñada[2]

Abstract

This article develops two hypotheses about economically-relevant values of Christian believers, according to which Protestants should work more and more effectively, as in the "work ethic" argument of Max Weber, or display a stronger "social ethic" that would lead them to monitor each other's conduct, support political and legal institutions and hold more homogeneous values. Tests using current survey data confirm substantial partial correlations and possible different "effects" in mutual social control, institutional perfor-

[1] The author acknowledges the comments received from Doug Allen, Manuel Bagüés, Robert Barro, Lee Benham, Albert Carreras, Nuno Garoupa, Dean Lueck, Phillip E. Keefer, Rachel McCleary, Debin Ma, Eduardo Melero, Lewis S. Mudge, Andrew Scott, Paul Zak, Luigi Zingales, three referees and seminar participants at Berkeley, FAES, Harvard, Instituto de Empresa, ISNIE, UAM, UPF and Washington University, as well as the research assistance of Petar Balachev. The usual disclaimers apply. The author acknowledges financial support from the Barcelona GSE Research Network and the Government of Catalonia; the Spanish Ministry of Science and Innovation, through grant ECO2008-01116; and the European Commission, through the Integrated Project "Reflexive Governance in the Public Interest". The data utilized were documented and made available by the Zentralarchiv für Empirische Sozialforschung, University of Cologne, and were collected by independent institutions in each country. Neither the original collectors nor the Zentralarchiv bear any responsibility for the analyses or interpretation presented here.

[2] Pompeu Fabra University and Barcelona GSE. Trias Fargas, 25. 08005-Barcelona (Spain). E-mail: benito.arrunada@upf.edu.

mance and homogeneity of values but no difference in work ethics. Protestantism therefore seems conducive to capitalist economic development, not by the direct psychological route of the Weberian work ethic but rather by promoting an alternative social ethic that facilitates impersonal trade.[3]

Keywords: Religion, values, Weber, institutions, enforcement.

1. Motivation

This article compares the economically-relevant values of Catholics and Protestants based on predictions that stem from differences in the theology, church organization and social practice of the two religions. In particular, it argues that different behaviours and values between Catholicism and Protestantism fit in with differences in beliefs and in the enforcement mechanisms that have characterized these two religions since the Reformation. Catholicism relied on the theology of salvation by works and the role of the Church as intermediary and enforcement agent. Protestantism, on the other hand, relied on salvation by divine grace and enforcement through social interactions. Both differences affected a number of factors that impinge on individual success and how institutions and the economy work. In particular, while Protestantism favours the emergence of anonymous trade and thus markets, Catholicism is more conducive to developing personalized trade. From this line of reasoning two hypotheses — according to which the two religions produced different work and social ethics — and a number of specific predictions are drawn and then tested on data from the 1998 ISSP survey, which covers 32 countries, thus making it possible to account for country fixed effects and to purge the effects of religion from country-level unobserved heterogeneity.

---

[3] Appendix with Figures online available at: http://www.uni-erfurt.de/finanzwissenschaft/

Numerous empirical studies have been carried out on the economic effects of religion (Iannaccone, 1998). Within the sociology and economics of religion, most works focus on real variables, trying to explain the relationship between religious traits such as affiliation or participation and diverse measures of behaviour and achievement at the individual level. Connections have been found, among others, between religiosity and wages (Chiswick, 1983), school attendance (Freeman, 1986), health (Ellison, 1991), and criminal behaviour (Evans *et al.,* 1995). However, it is understandably hard to draw general conclusions from individual observations within a single country. Cross-country studies have also found connections between religious characteristics or country background and a variety of country-level economic characteristics, such as values assumed to be conducive to capitalist development, as well as historical or recent economic performance. Thus, La Porta *et al.* (1997) and Inglehart (1999) find that trust is lower in Catholic countries; Blum and Dudley (2001) estimate that wages increased more in Protestant European cities between 1500 and 1750; Stulz and Williamson (2003) argue that predominantly Catholic countries tend to offer less protection to lenders because of an alleged Catholic bias against usury; Barro and McCleary (2003, 2006) show that growth relates positively to beliefs and negatively to church attendance, suggesting that the effect of religion depends on efficiency in the production of belief; Inglehart and Norris (2004) confirm that the authority of established religions tends to decrease in wealthy countries. However, studies that use country measurements and averages within a cross-section of countries find it difficult to identify the effects of religion as it is mixed up with other institutional factors.

The methodology of this article is similar to that used by Glaeser and Glendon (1998), Sacerdote and Glaeser (2008), and Guiso, Sapienza and Zingales (2003) in relying on an international collection of survey data at the individual level and controlling for fixed country effects, as well as several personal characteristics. This within-country analysis, by controlling for most potential causes, comes closer to identifying the effects of religion. In fact, with the inclusion of country controls, the effect of religion might be underestimated to the extent that it has become embedded in national traits.

Overall, its findings provide little support for Weber's "work ethic" hypothesis, whereby Protestants tend to work more and more effectively than Catholics. They support, however, a "social ethic" hypothesis, as Protestant values shape individuals to be more active in mutual social control, more supportive of institutions, less bound to close circles of family and friends and to hold more homogeneous values.

These results are in line with Glaeser and Glendon (1998) who, after modelling the incentives in Calvinist predestination, confirm empirically that Catholicism and Protestantism associate with different social interactions; and with Guiso, Sapienza and Zingales (2003), who also find that Catholicism and Protestantism offer pros and cons with respect to economic attitudes. The argument is partly similar to that of Becker and Woessmann (2009), who argue that Protestant regions grew faster because Protestant emphasis on reading the Bible led, as a side effect, to greater investment in literacy and human capital. My argument is also one of side effects but related to the development of a social ethic that favoured market transactions and market-enhancing institutions.[4]

The present work differs from, and complements, previous works in several important ways. First, some previous works supply heterogeneous empirical correlations between religion and economic

---

[4] Ekelund et al. (2006: 189-231) discuss other possible reasons, such as simpler churches and liturgies, and fewer holidays and pilgrimages, as to why the Protestant Reformation may have affected economic growth.

performance or attitudes. As a consequence, their findings are hard to evaluate whereas the empirical tests in this article are developed from an analytical framework that allows a set of testable hypotheses to be drawn up, painting a more systematic and theoretical picture of the links between alleged causes and effects, which comes closer to examining cultural innovation instead of taking culture as given. Second, the effect of religion is estimated not only on values but also on personal outcomes such as working hours, education and personal success. Third, using data from the 1998 International Social Survey Programme (ISSP) surveys conducted in 1998 and 1999 in 32 countries allows estimation of the effects of religion when strong believers allegedly played a greater role in society.

The rest of the article is structured as follows. Section 1 develops a framework to analyze the economic impact of religions, based on a typology of enforcement systems, applies it to the changes introduced by the Protestant Reformation and defines on this basis two testable hypotheses according to which Protestantism favours a more productive work ethic or a stronger social ethic that leads Protestants to exert greater social control, support the rule of law more and hold more homogeneous values. Section 2 describes the ISSP data, the specific variables employed and the statistical regressions used to test the hypotheses. Section 3 presents and discusses the results, according to which Protestantism promotes values favourable to capitalist relations based on impersonal trade, with no perceptible impact on the work ethic. Section 4 concludes.

2. Analytical Framework

2.1 The Effect of Religion on Enforcement and Growth

In all societies, individual behaviour is constrained by norms and rules that humans define and enforce by different means. Religion is one of these means. To analyze the effects of Christian religions,

I will distinguish three types of structures according to which party is responsible for enforcing the more or less implicit terms of exchange in a given interaction. Under "first party" enforcement, the obliged individuals evaluate their own conduct in relation to their own reading of a moral code, a code that includes many economically-relevant preferences, towards effort, thriftiness, and so on. In accordance with this evaluation, individuals sanction themselves with some psychological compensation, which in Christianity is related to the idea of "salvation" and eternal life in heaven. "Second party" enforcement is based on verification and sanction by the party suffering the consequences of breach. In addition to partners in a standard economic exchange, peers in groups are also second parties to the extent that they exert pressure on noncompliant members through diverse means, from shaming to ostracizing or even killing them. Lastly, under "third party" enforcement, more or less specialized agents, such as political rulers, judges and police forces, verify the behaviour of group members and punish those who do not follow the rules.

Religion obviously influences first party enforcement. For example, relative to the more individualistic pagan views prevalent at the time of the Roman Empire, Christianity greatly reinforced first party enforcement by imposing on believers the then novel moral duty of helping their neighbours (Stark, 1996). In this Christian spirit, natural feelings of compassion, which Roman patricians were educated to suppress, were the cornerstone of Adam Smith's moral conception in his *Theory of Moral Sentiments* (1759). Less obviously, religion also affects the functioning of second and third party enforcement. In primitive societies, there is even little separation between religious and civil law. In more developed theocratic regimes, religious authorities also take over or dominate political rulers, and there is little or no separation between religious and civil law. Christianity followed a long and tortuous path along these lines. It started as a minority cult whose views conflicted with those that were politically correct at the time, but became the State religion in the last centuries of the Roman Empire. During the late Middle Ages, and especially on the eve of the Reformation, the Church was not only the monopoly supplier of religious services but also the main provider of educational, legal, bureaucratic and welfare services; it commanded substantial military forces; the papal state constituted a political power in itself; and churchmen were the main political officials all across Europe (Cameron, 1991).

2.2 Comparative Analysis of Christian Moral Enforcements

In this context, the Protestant Reformation radically modified both the contents of moral rules and the enforcement mechanisms of moral and civil rules alike. The Reformation directly affected the three enforcement systems:

First, reformers altered the structure of beliefs on salvation, switching from Catholic salvation by works to salvation by divine grace alone. Following Max Weber's *The Protestant Ethic and the Spirit of Capitalism* (1904-1905), many writers have considered that this change in beliefs improves economic incentives, especially in the Calvinist version that emphasizes predestination but also in the common Protestant focus on ordinary labour and vocation. The argument goes that even though good works do not warrant salvation, they serve as a signal to the believer, who is therefore moved to constant self-examination, with increased moral awareness. Worldly success is also seen as a positive signal when coming from disciplined work and not resulting in excessive consumption. Reformers thus modified the contents of the moral code in some dimensions with two potentially crucial economic consequences: by giving a more positive moral meaning to worldly activities, they encouraged a work ethic that favoured effort; and, by frowning on excessive consumption, they encouraged savings. According to this argument, the consequences to be expected are that both the laity and the clergy will focus on productive activities and abandon unproductive ones. A sort of secular asceticism should develop, in which individuals comply with divine plans by punctually performing their earthly duties.

However, the degree of motivation provided by Protestant theology in Weber's interpretation is open to doubt for a variety of reasons. First, there is a psychological inconsistency in that Protestant believers are saved by God, with good works contributing nothing. Even 16th century reformers soon realized how difficult it was to "persuade their flocks to be religious, while also teaching that 'good works' of piety were worthless to earn salvation" (Cameron, 1991: 400). Second, Protestant believers could easily deceive themselves when relying on self-examination. In contrast, Catholic enforcement was grounded on confession of sins to a priest, which suffers greater agency costs but offers specialization advantages (Arruñada, 2009). Third, empirically, predestination may trigger very different responses, as shown by its role in Islam (Rodinson, 1974). Lastly, Catholicism may have been more hospitable to capitalism, at least originally (e.g., Dickens: 178-79; Berman, 1983: 337-39).

Second, the Reformation dismissed the role of the Church as an intermediary between God and believers, a role that made lay people passive religious subjects. In the Medieval Church, the Bible was interpreted and validated by the Church, and the laity was discouraged from reading it; theologists debated in closed academic circles, not allowing the laity to know about their controversies; and priests had the power to forgive sins in private sacramental confession, thereby ruling on believers' salvation. The reformers minimized this intermediary role of the Church by setting the Bible as the only source, even as the rule according to which to judge the Church; and correspondingly empowering the laity, encouraging them to read the Bible, and holding theological debates in the open.[5] They also abolished the old penitential system, eliminating the power of the Church to forgive sins. Most visibly, they eliminated barriers to entry by using the vernacular instead of Latin for liturgy and writing.

This broad empowerment of the laity came with corresponding duties: lay people had to know more and, especially, fill the vacuum left by the disappearance of private confession. These changes should make lay people abandon their previous passivity, becoming more vigilant of their neighbours' conduct and worrying more about how their own deeds will affect their neighbours' opinions on them. Mutual social control thus avoided the obvious risk that self-examination might result in more lenient standards of conduct. These consequences were more explicit in stricter communities. For example, the Geneva of Calvin adopted many intrusive social controls, such as "family visitations," by which two elders regularly visited each home to discuss the spiritual health of each family. Another classic account of these practices in mutual control was also given by Weber in his description of American sects (1920).

Third, in contrast to the more independent Catholic Church, reformers were more supportive of political and legal institutions, often because they needed political support in their fight against Catholicism. The Medieval Church had been an international power that held very substantial wealth and limited the power of political rulers, frequently opposing them. Where the Reformation succeeded, most Church property was soon seized by political rulers, and the previous Church privileges were removed. Furthermore, lay rulers rapidly asserted their domination of religious affairs. Consequently, many Protestant churches rapidly became appendices of local or

---

[5] See Becker and Woessmann (2009) on the consequences of Protestant emphasis on reading the Bible.

national rulers. Moreover, in contrast to the ambivalent support provided by the Catholic Church to political rulers and the nuanced advice the Church gave to the laity for dealing with rulers, reformed churches more flatly affirmed that believers had to obey their rulers, as Luther exhorted very early on (1523). Such concentration of political power may have and often did result in tyranny. However, in a similar fashion to self-control, it also tended to be restrained by more active mutual social control.

In addition, the changes introduced by the Reformation also made values more homogeneous among believers. This should lower the transaction costs of impersonal trade, the sort of trade between strangers that has been considered crucial in capitalist economic development at least since North and Thomas (1973), and by authors in different disciplines, such as Granovetter (1985) and Seabright (2004). The two religions provide markedly different setups in this regard:

Primarily, Catholic practice favours more diverse moral standards because of both the contents and its moral code and, mainly, its enforcement mechanisms. With respect to the code, its prioritization of the family encourages selective charity and reinforces in believers their natural tendency to favour their relatives and possibly friends over strangers. It therefore enhances the use of double standards. With respect to enforcement, both the theology of salvation by works and the practice of private confession of sins to a priest support heterogeneous standards. First, salvation by works involves an element of individual fine-tuning because works cannot be evaluated without considering the possibilities of each individual and moral standards are adjusted to specific circumstances. In fact, medieval theologists had minutely devised prescriptions for each case, developing the body of "casuistry" literature. Private confession also adjusted moral standards to each individual: priests were trained to adapt the moral code to the strength of the penitent, even negotiating penance with them. In addition, the theology of Purgatory made it possible for merits to be traded amongst believers and with the Church, which reinforced inequality (Arruñada, 2009). The sale of indulgences also caused greater moral disparity among believers (in addition to considerable rent-seeking, as emphasized by Ekelund *et al.* (1992, 1996, 2002, 2006).

Conversely, greater homogeneity in the moral standards of Protestantism derives from its emphasis on universal charity and its greater reliance on "external" sources for enforcement, both second parties and legal institutions. First, the Protestant ideal tends to place obligations to strangers on a par with those to family members (McCleary, 2007). Second, compared to the secret judgments of the confessional, reliance on external enforcement is likely to produce more equal treatment, as modelled by Glaeser and Glendon (1998). Examples abound, starting with John Calvin's insistence on treating all believers equally, or the community responsibility system practiced by the American sects described by Weber (1920), which is somehow similar to the late medieval system analyzed by Greif (2002). In this extreme case, as individuals are liable for the debts of their colleagues, they will insist that they meet the standards of the group, both on admission and later on. Third, more generally, legal enforcement applies the same principle on a larger scale, by providing impartial enforcement of obligations without paying attention to who the parties are and, in particular, regardless of whether they are locals or outsiders.

Summing up, the analysis supports two distinctive hypotheses. The *work ethic* hypothesis predicts that Protestant believers work more and more effectively than Catholics. The *social ethic* hypothesis predicts that Protestants show greater concern for social interactions, in terms of at least social control, rule of law and homogeneity of values.

3. Data and Tests

3.1 Data

The tests will rely on several econometric models built with cross-section data from the 1998 religion module of the International Social Survey Programme (ISSP) Survey. The ISSP is a continuing program of cross-national collaboration on surveys covering topics of importance for research in the social sciences. The surveys were conducted in 1998 and 1999 (8 countries) in a total of 32 countries, most of them developed countries, with sample sizes between 804 and 2,488, and a total of 39,034 observations. After dropping observations with missing values in the independent variables, 19,246 observations on Protestants and Catholics remain, which are distributed across countries as summarized in 1. In each of these national surveys, the questionnaires of the religion module included at least 72 questions about the respondents' feelings (for instance, their happiness), values (tolerance of homosexuality, confidence on parliaments, trust in strangers and so on), religious beliefs (in heaven, in hell, etc.) and practice (church attendance), social habits (different volunteer activities), and opinions (government responsibilities), etc.; as well as a full set of demographic variables (sex, marital status, education, earnings, etc.). Detailed explanation of all variables is given in 1 in the Annex.

These surveys have been used in many other studies.[6] Using ISSP data instead of the World Values Survey reduces sample size and the number of countries and variables. It provides, however, a more detailed measurement of the intensity of beliefs, which allows me to estimate its impact and to distinguish the fixed effect of "belong-

[6] Full information on the ISSP surveys is available at http://www.issp.org (accessed January 13, 2009), including data and codebooks for the religion 1998 module and a list of the thousands of studies using the ISSP data.

ing" to a religion from the variable effect of "believing" its doctrine more or less strongly.

2 summarizes the empirical exercise, in which several tests are used in parallel for each of the predictions. These tests rely on several econometric models examining differences in values and actions between Protestants and Catholics. For simplicity, observations for members of other religions are dropped. In addition, for the Netherlands, data on individual earnings are estimated as the predicted values of an OLS regression of available individual earnings on family income, family size and education level. Family income is also assumed to be income by other family members in the 635 observations for which asserted family income is lower than individual earnings. Lastly, given that the surveys provide highly correlated questions for some issues, only one variable was used in such cases. When the variables are not so heavily correlated, indexes were constructed by using the first principal components of the variables are used (2 to 6 in the Annex). Results do not materially change as a consequence of these imputations and simplifications.

3.2 Work Ethic

The work ethic hypothesis will be tested by examining how Protestants and Catholics compare in two indicators: (1) the number of weekly *Working hours*, used as a proxy for the willingness to exert effort; and (2) an index of personal *Success*, built as the first principal component of four variables (individual earnings standardized within each country, working as a supervisor, being self-employed and each respondent's subjective social class).

The predictions are that, within each country and controlling for demographic variables, Protestants should work more hours and achieve greater success than Catholics. The reason lies in both the emphasis of the Protestant moral code on asceticism and methodical work, and the greater motivation supposedly produced by its theology of salvation.

3.3 Social Ethic

Predictions of the social ethic hypothesis will be tested in three distinctive areas: social control, rule of law and homogeneous values.

3.3.1 Social Control

According to the social ethic hypothesis, Protestants should exert a greater effort in mutual social control than Catholics. This prediction will be examined in three ways: First, by directly testing if Catholics *Volunteer* less than Protestants. The assumption here is that respondents' volunteering is correlated to their willingness to informally monitor and sanction the behaviour of others. This assumption is plausible because mutual control is another form of unrewarded volunteering. In addition, some volunteer activities act as enforcement mechanisms themselves, because enjoying membership is conditional on complying with a certain pattern of behaviour. Volunteer work is gauged with an index built as the first principal component of four variables measuring volunteering in political, charitable, religious and other activities.

Second, by testing if greater levels of education affect differently for Protestants and Catholics how much confidence people have in the Church and religious organizations (*Trust Church*). The hypothesis predicts that, whatever the effect of education, it will be smaller or even negative for Catholics, because most reformed churches relinquished some of their functions in moral enforcement, correspondingly empowering individuals and encouraging them to learn. Therefore, substitution between education and church enforcement was accomplished by Protestants centuries ago, while the Catholic Church has retained a more active role in moral enforcement. As a consequence, education should be a complement of religion for Protestants but a substitute for Catholics.

Lastly, by similarly testing if greater levels of education affect *Religious practice* differently for Catholics and Protestants, where *Religious practice* is an index built with four variables measuring prayer frequency, participation in church activities, self-description as a religious person and frequency of attendance at religious services. Considering the results in the literature (Iannaccone, 1998: 1470), greater education is expected to increase religious participation. However, the prediction concerns only differences between religions — in particular, it predicts that this effect will be significantly smaller for Catholics than for Protestants. The rationale is the same as for confidence in the Church.

3.3.2 Rule of Law

In terms of the rule of law, the social ethic hypothesis predicts that Protestants support political and legal institutions more than Catholics. It will be tested by examining how Protestants and Catholics compare with respect to three variables: First, their *Tolerance of tax fraud*. The fact that taxes are necessary for operating political and legal institutions upholds the notion that less tolerance of tax fraud is related to greater support of such institutions. In addition, the Catholic Church has been relatively lenient with respect to tax fraud, not considering it as a serious sin, perhaps as a remnant of the medieval times when it competed for tax money with civil rulers. Given the greater support historically given by Protestant churches to political rulers, it is predicted that within each country and also controlling for a full set of demographic variables, Catholics will be more tolerant of tax fraud.

Second, their willingness to *Cover up for friends*, measured through respondents' reactions to the hypothetical case in which they are riding in a car driven too fast by a close friend who hits a pedestrian, and this friend asks the respondent to tell the police that he was obeying the speed limit. The variable therefore measures individuals' unwillingness to voluntarily cooperate with the legal system and its representatives when this cooperation conflicts with friendship ties. It is assumed to indicate how much support respondents provide to third party enforcement. Also in this case, it is predicted that Catholics will be more willing to cover up for their friends.

Lastly, I will examine respondents' confidence in political and legal institutions, measured with the index *Trust institutions*, which combines confidence in the parliament, and the court and legal system. The logic behind these proxies is straightforward, as Parliament establishes the legal rules and courts enforce them. Our prediction is that Catholics will be less confident of their political and legal institutions.

3.3.3 Homogeneous Values

Lastly, the social ethic hypothesis predicts that Protestants hold more homogeneous values than Catholics. It will also be examined in three ways: First, the homogeneity of moral standards within the Protestant and Catholic religion will be directly tested by comparing the residuals of the regressions on values between the two groups, expecting a higher variance among Catholics.

Second, homogeneity of values will be tested indirectly by examining how Protestants and Catholics compare with respect to a measure of interpersonal generalized trust, given by responses to the question, "Generally speaking, would you say that people can be trusted or that you can't be too careful in dealing with people?" (*Trust strangers*). This variable is often related to "social capital" (Putnam, 1993) and is thought to convey trust in strangers (Knack and Keefer, 1997). Its connection to homogeneity is clear if people trust strangers more in homogeneous societies, as argued by Alesina and LaFerrara (2000, 2002), an idea grounded both on social (Tajfel and Turner, 1979) and evolutionary psychology (Trivers, 1971). The prediction is that Catholics should trust strangers less than Protestants.

Complementarily, I will finally check the importance individuals give to their family, to examine the argument put forward by Putnam (1993), Fukuyama (1995) and others that there is substitution between the strength of family ties and formal institutions. Lacking direct measures, I will use as a proxy the difference in individuals' stated tolerance of heterosexual relations before and after marriage. The prediction is that this index of *Importance of family*, measured as the gap between tolerance of premarital sex and adultery, will be greater for Catholics.

3.4 Models

3.4.1 Main Model

To perform most of these tests, the following equations will be estimated:

$$
\begin{aligned}
Y_i = \alpha_0 \quad & + \alpha_{0c}\, Catholic \\
+ \beta_1\, Faith \quad & + \beta_{1c}\, Catholic \times Faith \\
+ \beta_2\, Religious\ upbringing \quad & + \beta_{2c}\, CatholicR \times Religious\ upbringing \\
+ \beta_3\, Education \quad & + \beta_{3c}\, Catholic \times Education \\
& + \Sigma_t\, (\beta_t\, Control_m \text{ variables}) \\
& + \Sigma_r\, (\beta_r\, Country_n \text{ dummies}) \quad (1)
\end{aligned}
$$

where each dependent variable, Y_i, represents a value or action, as stated by respondents to the survey, from their weekly working hours to their trust in strangers. Half of the dependent variables are expressed in terms of categories with a natural order. Ordered *probit* models are estimated in these cases, and ordinary least squares are used for the rest. The regressions of *Working hours* and *Positive working hours* are *tobit* and *probit* models. All equations were estimated using weight adjustments with robust (Huber-White) standard errors. Neither the choice of model nor the use of survey estimation materially affect the results.

Independent variables are as follows:

- *Catholic* is a binary variable that takes value one for respondents who state that they belong to the Catholic religion, zero otherwise. The default category is Protestant.

- *Faith* is an index measuring the intensity of respondents' faith. Simplicity plus the substantial collinearity among the three belief variables (in the afterlife, heaven and hell) advise using a composite index of belief intensity, built as the first principal component of the three variables.
- *Upbringing* measures the degree of religious indoctrination that respondents received during their childhood. This is taken directly from a survey question asking respondents how often they attended religious services when they were around 11 or 12 years old.
- *Education* measures the highest degree of education reached by respondents.
- *Interactive variables*, built as products of *Catholic* times *Faith*, *Upbringing* and *Education*, are introduced to test differences in the effects of faith, upbringing and education between the two religions. *CatholicR* is a dummy that takes value one for those raised as Catholics.
- Control variables were introduced for the sex of respondents, their age and age squared, and their marital status (through three dummies for widows, divorced and separated and single), as well as country dummies.

3.4.2 Fixed and Variable Effects of Religion

Model (1) distinguishes between fixed and variable "effects" of the two religions on values and behaviour. Fixed effects are related to membership or, more broadly, to "belonging" to a particular religious group, and do not vary across believers of a given faith. In our case, their coefficients (α_{0c}) estimate the difference between belonging to Catholicism and Protestantism, because observations for other religions have been dropped. Furthermore, given that *Faith*, *Upbringing* and *Education* have been standardized within the sample, these fixed effects measure attitudes for the average person in the whole sample of Catholics and Protestants (average not only in terms of the demographic controls but also in terms of *Faith*, *Religious upbringing* and *Education*). Their estimates are given in the first row of 4.

In addition to these fixed or belonging effects, the two religions provide different structures of beliefs and enforcement that are predicted to lead to different variable effects, meaning in our case that the intensity of belief, the degree of religious upbringing and the degree of education should affect values and actions for Protestants and Catholics differently. In the equations, we take Protestants as the omitted category, estimating Protestant variable effects with coefficients β_j, and the differential impact of Catholic *Faith*, *Upbringing* and *Education* with coefficients β_{jc}, with $j = 1, 2, 3$, respectively. Their estimates are given in the rows corresponding to the interactive variables in Panel A of 4. In the case of education, estimating variable effects is useful to test the social control hypothesis whereas, for faith and upbringing, estimated variable effects give us a glimpse into the effects that religion may have exerted in the past, when both the intensity of religious belief and the degree of religious indoctrination can be assumed to be greater then they are now in most societies.

Complementarily, the overall effect of "being Catholic" will be estimated with a simplified version of model (1) in which the variables *Faith*, *Upbringing*, *Education* and their interactions are excluded, such that the new coefficients of the *Catholic* variable estimate how average Catholics in the sample differ from average Protestants after controlling for demographic and country effects but not for the intensity of their faith, upbringing and education. Estimates of these average effects are given in the first row of Panel B in 4.

4. Results

3 presents summary statistics of the data used for the analysis. Most differences in means and standard deviations for Protestants and Catholics are consistent with the hypotheses. 4 presents the main results, obtained by estimating the effects of the two religions on a variety of values, conducts and facts. Catholicism is represented by a dummy binary variable, with Protestantism as the omitted category. Results for constants, control variables and country dummies are omitted but their use is supported by their statistically significant correlations with the dependent variables and the fact that most control variables show the expected signs. The Table contains two panels. Panel A shows the results for models in equation (1), with variable effects, while Panel B presents the average effects obtained with the simplified model.

4.1 The Work Ethic Hypothesis

Results hardly provide any support for the work ethics hypothesis. Despite the fact that on average Protestants work 8.5% more hours and show greater personal success, the significance of these differences disappears after controlling for demographic and country effects according to the non-significant coefficients of fixed effects in 4, both for the standard person in the sample (panel A) and for the standard member of each religion (panel B).

Results on working hours, a variable that measures working time at all jobs, but not time worked at home, are slightly ambiguous with respect to the differential effects of the intensity of religious belief and upbringing between Catholics and Protestants. As shown in panel A, for Catholics, stronger faith and religious upbringing are associated with fewer working hours (equation [1]). However, this result seems to be driven by the fact that the only working hours considered are those worked in jobs. Catholics are indeed less likely to report positive working hours (equation [2]). However, for those Catholics with positive working hours, belief intensity is associated with a greater number of working hours (equation [3]), a result driven fully by Catholic women. Overall, the results seem to reflect a difference between the two religions as to occupational patterns, which cannot be fully clarified without knowing how many hours the two types of respondents work outside their jobs. With the data available, the observed difference—which refers only to the effect of faith and upbringing—cannot be ascribed to a differential willingness to exert effort. It seems more likely to respond or at least be heavily influenced by different priorities in allocating time between the family and the outside world, an interpretation that fits in well with the greater importance that Catholics grant to the family (section 3.2.3).

Results for personal success are even clearer, with no significant differences being observed when controlling for demographic and country variables, neither in the fixed effect of belonging to a religion nor in the variable effects of religious belief intensity or upbringing.

4.2 The Social Ethic Hypothesis

4.2.1 Social Control

Results confirm the three social control predictions. First, average Catholics not only volunteer work significantly less than Protestants (on average, about .159 standard deviations) but volunteering increases with faith and upbringing less than half for Catholics than what it does for Protestants. Catholic values are thus more weakly linked to volunteering and therefore are allegedly less conducive to mutual control, to the extent that mutual control relies on volunteer enforcement work and many organizations based on volunteer work also act as enforcement devices by, for example, screening access to social networks.

Second, the data show an acute contrast in the relationship between education and confidence in churches and religious organizations: better-educated Protestants trust them more whereas better-educated Catholics trust them less (from a rate of .074 standard deviations of trust for each deviation in education for Protestants to -.090 deviations for Catholics). Catholics also show more confidence in their Church, and their confidence increases with their faith and religious upbringing. However, greater confidence can be interpreted in different ways.

Third, education has a similarly contrasting effect on religious practice because, even if in this case education has for Catholics a slightly positive instead of a negative effect, this attenuation probably is at least partly driven by the likely presence of a social element in the demand for religious practice, as argued by Sacerdote and Glaeser (2008).

These contrasting effects of education support the idea that for Protestants education complements religion whereas for Catholics education substitutes for religion. It therefore seems that the Catholic Church is less in tune with its more educated laity, possibly due to the greater role the Catholic Church plays as an enforcer, which conflicts more with educated laity.

4.2.2 Rule of Law

Results clearly confirm two of the three predictions according to which Protestants support political and legal institutions more than Catholics.

First, Catholics are significantly more tolerant of tax fraud than Protestants, in line with Guiso, Sapienza and Zingales (2003). Furthermore, even if strong Catholic beliefs are associated with less tolerance of tax fraud, this association is about a third weaker than among Protestants. The result therefore confirms that, as predicted, Catholic values are less supportive of those political and legal institutions that are financed with taxation.

Second, Catholics are also more willing to cover up for their delinquent friends in dealings with the police, and strong Catholic beliefs have a similarly positive but weaker effect. This result confirms that Catholic values elicit less cooperation from citizens in the functioning of legal institutions when they conflict with smaller social circles, such as the ones defined by friendship ties.

Third, no significant differences are observed between Protestants and Catholics with respect to their confidence in political and legal institutions, measured through the index of *Trust institutions*. Strong Catholic believers even show more confidence than strong Protestant believers, with Catholic faith showing almost twice the effect of Protestant faith, in line with Guiso, Sapienza and Zingales (2003), who find Catholics trust both the Government and the legal system more than Protestants.

The results for this third proxy of institutional support might be reconciled with those for the two other proxies by considering that citizens' uncritical confidence in political and legal institutions does not improve the functioning of these institutions. According to this argument, by empowering individuals, Protestantism has ended up encouraging a relatively more sceptical view on institutions and not only on the institutionalized Church. Protestants are more willing to contribute to the public good by punishing tax fraud socially, denouncing misbehaviour even at the cost of losing friends and holding a sceptical view of institutions.

This interpretation emphasizes the empowerment of individuals which was used mainly to justify the social control hypothesis, and therefore reinforces the social control hypothesis to the detriment of the rule of law hypothesis, grounded on the direct political prescriptions of Protestant churches.

4.2.3 Homogeneous Values

Different versions of our two tests confirm that Protestants hold more homogeneous values than Catholics.

First, most standard deviations are significantly smaller for the Protestant sub-sample, both in the original data (3) and, more revealingly, in the residuals of the regressions (5). This greater homogeneity should reduce the exchange costs faced by members of the more homogeneous group, both within and outside the group, by easing coordination tasks. This effect on coordination would be enhanced by the fact that such homogeneity is present in all unobservable variables, while the only significant exceptions (personal success and volunteer work) are easy to observe and, therefore, are of lesser consequence for trade. This result is reaffirmed when comparing the standard deviations of residuals obtained in regressions of the unobservable on all observable variables (as done in 7 in the Annex).

Both religions may thus be suitable for supporting human interaction in different kinds of environment and transaction. In comparison with the more homogeneous Protestant ethic, the more diverse Catholic moral standards may increase transaction costs in impersonal trading but also make personal trade easier, by better adapting moral incentives to the diverse situations faced by believers. These well-adapted incentives and standards probably perform better than more general solutions in the self-control sphere. This is so because, when parties know each other, they can use additional information when transacting. This is more likely to happen in rural environments and, more generally, for friends and family-related interactions. With its relatively more homogeneous standards, Protestantism seems, however, better adapted for impersonal trading between anonymous parties, such as those in commerce, finance and industry, a conclusion in line with that of Blum and Dudley (2001).

Second, average Catholics trust strangers less, confirming the findings of Guiso, Sapienza and Zingales (2003) with individual data, the cross-country results of La Porta *et al.* (1997) and Inglehart (1999), and the prediction of Putnam (1993), even though no differences between Catholics and Protestants are observed with respect to how their intensity of religious beliefs or upbringing affect their trust in strangers. It also remains an open question to what extent this greater trust might result from greater homogeneity. However, whatever its origins, greater trust would have important economic consequences, given its role in conforming initial expectations that are crucial in making cooperative strategies viable in repeated games, for instance when implementing a "tit for tat" strategy, and the correlation established between trust and economic growth (Knack and Keefer, 1997; Zak and Knack, 2001).

Third, Catholics not only give more importance than Protestants to family ties, but Catholic beliefs and upbringing are also positively related to the proxy of family importance, which is in line with the argument of Putnam (1993). This greater importance of the family tallies with the propensity shown by Catholics to take occupational choices that favour "production" within the family and might hinder the functioning of institutions, for example through nepotism. When adding the greater proclivity of Catholics to cover up for their friends and their lesser trust in strangers, the "social ethic" of Catholicism seems to favour personal exchange to the detriment of impersonal exchange.

4.3 Discussion

These results suffer several limitations. First of all, finding significant correlations does not necessarily imply causation. It is possible that hidden variables may be affecting both the religiosity and other values. The analysis attenuates this problem by relying on within-country variation and by estimating fixed and variable effects, as it can be assumed that the fixed effects are relatively more exogenous. In addition, as argued by Guiso, Sapienza and Zingales (2003, 2006), the significance of the religious upbringing variable supports the notion that causality runs from religion to values.

Second, the data are built from statements on values instead of observations on actual behaviour. Given the nature of some of the questions (for example, whether one tolerates tax fraud), one should expect some bias caused by a certain tendency to lie because of "political correctness". However, given that the analysis here focuses on differences between Catholics and Protestants, this bias should matter only to the extent that the proclivity to lying varies systematically between both religions.

Third, many of these tests use values to test hypotheses about actions. Some support for this approximation is given by empirical tests showing that, when responding on values, people tend to convey information on their own predispositions. For instance, self-reported trust has also been shown to be a good proxy of trustworthiness actions in an experimental setting (Glaeser *et al.*, 2000).

Fourth, given that these results have been obtained with current data, it could be claimed that the two theologies of salvation in Catholicism and Protestantism did provide different work ethics effects in the past but these differential effects have now disappeared. Such dilution of differences seems unlikely, however, when considering that social norms change slowly; therefore, current values may inform us on the effects of past values. As Glaeser and Glendon put it, "current social norms may still be the legacy of prior religious beliefs" (1998: 431). Moreover, if we take the differential effects of intense beliefs as a proxy for the differential effects that both religions may have had in a more religious past, the estimates lend more support to the social ethic than to the work ethic hypothesis. Even the differences observed in working hours seem to reflect occupational choices that are more consistent with the social ethic hypothesis.

Lastly, large sample size tends to cause statistical significance even with slight substantive effects. However, in this case, when evaluating substantive significance, it must be remembered that the effects of religions are underestimated because only within-country variation is considered. Much of the influence that religion has exerted throughout history has been through changes in the fabric of different societies. This effect is embodied here in the country dummy variables. This ensures that observed differences are not wrongly attributed to religion, but it also reduces the apparent explanatory power of religion. The overall consistency of results, both internal — between the battery of variables used in the paper — and external — with respect to those in the literature —, also rules out the possibility that they might be driven by mere chance, in the spirit of Meehl (1978).

5. Concluding Remarks

Overall, the article finds little support in survey data on currently held values for Weber's "work ethic" hypothesis in "The Protestant Ethic," by which Protestants would tend to work more and more efficiently than Catholics. It finds substantial support, however, for an alternative "social ethic" argument, as Protestant values are shown to shape a type of individual who exerts greater effort in mutual social control, supports institutions more and more critically, is less bound to close circles of family and friends and also holds more homogeneous values. In Weberian terms, the data are therefore more supportive of Weber's view in "The Protestant Sects," with its emphasis on mutual social control.

In line with these results, the economic contribution of the Protestant Reformation would have been connected not to the psychology of individuals regarding economic activity but to their empowerment as citizens vis-à-vis other citizens, the community and the State, affecting the relative effectiveness of alternative enforcement systems. The consequences for economic growth and the development of Capitalism would be related, first, to the greater effort that individuals are willing to exert in informal social enforcement; second, to the contribution that having more independent individuals makes to the design and functioning of political and legal institutions; and, lastly, to the greater homogeneity of values among individuals. All these features work in favour of anonymous markets, as they facilitate legal enforcement and reduce the cost of impersonal exchange.

References

Arruñada, B. (2009). 'Specialization and rent-seeking in moral enforcement: The case of confession', *Journal for the Scientific Study of Religion*, vol. 48(3), pp. 443-61.

Alesina, A. and La Ferrara, E. (2000). 'Participation in heterogeneous communities', *Quarterly Journal of Economics*, vol. 115(3), pp. 847-904.

Alesina, A. and La Ferrara, E. (2002). 'Who trusts others?', *Journal of Public Economics*, vol. 85(2), pp. 207-34.

Barro, R. J., and McCleary, R. M. (2003). 'Religion and economic growth across countries', *American Sociological Review*, vol. 68(5), pp. 760-81.

Barro, R. J., and McCleary, R. M. (2006). 'Religion and political economy in an international panel', *Journal for the Scientific Study of Religion*, vol. 45(2), pp. 149-76.

Becker, S. O., and Woessmann, L. (2009). 'Was Weber wrong? A human capital theory of Protestant economic history', *Quarterly Journal of Economics*, vol. 124(2), pp. 531-96.

Berman, H. J. (1983). *Law and Revolution: The Formation of the Western Legal Tradition*, Cambridge MA: Harvard University Press.

Blum, U., and Dudley, L. (2001). 'Religion and economic growth: Was Weber right?', *Journal of Evolutionary Economics*, vol. 11(2), pp. 207-230

Cameron, E. (1991). *The European Reformation*, Oxford: Oxford University Press.

Chiswick, B. R. (1983). 'The earnings and human capital of American Jews', *Journal of Human Resources*, vol. 18(3), pp. 313-36.

Dickens, A.G. (1966). *Reformation and Society in Sixteenth Century Europe*, London: Thames and Hudson.

Ekelund, R. B., Jr., Hébert, R. F., and Tollison, R. D. (1992). 'The economics of sin and redemption: Purgatory as a market-pull innovation?', *Journal of Economic Behavior and Organization*, vol. 19(1), pp. 1-15.

Ekelund, R. B., Jr., Hébert, R. F., and Tollison, R. D. (2002). 'An economic analysis of the Protestant Reformation', *Journal of Political Economy*, vol. 110(3), pp. 646-71.

Ekelund, R. B., Jr., Hébert, R. F., Tollison, R. F., Anderson, G. M., and Davidson, A. B. (1996). *Sacred Trust: The Medieval Church As an Economic Firm*, New York and Oxford: Oxford University Press.

Ekelund, R. B., Jr., Hébert, R. F., and Tollison, R. D. (2006). *The Market for Christianity*, Cambridge, MA: MIT Press.

Ellison, C. G. (1991). 'Religious involvement and subjective well-being', *Journal of Health and Social Behavior*, vol. 32(1), pp. 80-99.

Evans, T. D., Cullen, F. T., Dunaway, R. G., and Burton, Jr., V. S. (1995). 'Religion and crime reexamined: The impact of religion, secular controls, and social ecology on adult criminality', *Criminology*, vol. 33(2), pp. 195-224.

Freeman, R. B. (1986). 'Who escapes? The relation of churchgoing and other background factors to the socioeconomic performance of black male youths from inner-city tracts', in (R. B. Freeman and H. J. Holzer, eds.), *The Black Youth Employment Crisis*, pp. 353-76, Chicago and London: University of Chicago Press.

Fukuyama, F. (1995). *Trust: The Social Virtues and the Creation of Prosperity*, New York: Free Press.

Glaeser, E. L., and Glendon, S. (1998). 'Incentives, predestination and free will', *Economic Inquiry*, vol. 36(3), pp. 429-43.

Glaeser, E. L., Laibson, D., Scheinkman, J. A., and Soutter, C. L. (2000). 'Measuring trust', *Quarterly Journal of Economics*, vol. 115(3), pp. 811-46.

Granovetter, M. (1985). 'Economic action and social structure: The problem of embeddedness', *American Journal of Sociology*, vol. 91(3), pp. 481-510.

Greif, A. (2002). 'Institutions and impersonal exchange: From communal to individual responsibility', *Journal of Institutional and Theoretical Economics*, vol. 158(1), pp. 168-204.

Guiso, L., Sapienza, P., and Zingales, L. (2003). 'People's opium? Religion and economic attitudes', *Journal of Monetary Economics*, vol. 50(1), pp. 225-82.

Guiso, L., Sapienza, P., and Zingales, L. (2006). 'Does culture affect economic outcomes?', *Journal of Economic Perspectives*, vol. 20(2), pp. 23-48.

Iannaccone, L. R. (1998). 'Introduction to the economics of religion', *Journal of Economic Literature*, vol. 36(3), pp. 1465-95.

Inglehart, R. (1999). 'Trust, well-being and democracy', in (M. Warren, ed.), *Democracy and Trust*, pp. 88-120, New York and Cambridge UK: Cambridge University Press.

Inglehart, R., and Norris, P. (2004). *Sacred & Secular: Religion and Politics Worldwide*, Cambridge UK: Cambridge University Press.

Knack, S., and Keefer, P. (1997). 'Does social capital have an economic payoff? A cross-country investigation', *Quarterly Journal of Economics*, vol. 112(4), pp. 1252-88.

La Porta, R., Lopez-de-Silanes, F., Shleifer, A., and Vishny, R. W. (1997). 'Trust in large organizations', *American Economic Review*, vol. 87(2), pp. 333-38.

Levene, H. (1960). 'Robust tests for equality of variances', in (I. Olkin, ed.), *Contributions to Probability and Statistics*, pp. 278-92. Stanford, CA: Stanford University Press.

Luther, M. (1523). *Secular Authority: To What Extent it Should Be Obeyed*, January, in *Martin Luther's Basic Theological Writings* (T. F. Lull, ed.), 1989. Minneapolis: Fortress Press.

McCleary, R. M. (2007) 'Salvation, damnation and economic incentives', *Journal of Contemporary Religion*, vol. 22(1), pp. 49-74.

Meehl, P. E. (1978). 'Theoretical risks and tabular asterisks: Sir Karl, Sir Ronald, and the slow progress of soft psychology', *Journal of Con-*

sulting and Clinical Psychology, vol. 46(4), pp. 806-34.

North, D. C., and Thomas, R. P. (1973). *The Rise of the Western World: A New Economic History*, Cambridge UK: Cambridge University Press.

Putnam, R. (1993). *Making Democracy Work: Civic Traditions in Modern Italy*, Princeton, NJ: Princeton University Press.

Rodinson, M. (1974). *Islam and Capitalism*, London: Allen Lane. (English translation by Brian Pearce).

Sacerdote, B. I., and Glaeser, E. L. (2008). 'Education and religion', *Journal of Human Capital*, vol. 2(2), pp. 188-215.

Seabright, P. (2004). *The Company of Strangers: A Naturals History of Economic Life*, Princeton and Oxford: Princeton University Press.

Smith, A. (1759). *The Theory of Moral Sentiments*, Indianapolis: Liberty Fund (1982).

Stark, R. (1996). *The Rise of Christianity: A Sociologist Reconsiders History*, Princeton: Princeton University Press.

Stulz, R. M., and Williamson, R. (2003). 'Culture, openness and finance', *Journal of Finance Economics*, vol. 70(3), pp. 313-49.

Tajfel, H., and Turner, J. (1979). 'An integrative theory of intergroup conflict', in (W. G. Austin and S. Worchel, eds.), *The Social Psychology of Intergroup Relations*, pp. 33-47. Monterrey, CA: Brooks/Cole.

Trivers, R. L. (1971). 'The evolution of reciprocal altruism', *Quarterly Review of Biology*, vol. 46(1), pp. 35-57.

Weber, M. (1904-1905). *The Protestant Ethic and the Spirit of Capitalism*, Routledge, London and New York, 1992. Translated by Parsons, T., 1930, from the revised version originally published in the series *Gesammelte Aufsätze zur Religionssoziologie*, 1920. Tubingen: J. C. B. Mohr (Paul Siebeck).

Weber, M. (1920). 'The Protestant sects and the spirit of capitalism', http://www.ne.jp/asahi/moriyuki/abukuma/weber/world/sect/sect_frame.html, accessed January 19, 2009.

Zak, P. and Knack, S. (2001). 'Trust and growth', *Economic Journal*, vol. 111(470), pp. 295-321.

The economic impact of Reformation in the light of different concepts: economic spirit, economic system, economic style (Weber, Sombart, Müller-Armack)

Günther Chaloupek

1. Introduction

For more than a century - the first part of Max Weber's celebrated essay appeared in the 1904 volume of the *Archiv für Sozialwissenschaften* - the question whether and to what extent the rise of capitalism can be attributed to a change in the minds of men originating from the sphere of religion has been a major issue in the historical as well as in the social sciences. In view of the vast range of the debate which has been sparked off by this and later contributions by Weber on the relationship between protestant ethic and the spirit of capitalism[1], the aim of this contribution is a rather limited one: to present a comparative analysis of Weber's essential findings,

---

[1] The question does not appear to be "settled" in the sense of a broad consensus among historians and social scientists. According to Otsuka (1982), who refers to the older comments only, "economic historians have been overwhelmingly negative about Weber's stand." (p. 61) My impression is, that even among more recent comments by historians a majority is more critical than sympathetic with Weber's theses. Van Dülmen (1981, p. 17) concedes that Protestantism "was favourable for a milieu which promoted the rationalization of life", while he also denies explicitly that the spirit of capitalism had its roots in ascetic Protestantism. According to Schröder (1995), most of Weber's fundamental relationships between Puritanism and capitalism are unfounded or erroneous. In contrast, in H. Trevor-Roper's view, Weber's thesis has by and large held its own (1970, p. 18). On this point, see also section 4 of the present contribution.

first with those of Werner Sombart, certainly the most famous contemporary social scientist writing on the same subject, who was at the same time his combatant with respect to method and general approach, his critic in important respects, and his rival. Thereafter, I will discuss the issue under the aspect of the concept of "economic style" ("*Wirtschaftsstil*") on which Alfred Müller-Armack based his study of the impact of Reformation on economic development in Europe since the 16th century.

According to Sombart (1925/2002, p. 289ff), "spirit" is one of three basic elements of the concept of "economic system", while "form" and "technology" are the other two. With spirit Sombart means the fundamental ideas towards which the minds of economic agents are orientated. Form is "regulation and organization of economic life", its legal and political framework. Sombart's concept of technology comprises the methods which are applied in the process of production and distribution of goods.

Max Weber has not explicitly developed his own, nor has he endorsed Sombart's concept of economic system, but it is evident that he was thinking in essentially the same categories when he assigned a major, though not necessarily decisive role to the "capitalist spirit" in the formation of the system of capitalism: "...we have no intention whatever of maintaining such a foolish and doctrinaire thesis as that the spirit of capitalism ... could only have arisen as the result of certain effects of the Reformation, or even that capitalism as an economic system is a creation of the Reformation". Weber also uses the concept of form when he says that "certain important forms of capitalistic business organization (emphases added, G. Ch.) are known to be considerably older than the Reformation". (Weber 1920/1930, p.91) [2] If technology does not seem to have at-

[2] Weber uses the term "economic system" in a similar context e.g. in his reply to Rachfahl, (Weber et al 1982, p. 170), and also in *Wirtschaft und Gesellschaft,* in sections where he refers to the capitalist system (pp. 368f, 647f).

tracted Weber's attention to any major degree, he is aware of its importance when - if only in a footnote - he refers "to the place of the Scotch in science, literature, and technical invention ... We cannot speak here of its (i.e. Puritanism's, G.Ch.) significance for the development of technique and the empirical sciences."(ibid., p.275)

Therefore, it appears justified to discuss differences between Weber's and Sombart's views on the economic impact of Reformation with respect to economic spirit (section 2), form and technology (section 3) in the context of an overarching concept of economic system. Economic style, although developed from and closely related to economic system, is quite different in that it apportions - as will be shown in section 5 - rather unequal weights to the three principal elements.

2. Weber and Sombart on the relevance of Reformation for the development of the spirit of capitalism

In his famous replies to the first detailed critiques of his 1904/05 essays by Fischer and Rachfah, Weber's main task was to clear up misunderstandings that he was suggesting Reformation as the single cause for the rise of capitalism, and also to reaffirm his claim for a treatment of the issue under a theoretical perspective against the usual approach of historians based on mere story-telling, casuistry and vulgar psychology. Compared to these early critiques, Sombart proposed an alternative view within the same - or at least very similar[3] - conceptual framework which presented a considerably more serious challenge for Weber's theses.

---

[3] Apart from spiritual, political-institutional, technological, geographical factors of influence Sombart (1911, 1913) also mentions biological disposition ("blood") which may facilitate or impede a nation's ability to adopt the capitalist system.

Weber and Sombart are more or less in agreement as regards the essence of capitalist spirit. In Weber's words, capitalism is "pursuit o profit, and forever renewed profit, by means of continuous, rational capitalistic enterprise ... In a wholly capitalistic order of society, an individual capitalistic enterprise which did not take advantage of its opportunities for profit-making would be doomed to extinction." (1920/1930, p. 17) Likewise, Sombart (1925/2002, p. 312f) mentions profit-orientation (*"Erwerbsprinzip"*), individualism and economic rationalism as principal ingredients of the spirit of capitalism.

The differences between Weber and Sombart on the relevance of Reformation for the development of the capitalist spirit mainly concern

(i) the origin of what both call economic rationalism;

(ii) the special role of protestant sectarian movements, especially of Puritanism, in the development of capitalism.

ad (i) In Sombart's view, traces of economic rationalism can be found in many ancient writings. In the teachings of the medieval schoolmen all the essential elements of economic rationalism such as calculation, modesty, foresight, caution, etc., are present. He finds bourgeois virtues "fully developed" in the Italian Leon Battista Alberti's (1404-1472) book on household management *Della famiglia* "several hundred years before Puritanism existed. In as far as a religious system is responsible for their formation, it is the Catholic system. The Protestant ethic only had to take over what Thomas Aquinas had created." (Sombart 1913, p. 334) If Sombart, on the one hand, emphasizes the importance of moral convictions rooted in religious beliefs particularly in the early, formative period of capitalism, on the other hand, he gives equal credit to the philosophy of late antiquity and to "all three religions", i.e. to the catholic, the protestant and to the Jewish religion. (ibid., p. 355)[4]

In his reply, Weber (1920/30) explicitly denies Sombart's contention that Benjamin Franklin's maxim "time is money" had been nearly literally anticipated by Alberti. In his book *Der Bourgeois* which Weber considers "by far the weakest of his larger works" (ibid., p. 191) Sombart, according to Weber, has failed to comprehend the essential difference between Alberti's the nobleman's principles of household management whose ultimate end was to achieve "*tranquillità dell' animo*", and the relentlessly acquisitive attitude advocated by Franklin and other Puritans. Alberti's "dislike of any office as a source of unrest, ... the ideal life in a country villa of, his nourishment of vanity through the thought of his ancestors ... - all these things would in the eyes of any Puritan have been sinful idolatry of the flesh, and in those of Benjamin Franklin the expression of incomprehensible nonsense." (ibid.) Such an orientation, "with all its resemblance to the current Christian ethic, ...was to a large extent of the antique pagan character." (ibidem, p. 197)

ad (ii) To be sure, Sombart, at certain instances, acknowledges that "in their progressing from parsimony to stinginess (*parvificentia*) lies perhaps the greatest contribution to the bourgeois spirit embodied in capitalism which the Puritan and the Quaker ethic can claim for themselves." (Sombart 1913, p. 333) But at the same time, he plays down the relevance of this contribution by putting heavy emphasis on the ethical restrictions which the teachings of the Puritan theologists imposed on the conduct of business. In his view, Puritanism cannot be held responsible for "the limitless expansion of the drive for acquisition, for senseless moneymaking, for the idiosyncrasy of business, which characterizes mature capitalism". Nei-

---

4 The corresponding passages in Sombarts „*Moderner Kapitalismus*“ are in Vol. II/1, pp. 29ff., where Sombart also points to the new aspect (compared to „Bourgeois“) of reliability of contract („*Vertragstreue*“).

ther can Puritan ethics be charged for advocating "ruthless acquisition. In this respect, because it gives approval to acquisition by honest means only, there is no difference at all to Thomistic business morals". (ibid, p. 334) For Sombart, in the formative period of capitalism both religious confessions present an impediment of equal strength to the unfolding of acquisitive drives. (ibid, p. 355)

In Weber's view, Sombart makes the error of taking his sources at their face value while the real, if originally unintended effects of Puritan ethics on the minds of men were quite different. Instead of referring to what was theoretically and officially prescribed in learned books or popular sermons and tracts, for Weber the focus had to be directed towards "the influence of those psychological sanctions which, originating in religious belief and the practice of religion, gave a direction to practical conduct and held the individual to it." (1920/30, p. 97) It is social achievements which, according to Calvinist teachings, indicate who are the elected to whom the premium of salvation is granted. In contrast, "Sombart ... continually cite(s) the ethical writers (mostly those of whom they have heard from me) as codifications and rules of conduct without ever asking which of them were supported by effective religious sanctions." (ibidem, p. 217)[5]

In his book *Die Juden und das Wirtschaftsleben* Sombart points to Judaism as a posssible source of Puritanism. In his view, there are many indications for a "nearly complete coincidence of Jewish and puritan perceptions" for which he mentions as prominent examples " the predominance of religious interests, the idea of trial and proof (“*Bewährungsgedanke*”), above all the rationalization of the conduct of life, the connecting of religious concepts with acquisitive

---

[5] Parsons' translation is not entirely accurate here – compare the German original: “... ohne zu fragen, für welche von diesen denn die psychologisch allein wirksamen *Heilsprämien* gegeben waren.” (Weber 1979, p. 191 – emphasis original)

interests, ..." (Sombart 1913b, p 292). If "Puritanism **is** (emphasis original, G.Ch.) Judaism" (ibidem. p. 293), this does not imply that there has in fact been an influence of Judaism on Puritanism, for which Sombart does not see sufficient evidence yet.

Weber strongly denies any such kind of intimate relationship between Judaism and Puritanism. While he admits that "Old Testament morality was able to give a powerful impetus to the spirit of self- righteous and sober legality which was so characteristic of the worldly asceticism of this form of Protestantism" (1920/30, p. 165), he cautioned against drawing parallels. In the middle ages, Weber argued, Jews were "an outcast people", whose position" may be compared sociologically with an Indian caste in a world otherwise free from castes". At best, they were accepted as a "guest people", but they could not participate either in the society nor in the economy of cities and towns on an equal footing. Moreover, "Judaism maintained the originally universal dualism of internal and external attitudes, under which it was permissible to accept interest from foreigners who did not belong to the brotherhood or established association. Out of this dualism followed the sanctioning of other irrational economic affairs, especially tax farming and political financing of all sorts. In the course of centuries the Jews acquired a special skill in these matters which made them useful and in the demand. But all this was pariah capitalism, not rational capitalism such as originated in the west". (Weber 1923/2003, pp. 358ff)

What becomes evident from these quarrels is that Sombart uses a more general concept of "rationalization" which, in Weber's view, lacks the necessary precision. The specific contribution of Reformation to the emergence of the sprit of capitalism is obscured if Reformation is only understood as a stage in the development from ancient and medieval rationalism to Voltaire's worldly rationalism of the 18th century. "This is by no means the soil in which that relationship of a man to his calling as a task, which is necessary to capitalism, has pre-eminently grown." If "rationalism is a historical concept which covers a whole world of different things", it is Weber's intention to elaborate "whose intellectual child the particular form of rational thought was, from which the idea of calling ("*Beruf*") has grown, which is ... so irrational from the standpoint of purely eudaemonistic self-interest, but which has been and still is one of the most characteristic elements of our capitalistic culture." (Weber 1920/30, pp. 76ff)

In still another respect, Sombart points to the traditional attitudes which characterized the conduct of small businesses in trade as well as in handicraft up to the 18th century and in some instances even beyond, irrespective of the religious orientation of a country. "Honourable" conduct of business implied that price setting had to observe the idea of "just price", the imperative to refrain from extortion of customers, but also from aggressive competition against the other market participants, especially through price cutting and advertising, the impediment of technical change through prohibition of new and more powerful methods of production, and also of new products. (Sombart 1919, Vol. II/1, pp. 36ff) Sombart also mentions the gradual dissolution of traditional views and attitudes, such as the replacement of traditional, normative price theory based on ethical principles by objective-causal theories which liberated price setting from ethical constraints. (ibid., pp. 41ff) At the same time, he maintains that "the normative view retains the upper hand" in the sense that ethically motivated rules still had to be obeyed while the market constellation was only one of the circumstances which had to be considered. Weber, who would not deny the power which traditional ideas exerted over the minds of businessmen, nonetheless in this context emphasizes the other aspect: that it was the protestant ethic which induced the change in attitudes of a growing number of owners of small businesses that they made use of chances to increase their sales by reducing their prices or by offering new, changed products, and that it was their moral duty to act in this way. (Weber 1923/2003, pp 267f)

3. The relevance of Reformation for "form" and "technology"

In his essay on the protestant ethic Weber deliberately chose to focus on the spirit of capitalism. At the same time, Weber repeatedly emphasized that this narrowing of the subject does not mean that the other dimensions of economic development are less relevant. But, apart from occasional side remarks[6], he did not elaborate in these aspects in any greater detail. Even in his "General Economic History" whose authenticity is limited[7] he confines himself to remarks of a rather general nature.

Weber identifies several areas of economic policy where Reformation had a major impact on structural forms which were newly developed as complements of the emerging spirit of capitalism:

- Whereas France under the system of Colbert, the absolutist regimes on the continent, and originally also England under the Stuarts used the form of exclusive monopolies to secure government revenues and to stimulate production, England took a different course. In the so-called "long parliament" (1640-1660) the petty-bourgeois class of owners of small businesses most of whom were Puritans who were fierce enemies of monopolies broke the political power of the feudal classes. (Weber 1923/2003, pp. 349f) Capitalistic development was not an outgrowth of national mercantilism. "The course of events was that a stratum of entrepreneurs

[6] 1920/30, p. 67, 91, 213, etc.

[7] As a book, Weber's General Economic History was reconstructed after his death from lecture notes – partly his own notes, but also from notes taken by students who attended his lectures.

which had developed in independence of the political administration secured the systematic support of Parliament in the 18th century, after the collapse of the fiscal monopoly policy of the Stuarts. Here for the last time rational and irrational capitalism faced each other in conflict, that is, capitalism in the field of fiscal and colonial privileges and public monopolies, and capitalism oriented in relation to market opportunities which were developed from within by business interests themselves on the basis of saleable services." (ibidem, p. 350)

- Concerning the organization of economy and society in the colonies, the Dutch and the English (protestant) entrusted private companies with the exploitation (p. 298), whereas for the traditional governments of catholic Spain and Portugal the exploitation of colonies primarily served the purpose of extracting state revenues.
- It was under the influence of Puritanism that relief and support for the poor was increasingly tied to their willingness to accept work, and that "anyone who did not take a job voluntarily was thrust into the workhouse with its strict discipline." (p. 307)
- With respect to technology, economic rationalism produces rational technology, "that is, one reduced to calculation to the largest possible degree, which implies mechanization" (p. 277), and therefore the abolition of traditional impediments of innovations.

Due to the nature of Weber's posthumously published lectures on economic history, these subjects are not elaborated with the support of empirical illustrations and evidence that could compare with Sombart's Modern Capitalism.

In Sombart's *magnum opus* explicit references to Reformation are scarce. In accordance with his general thesis, that catholic and protestant religion have made equal contributions to the development of the spirit of capitalism, he tries to give a comprehensive, overall description and analysis of the formation of the new economic order and of a progressive technology by concentrating on main trends and their determining factors. As a consequence, Sombart is less interested in comparisons between countries which would highlight differences resulting from different starting positions, from different external influences on the economic system, and also from different decisions at crossroads.

In his broad picture of the evolution of capitalism as a system Sombart assigns a prominent role to the formation of the "modern" state which strives to augment its absolute powers through rational means. Due to rivalry among European national states a growing part of economic resources is devoted to warfare and also to competitive display of splendour and ostentatious luxury consumption. War and "*Luxus*" (demand for luxuries) are therefore the principal demand-side forces that promote capitalist production. On the supply side, for the development of capitalist production the creation of big enterprise through monopolistic privileges is of no lesser importance than the growth of new industries through the multiplication of small businesses.

In the section on entrepreneurs, Sombart treats the relevance of Reformation for the formation of new bourgeois strata under the headings of "heretics" and "aliens".[8] Thus he de-emphasizes the importance of the protestant roots of their mental attitudes in the conduct of business, while he prefers the unfavourable circumstances resulting from the disadvantaged status of minorities as an explanation for their extraordinary ambitiousness and diligence.

---

8 "*Ketzer*" and "*Fremde*", Vol. I/2, pp. 877ff and pp. 883ff.

Weber, in his counterargument, found Sombart's theses concerning the contributions of war and

luxuries to economic development in early capitalism grossly exaggerated. "The decisive impetus toward capitalism could only come from one source, namely a mass market demand, which again could arise only in a small proportion of the luxury industries through the democratization of the demand." (Weber 1923/2003, p. 310)

4. Spirit as cause or/and as effect

Finally, there is the difficult issue of cause and effect, or, if there are influences in either direction as both Weber and Sombart are convinced, where the main direction of influence ran. Sombart makes the "strong" statement that the acknowledgement of bourgeois conduct of life by Puritanism was conceded under the pressure and power of economic circumstances[9]. If, on the other hand, the bourgeois spirit became an important promoter of capitalism as it became more deeply ingrained in the minds of men, this influence is a secondary phenomenon.

Weber takes a more differentiated position on this issue. On the one hand, he rejects any monocausal explanation of the system of capitalism as the product of spirit which itself had been changed by Reformation. On the other hand, Weber considered any assumption of precedence of economic or technological factors over spiritual factors as premature. "In view of the tremendous confusion of interdependent influences between the material basis, the forms of social and political organization, and the ideas current in the time

[9] „Dass der Puritanismus schließlich die bourgeoise Lebensführung anerkannte als eine dem Gnadenstande verträgliche, ist ihm von der Macht der wirtschaftlichen Verhältnisse a b g e r u n g e n und a b g e z w u n g e n worden." (Bourgeois p. 351)

of the Reformation, we can only proceed by investigating whether and at what points certain correlations[10] between forms of religious belief and practical ideas can be worked out. At the same time we shall as far as possible clarify the manner and the general direction in which, by virtue of those relationships, the religious movements have influenced the development of material culture. Only when this has been determined with reasonable accuracy can the attempt be made to estimate to what extent the historical development of modern culture can be attributed to those religious forces and to what extent to others." (p. 91f)

Weber emphasizes several instances where the causality runs from spirit to material culture.

The environment for Benjamin Franklin's plea for restless activity and frugality was not a highly commercialized let alone industrialized economy and society. "... in the backwoods small bourgeois circumstances of Pennsylvania in the eighteenth century, where business threatened for simple lack of money to fall back into barter, where only the earliest beginnings of banking were to be found, the same thing was considered the essence of moral conduct, even commanded in the name of moral duty. To speak here of a reflection of material conditions in the ideal superstructure would be patent nonsense". (1920/30, p 74f)

If in the cases of the Pietism of the Continent of Europe and the Methodism of the Anglo-Saxon peoples, as well as milder forms of the consistent ascetic ethics of Puritanism, "one wished to interpret these religious conceptions as only exponents or reflections of capitalistic institutions, just the opposite would have to be the case." (ibidem, p. 252)

---

[10] "Correlations" is Parsons' translation for "Wahlverwandtschaften" (Weber 1997, p. 77)

"In the Puritan concept of the calling the emphasis is always placed on this methodical character of worldly asceticism, not as with Luther, on the acceptance of the lot which God has irretrievably assigned to man" (p. 162) - "this sort of religious ethics cannot be regarded as a reflex of economic conditions. The specialization of occupations had, if anything, gone further in medieval Italy than in the England of that period." (p. 266)

Such statements, in combination with Weber's general approach to the subject, have induced many critics to suggest that Weber was proposing a wholly or predominantly idealistic interpretation of the history of capitalism. If Weber rejects a wholly materialistic concept of history[11], he does not deny, and in several respects explicitly recognizes the influence of "material" factors. But on the whole, he leaves the question open and reserves final judgement for further research.

Alfred Müller-Armack, who later proposed an idealistic interpretation of capitalistic evolution (see the following section), regretted that Weber, at a crucial point, did not pursue his idealistic approach far enough and thus failed to give religious movements their due weight. In his view, Weber was too modest in contenting himself with mere "correlations" between religious dogma and economic attitudes. What was missing in his studies on the Protestant ethic is "the demonstration of intermediate stages in through which the idealistic approach transforms into specific political and economic forms and eventually determines economic attitudes". (Müller-Armack 1941, p. 81)

According to Richard H. Tawney, more light can be cast upon the question of causation by recognizing that, from its beginnings, Cal-

---

[11] This, of course, produced a substantial literature from Marxist social scientists. For a selection of contributions from this side see Seyfarth/Sprondel 1973.

vinism and also Puritanism had a double message concerning conduct and attitudes of their believers in economic and social life. On the one hand, many rules of rigorous collective religious discipline followed traditional medieval thinking and were inimical towards acquisitive attitudes, while on the other hand the individualistic orientation of the new doctrine prepared the ground for capitalism. "The really significant question is that of the causes of the change from one standpoint to the other, a question which Weber appears to ignore". (Tawney 1926/1947, p. 262) The change occurred when "the Puritan movement came to power with the consequence that "these two elements flew apart. The collectivist, half-communistic aspect , which had never been acclimatized in England, quietly dropped out of notice ... The individualism congenial to the world of business became the distinctive characteristic of the world of a Puritanism which had arrived, and which, by becoming a political force, was at once secularized and committed to a career of compromise. Its note was not the attempt to establish on earth a 'Kingdom of Christ', but an ideal of personal character and conduct, to be realized by the punctual discharge both of public and private duties. Its theory had been discipline; its practical result was liberty". (ibidem, p. 194f)

With this resolution of the conflict, it seems fair to say that Tawney's position is somewhere in between an idealistic and a materialistic explanation. Clearly, the new religious doctrines originate from the sphere of religion, whereas their effects on the attitudes of men come from economic and political reality.

5. Reformation in the light of Alfred Müller-Armack's concept of "economic style" (*"Wirtschaftsstil"*)

The concept of "economic style" was derived from Sombart's concept of economic system. Sombart himself uses the term "economic style" in the introductory part of his essay *"Die Ordnung des*

Wirtschaftslebens" where he emphasizes the need for a concept which is capable of "comprehending the totality of economic life"[12], but in the text that follows he switches to the more precise term "economic system". Heinrich Bechtel was the first who applied the concept of economic style in the field of economic history in his monograph on a specific epoch: *Wirtschaftsstil des deutschen Spätmittelalters* (1930)[13]. In his contribution to the *Festschrift* presented to Werner Sombart at the occasion of his 70th birthday Arthur Spiethoff set out to develop in general terms a concept of economic style which would eliminate some of what he considered shortcomings of Sombart's economic system and thus encompass and express "the characteristic shape of economic life" more comprhensively[14]. To fulfill this intention, Spiethoff proposes to enlarge Sombart's three principal dimensions spirit, form and technique by two additional ones: social order and economic process[15].

But it was Alfred Müller-Armack (1901-1978)[16] who first applied the concept of economic style to Weber's and Sombart's central subject. If style in general represents the unity of expression and attitude which is visible in the different areas of life at a certain time,

---

[12] „Diese Stilidee der Wirtschaftswissenschaft (wie wir einstweilen in Anlehnung an die Terminologie der Kunstwissenschaft sagen wollen) muss nun offenbar die Ganzheit des wirtschaftlichen Lebens zu umfassen trachten, muss Geist, Form und Ordnung in ihrer Besonderheit zu bestimmen imstande sein, ist also umfassender als die (praktischen) Ordnungsideen der Wirtschafts- und Betriebsordnung." (1925/2002, p. 272)

[13] In the introductory chapters, Bechtel discusses in detail the relationship of the concept of economic style to the concept of style as it was originally used in art history.

[14] Wirtschaftsstil „ist der Inbegriff der Merkmale, die eine arteigene Gestaltung des Wirtschaftslebens zur Verkörperung bringen." Spiethoff 1932, p. 56.

[15] *„Gesellschaftsverfassung"* und *„Wirtschaftslauf"*. He also adds natural conditions to technology. Ibidem, p 76f.

[16] For a brief, comprehensive survey of his writings see Hoffmann/Watrin 1961.

economic style comprehends the uniform character of economic and social phenomena. (Müller-Armack 1941, p. 14). As an ideal-type concept, economic style is applicable only in cases where in a certain period in a certain country the real economy and society conforms to an ideal type, whereas in reality we usually encounter a mixture of styles for which Müller-Armack reserves the concept of economic system (ibidem, p.15) He gives Sombart credit for having used economic spirit as dominant principle for classification of systems and epochs, but Sombart "did not succeed in propelling analysis of style far enough to expose a uniform principle of style." (p. 70)

The dominant role of religion in Müller-Armacks study of economic styles becomes evident from his brief sketch of economic styles which preceded the economic style of the modern age: magic world view, animistic epoch, polytheism, monotheism. The economic style of the middle ages was still a variant of monotheism. "The penetrating power of Europe's economic culture comes to the fore only with the use of capitalistic methods in the 16th century." (p. 44) Instead of the ambiguous term "capitalism" Müller-Armack prefers "modern age economic style" (*"neuzeitlicher Wirtschaftsstil"*) which did not emerge simultaneously in all of Western Europe but spread across countries with different speed. As a consequence, Europe did not share a common economic style from the 16th to the 18th century. The essence of modern age economic style is the formation of an "overall dynamic system" (*"gesamtdynamisches System"*)[17] based on the "creation of a rational organization of enterprise with the aim of making possible permanent technical progress, (and) on the liberation of markets which are geared towards permanent economic progress." (p. 72f)

---

[17] For a theoretical exposition of these „overall dynamics" Müller-Armack refers to his book *Entwicklungsgesetze des Kapitalismus* published in 1932.

But the economic style of the modern age does not originate from the economic sphere. "It receives its stamping from the change of world view, of the structure of the state, of scientific knowledge." (p. 70f) Starting point for Müller-Armack's treatment of capitalism of the modern age is Weber's analysis of the relation of Reformation and especially the Calvinist version of Protestantism to the formation of the spirit of capitalism. Going far beyond Weber, Müller-Armack traces all the essential changes that brought about the transformation to the capitalist economic system in its dimension of form and technology from Calvinist religious spirit. In contrast to Sombart, Müller-Armack maintains that the development initiated by the protestant Reformation entailed a fundamental change of direction, whereas the movements of renaissance and humanism had produced only a relaxation of the framework of the medieval world view. (p. 81).

Of the elements of the Calvinist doctrine, it is not so much the doctrine of predestination as such, but its consequences which are essential for the formation of the economic spirit of the modern age. The negation of any kind of spiritual relief of the individual through sacraments given by the church as a mediator between man and god left the individual in complete solitude with his or her desire to obtain eternal salvation. The only escape from this depressing situation was asceticism in the form of obedience and practical work. (p. 82f) If studies in the sociology of religion have aimed at locating the decisive changes in the principles and commandments of economic ethics, this misses the central point in twofold respect. (p. 203ff) Müller-Armack is in agreement with Sombart when he states that there is very little change in the content of economic ethics, e.g. as regards price formation or usury, compared to the traditional doctrines of medieval schoolmen. More important, however, is the fact that as a consequence of Reformation religion lost control over the behaviour of its believers as the jurisdiction of the church over commercial life. The sacrament of confession, control of the institutions of education were abolished or transferred to the state. The main channel of influence of Protestant and especially of Calvinist religious thinking is through the creation of new forms of regulation and organization, and the stimulation of technical progress for which the new spirit provided the basis.

As a direct result of Reformation, the universal church ceased to exist in countries where the Reformation succeeded. Important powers such as jurisdiction and social policy were mostly transferred to the state. Cities, townships and guilds were subjected to the state's sovereignty. Whereas in catholic countries the church constituted a countervailing force to the secular prince, it was Reformation that made his power absolute. But the consequences for economy and society were different in Lutheran and in Calvinist countries. In the Lutheran territories of the German empire, the state came to dominate economy and society in important respects, which in turn had sweeping political consequences. It was Calvinist spirit which produced the essential forms of the modern economy and society, and also modern political institutions. The fundamentally anti-hierarchical, de-centralist character of Calvinist religious communities produced a sceptical or negative attitude of their members towards a strong state. Therefore,

- economic policies of Calvinist countries had a low preference for state regulation and for entrepreneurial activities of the state which were frequent in Lutheran countries.
- There was no institution in Calvinist countries which could substitute the old church as an important actor on the demand side of the economy (construction of churches and monasteries, altars, paintings, calices and other precious fittings, etc.)[18]

---

[18] This aspect is also emphasized by Nef 1964, p. 229f.

- "In England and in Holland, all the new enterprises which gained decisive importance for the development of the new economic style were primarily undertaken in private form." (p. 86f)
- As a consequence of the liberalization of government, privileges and monopolies which were rooted in traditional institutions such as the guild system were reduced or abolished.
- If for the Lutheran Protestants' perseverance in professional work is the ethical imperative and "fulfilment" is the principal motivation for man's active life, for the followers of Calvinism "success" becomes essential (p. 88), which must be achieved through the market which is governed by an anonymous, impartial mechanism.
- If, in its sober spirit, Calvinism rejects or suppresses the fine arts, it leads to a concentration of mental energies on natural sciences and on technical improvements. (p. 90f)

In the last part of his book ("The emergence of new economic forms", pp.205ff, of new forms of business enterprise, pp. 225ff, etc) Müller-Armack shows in detail how new economic institutional forms and regulations were developed on the basis of the new individualistic ethics.

- For the transformation of the urban handicraft system and the loosening of the restriction of the guild system the competition from new capitalistic enterprises was much less important than the erosion and dissolution of beliefs and attitudes on which the guild system was based. Whereas the medieval corporations were part of the Christian order of society whose ethics had distrusted restless work and whose social institutions had provided for the living of those who could not work, the new religious creed had little or no consideration for restrictions which limited competition or prohibited the invention of new products and production methods. (pp. 213ff)

- The emergence of the modern idea of insurance is seen as a consequence of the erosion and dissolution of traditional institutions of social support and poverty relief. With the increasingly individualistic orientation of man the idea emerged that he had to make his own provisions against the uncertainties of life. Traditional forms of security were displaced by newly established institutes which were based on rational, i. e. computational methods, by which insurance premiums, the likelihood of damages and losses of property, the requirements for financial reserves, etc. were calculated. (p. 232ff) In the Lutheran and especially in the catholic countries insurance companies were established with considerable time lag. If in England life insurance was introduced at the end of the 17th century. In Germany, where even J.H.G. Justi was repelled by the idea of calculating the value of man's life, the first company was founded only in 1827 (“*Gothaer*”).
- The first "workhouse" was established in Amsterdam where, as early as 1589 founded by the city council in the buildings of a monastery where vagrants, beggars and evildoers were locked up and put to work. The workhouses which were established in the following centuries in many countries as a combination of penitentiary and industrial factory are a typical creation of Calvinism. (p. 227ff)
- Another offspring of Calvinism was private corporate enterprise in the form of joint stock company. Facilitated by the abundance of capital, the essence of this new type of business enterprise was the rational calculation of its financial base. (p. 161)
- The idea of vocational schools ("Realschulen") originates

> from the Moravian brotherhood communities (Commenius). It was promoted by theologists rather than by businessmen. (pp. 259f)

With his method of "making inferences to find results which appear probable from the viewpoint of the tectonics in its totality" (p. 208f), Müller-Armack embarked on a speculative venture which Weber had deliberately tried to avoid by confining his statements "to relations in which an influence of religious ideas on the material culture is really beyond doubt. It would have been easy to proceed beyond that to a regular construction which logically deduced everything characteristic of modern culture from Protestant rationalism. But that sort of thing may be left to the dilettant who believes in the unity of the group mind and its reducibility to a single formula." (1920/30, p. 283f)

It was in reaction to Weber's self-imposed modesty that Müller-Armack, in an essay published several years after his book on *Genealogie der Wirtschaftsstile*, broke the narrowing fetters of the technical disciplines of economics and history by postulating "that the unity of style finds its perfect expression only in metaphysics." (1949, p. 513) He gives Sombart credit for having identified (in his book Modern Capitalism) spirit as true centre of a system which is the determinant force not only for minds and attitudes of men but also for the shaping of organizational forms and for technology. The concept of economic style, however, "is too narrow to comprehend the phenomenon in its full range. For that purpose, it might be more adequate to speak of cultural styles in order to better express the relationship of the style-concept to the full range of cultural phenomena." (p. 517)

In a certain sense, this statement marks the end of the German Historical School as a distinct current of the social sciences. In his earlier book on the "laws of capitalist development" Alfred Müller-Armack had based his analysis on Austrian economics in its

Schumpeterian variant. As it appears, he abandoned the idea of bridging the gap between modern-type economic analysis and historical approach towards economic phenomena - to become one of the leading theoreticians of the new political doctrine of Social Market Economy and ordoliberalism, and later to engage in politics by becoming a member of chancellor Adenauer's Christian-democratic government (as State Secretary for European affairs from 1958 to 1963).

References

Bechtel, Heinrich, Wirtschaftsstil des deutschen Spätmittelalters. München Leipzig, Duncker & Humblot, 1930.

Dülmen, Richard, van *Formierung der europäischen Gesellschaft in der Frühen Neuzeit,* in: Geschichte und Gesellschaft Vol. 7(1981), pp. 5-41

Hoffmann, Harriet, and Christian Watrin, *Wirtschaft, Gesellschaft und Kultur. Bemerkungen zum Werk Alfred Müller-Armacks.* In: Franz Greiß/Fritz W. Meyer (eds.), Wirtschaft, Gesellschaft und Kultur. Festgabe für Alfred Müller-Armack. 1961 Berlin Duncker & Humblot

Müller-Armack, Alfred, Genealogie der Wirtschaftsstile. 1941 Stuttgart Verlag W. Kohlhammer

Müller-Armack, Alfred, Entwicklungsgesetze des Kapitalismus. 1932 Berlin Junker und Dünnhaupt

Müller-Armack, Alfred, *Zur Metaphysik der Kulturstile.*In: Müller-Armack 1959, pp. 513-531

Müller-Armack, Alfred, Religion und Wirtschaft. 1959 Stuttgart Verlag W. Kohlhammer

Nef, John U., The Conquest of the Material World. Chicago and London 1964 Chicago University Press

Otsuka, Hisao, The Spirit of Capitalism. 1982 Tokyo Iwanami Shoten, Publishers

Schröder, Hans-Christoph, *Weber und der Puritanismus*, in: Geschichte und Gesellschaft Vol. 21(1995), pp. 459-478

Seyfarth, Constans, and Walter M. Sprondel (eds.), Seminar: Religion und gesellschaftliche Entwicklung. Studien zur Protestantismus-Kapitalismus-These Max Webers. 1973 Suhrkamp-Verlag Frankfurt

Sombart, Werner, Der Bourgeois. 1913 Munich and Leipzig Duncker & Humblot

Sombart, Werner, Der moderne Kapitalismus. Second edition, 2 Vol., 1919[3] Munich and Leipzig Duncker & Humblot

Sombart, Werner, Die Juden und das Wirtschaftsleben. 1911 Munich and Leipzig Duncker & Humblot

Sombart, Werner, /1925/ Die Ordnung des Wirtschaftslebens, in: Werner Sombart, Nationalökonomie als Kapitalismustheorie, pp. 265-376

Sombart, Werner, Nationalökonomie als Kapitalismustheorie. Ausgewählte Schriften, Eds. Alexander Ebner and Helge Peukert, Marburg 2002: Metropolis-Verlag

Spiethoff, Arthur, *Die Allgemeine Volkswirtschaftslehre als geschichtliche Theorie. Die Wirtschaftsstile*. In: Festgabe für Werner Sombart, ed. Arthur Spiethoff, special issue of Schmollers Jahrbuch 56-6(1933), pp. 51-84

Tawney, R.H., Religion and the Rise of Capitalism. 1947 Mentor Book The New American Library New York

Trevor-Roper, Hugh Redwald, Religion, Reformation und sozialer Umbruch. 1970 Berlin Propyläen-Verlag

Weber, Max, /1920/ The Protestant Ethic and the Spirit of Capitalism. Translated by Talcott Parsons, with a foreword by R.H. Tawney. London 1930.

Weber, Max, Die protestantische Ethik I. Eine Aufsatzsammlung. Ed. Johannes Winckelmann, 1979[5]. Gütersloher Verlagshaus Gerd Mohn

Weber, Max, et al., Die protestantische Ethik II. Kritiken und Antikritiken. Ed. Johannes Winckelmann, 1982[4]. Gütersloher Verlagshaus Gerd Mohn

Weber, Max, Wirtschaft und Gesellschaft. 1980[5] J.C.B. Mohr (Paul Siebeck) Tübingen

Weber, Max, Wirtschaftsgeschichte. Eds. S. Hellmann and M. Palyi, Munich and Leipzig 1923, Duncker & Humblot. English edition: General Economic History. Translated by F. Knight, 2003 Dover Publications, Mineola New York

Günther Chaloupek's "The Economic Impact of Reformation in the Light of Different Concepts: Economic Spirit, Economic System, and Style (Weber, Sombart, Müller-Armack)": *A Comment*

Ringa Raudla[1]

The paper by Günther Chaloupek certainly chooses an interesting prism for comparing the ideas of Werner Sombart and Max Weber: that of the "economic system" with its constitutive elements. Making use of such analytical lens is rather challenging, given that though Weber had intended to come back to analysing in a greater detail the other factors that had been conducive to capitalism (in addition to religion), he never really followed up on this intention.

To what extent Weber and Sombart in fact shared a similar conception of the different components of the economic system, is, however, not entirely clear. The tentative references made in the text by Chaloupek still leave the answer ambiguous, especially given that the citations by Weber refer to factors related to the *genesis* of the capitalist system rather than to the elements of a *formed* system. The contribution at hand essentially mixes together the *static* and the *dynamic* elements of the system. One could argue, however, that the factors leading to the *genesis* and the factors that characterise a *mature* system as an outcome would warrant differentiated attention.

Also, the contrast between "economic style" and "economic system" would need some further elaboration. The alleged difference

[1] Ringa Raudla (ringa.raudla@ttu.ee) is Research Fellow at the Chair of Governance, Department of Public Administration, Tallinn University of Technology.

amounts to economic style apportioning rather unequal weights to the principal elements. It can be argued, however, that the economic systems, as conceived by Weber or Sombart, did not attach completely equal weights to these components. From Weber's limited discussion on the other components – technology and form – it is rather difficult to deduce exactly the kind of weights he attributed to these factors.[2]

It was claimed in the contribution by Chaloupek that Weber and Sombart are more or less in agreement as regards the essence of capitalist spirit. That claim, however, would also warrant further consideration. It has sometimes been pointed out that their conception of capitalist spirit was different with regard to an important aspect. For Sombart, the capitalist spirit consists of two clearly distinguishable, perhaps even seemingly incompatible, components, both of which are, however, necessary parts of the capitalist spirit: a dynamic-adventurous component (also called the "entrepreneur" component) and a rationalist component (also called the "bourgeois" component).[3] Weber, on the other hand, emphasises that the main features of capitalist spirit are: the alignment to rules, the process of rationalisation, and the continuity of the accounting of efforts. According to Weber, the entrepreneurial spirit is not so close to the adventurous, speculative and risk-oriented attitude as the one delineated by Sombart (Prisching 1996, pp. 305, 322) Thus,

---

[2] As to the problem of the genesis of modern capitalism, Weber insists that any reasonably adequate account would have to include a vast matrix of causes, including material premises, institutional conditions, diverse and sometimes highly contingent flows of events. (Poggi 1982, p. 79)

[3] "The nature of the bourgeois and the nature of the entrepreneur are both necessary. Enterpreneurial spirit wants to conquer and to acquire, and bourgeois spirit wants to order and to preserve. The virtues which praise the bourgeois are: diligence, moderation, efficiency, contractual fidelity. It is the whole interwoven spirit composed of entrepreneurial and bourgeois attitude that is called capitalist spirit." (Prisching 1996, p. 311, citing Sombart)

while in Sombart's model these two components are equal and form a synthesis, Weber's focus is clearly more on the rational component.

In fact, what would also deserve further attention is whether there are differences in the way Sombart and Weber use the concept of "the spirit" as such. Weber himself suggests that by using the term "the spirit" he refers to a specific "ethos" and "ethik".[4] Sombart, however, also uses the terms "idea" or "soul", when he means "spirit" and uses the terms somewhat inconsistently (see Schneider 1996, p. 37).

It is claimed in the paper that the differences between Weber and Sombart on the relevance of Reformation for the development of the capitalist spirit mainly concern: i) the origin of what both call economic rationalism and ii) the special role of Protestant sectarian movements, especially Puritanism, in the development of capitalism.

When looking closer at what kind of arguments Sombart and Weber were making, it may turn out that the differences on these two questions may be smaller than what would seem at first sight. Also, what should be kept in mind when juxtaposing the ideas of Sombart and Weber is that in their discussions on the spirit of capitalism, Weber was in interested in a sociological theory, while Sombart's focus was on analysing a specific economic system (see vom Brocke 1996, p. 50).

---

[4] What precisely characterised this ethos? "The summum bonum of this ethic, the earning more and more money, combined with the strict avoidance of all spontaneous enjoyment of life … is though of … purely as an end in itself… Man is dominated by the making of money, by acquisition as the ultimate purpose to his life. " (Weber, 1930, p. 51). "The ethic specifies both an end, and a number of means to that end. Among these means are such virtues as industry, frugality, punctuality and honesty. The spirit of capitalism is a set of motivating ideas." (Lessnoff, 1994, p. 4)

With respect to the first difference regarding the origin of economic rationalism, it should be noted that Weber certainly did not make the claim that the roots of economic rationalism can only be attributed to the Puritan doctrine. Although Weber might have disagreed with some specific examples pointed out by Sombart, Weber's general standpoint did certainly not amount to the claim that he had established the only and exclusive connection between Calvinism (or Puritanism in general) and economic rationality. Sombart, also, took a rather differentiated view on the prevalence of economic rationality before Protestantism. As Sombart argues, "Any one who is at all acquainted with calculations in the Middle Ages knows that if you check the columns the general things is to find the totals incorrect. Mistakes in arithmetic were common occurrences. So was careless usage in calculating prices." (Sombart 1998 [1915], p. 18). Or, "Did the multitude live up to the high standard of the wise perceptors? Did every tradesman model his live in accordance to the schemes of virtues? ... From the complaints of the wise perceptors it rather looks as though they were prophets crying in wilderness." (p. 120)

With regard to the second difference, it is worth noting first that that it was from Sombart that Weber got the idea of concentrating on the influence of Protestantism in the first place (see vom Brocke 1996, p. 49). Also, when discussing the role of heresy as "a school for the capitalist spirit", Sombart points to both Protestants and Jews who, having been excluded from public life, put all their efforts into business. Sombart points out that Protestantism and capitalism are both based on the same new spirit: It is the spirit of heresy, the spirit of opposition to indolence, self-sufficiency, and muddling-on; in other words, it is the spirit of non-conformism which lays at the roots of church reform and economic reform (Prisching 1996, p. 319). Sombart also agreed with William Petty, who said that business spirit has not been connected with a certain religion, but with the heterodoxy of religious circumstances (Prisching 1996, p. 315). It would certainly be worth investigating further the possible connections between arguments made by Sombart about the importance of heretics and the arguments made by Weber with respect to "sects": that is, the connections between being "excluded" in the first place and then "excluding" others from the in-group as a result of that.

It should also be kept in mind that Weber certainly did not out-rule the influence and importance of other religions on the formation of the capitalist spirit. He did not even seek to establish a set of conditions sufficient to account for the rise of early capitalist entrepreneurship, let alone the larger phenomena of the genesis of modern capitalism (see Poggi 1982, p. 83). He does single out the influence of the Calvinist doctrine for analysis, but one should be, as Weber himself was, very careful in drawing any causative conclusions from that analysis.[5] Indeed, Weber's thesis should not be viewed as an effort to trace the causative influence of the Protestant ethic upon the emergence of capitalism, but "as an exposition of the rich congruency of such diverse aspects of a culture as religion and economics", "as a stimulating project of hermeneutics, a demonstration of interesting correlations between diverse cultural factors." (Fischoff 1991 [1941], p. 71) As pointed out by Fischoff (1991 [1944], p. 70), the misinterpretations of Weber's arguments have often been caused by the neglect of the methodological context where they were made, in particular his use of ideal-typical reasoning and his method of historical research "committed to the interpretative understanding of historical atoms, of particular emer-

[5] As Poggi (1982, p. 79) explains it, Weber identifies two distinct though compatible (and overlapping) processes through which Reformed Christianity assisted in the formation of the spirit of capitalism: the implications of Calvinist doctrine for the faithful's ethical posture, and the formation of sects generating in their members a need to prove themselves morally worthy in their everyday conduct.

gents chosen on the basis of their cultural significance and understood by a controlled intuitive method".

In Chaloupek's section on the spirit as a cause and an effect, more attention could have been paid to Sombart's ideas. In addition to discussing the Protestant or Puritan spirit as a cause, further analysis could look at what role the capitalist "spirit" as such played in the evolvement of capitalism and whether the role of the spirit differed in the different phases of the development of capitalism. As Sombart has put it: "In order to arrive at a right view of the cause and effects, one or two facts must be borne in mind. … In tracing the origins of capitalist spirit we must always bear in mind that the conditions vary fundamentally with each epoch of capitalist development. … In the early capitalist age the undertaker produced capitalism, in the perfected age capitalism produces the undertaker." (Sombart 1998 [1915], p. 197)

What would also be worth further discussion, in the light of Müller-Armack's views on the relations between the state and the development of capitalism, are Sombart's view on that issue. For Sombart, the princes, the state and the administration had often been important carriers of the early spirit of capitalism. As he points out, enlightened princes were often interested in economic activities and pushed the traditionalists towards more activities as well. Sombart also argues that sometimes there were outstanding talents in state administration and often the state was the only one who had enough capital at its disposal; furthermore, government had an advantage because it was supported by its organisational apparatus. As Sombart argues, private persons were forced or persuaded to adopt capitalism as administrators founded enterprises, installed production facilities, opened markets; the state even founded model enterprises for imitation. (Prisching 1996, p. 314) In discussing the beginnings of the "undertaking part" of the capitalist spirit, Sombart points to the importance of the state: "The whole life of the subject was circumscribed by the interests of the state. The state interfered with his private affairs and so got the average citizen accustomed to the idea of undertaking. By constantly striking at the stone, the state, as it were, produced sparks that gradually formed into a flame. How the spirit of enterprise must have nurtured by the needs of the state for centuries and centuries." (Sombart 1998 [1915], p. 61). "My object here is to call attention to the fact that ruling princes and their servants, the state officials, were among those who kept alive the spirit of capitalist undertaking; and that both played a role of no small significance among the earliest representatives of the modern economic outlook." (p. 84). "In those days, the civil servant represented the most important type of subsidiary capitalist undertaker, who by his special gifts made a lasting impression on the history of capitalism." (p. 87).

Müller-Armack's claim that, as a direct result of Reformation, social policies were mostly transferred to the state would require perhaps a closer examination in terms of the exact historical content. Regarding the example of life insurance brought out by Müller-Armack, whereby he claims that the emergence of the modern idea of insurance is a consequence of the erosion and dissolution of traditional institutions of social support and poverty relief and that Lutheran and especially in Catholic countries, insurance companies were established with considerable time lag), a case study could be cited. Zelizer (1978) analyses the development of life insurance in the US and points out that in early nineteenth-century Americans still saw it as sacrilege, or at best gambling, but by the late 1800s life-insurance had established itself as a breadwinner's obligation. She notes that the insurance industry, to achieve this transformation, made use of religious language and secured the support of clergy who urged their flocks the necessity of providing for family after death, making it a sacred duty. This personal connection seemed indispensable in attaching a ritual and symbolic significance to this otherwise rather bloodless commodity.

References

Fischoff, Ephraim. 1991 [1944]. "The Protestant Ethic and the Spirit of Capitalism: The History of a Controversy." *Social Research* 2: 53-77. Reprinted in *Max Weber: Critical Assessments*, *Vol. 2*, ed. Peter Hamilton. London: Routledge.

Lessnoff, Michael. 1994. *The Spirit of Capitalism and the Protestant Ethic. An Enquiry into the Weber Thesis.* Aldershot: Edward Elgar.

Poggi, Gianfranco. 1983. *Calvinism and the Capitalist Spirit. Max Weber's Protestant Ethic.* Amherst: The University of Massachusetts Press.

Prisching, Manfred. 1996. "The Enterpreneur and His Capitalist Spirit – Sombart's Pscyho-Historical model." In *Werner Sombart (1863-1941): Social Scientist. Vol 2. His Theoretical Approach Reconsidered*, ed. Jürgen Backhaus. Metropolis-Verlag: Marburg.

Schneider, Dieter. 1996. "Sombart or Spirit and Accountability of Capitalism as "Enthusiastic Lyricism". In *Werner Sombart (1863-1941): Social Scientist. Vol 2. His Theoretical Approach Reconsidered*, ed. Jürgen Backhaus. Metropolis-Verlag: Marburg.

Sombart, Werner. 1998 [1915]. *The Quintessence of Capitalism: A Study of the History and Psychology of the Modern Business Man.* London: Routledge.

Vom Brocke, Bernhard. 1996. "Werner Sombart, His Life, Works and Influence." In *Werner Sombart (1863-1941): Social Scientist. Vol 2. His Theoretical Approach Reconsidered*, ed. Jürgen Backhaus. Metropolis-Verlag: Marburg.

Weber, Max. 1930. *The Protestant Ethic and the Spirit of Capitalism.* London: Unwin.

Zelizer, Viviana. 1978. "Human values and the Market: The Case of Life Insurance and Death in 19th Century America." *American Journal of Sociology* 94 (3): 591-610.

Max Weber, the Protestant Ethics, and the Sociology of Capitalist Development

Alexander Ebner

1. Introduction

Recent debates on the dynamics of capitalist development have once again focused on the ideological underpinnings of the development process, thus highlighting the role of religion and specific world-views in shaping the institutional foundations of modern capitalism. Accordingly, to put it in the terms of Max Weber and fellow contemporary sociologists and economists, it may be argued that quest for the spirit of capitalism still provides a most relevant topic for major research endeavors. In particular recent advances in the domain of economic and social history have followed Weber in outlining the institutional specificity of the Western European economy as a birthplace of modern capitalism (North and Thomas 1973, Jones 1981, Rosenberg and Birdzell 1986, Mokyr 1990, Landes 1998, Lal 1998, North 2005). Proposed factors in the historically unique 'rise of the West' point at aspects such as the political competition among states, political freedom, property rights, the emergence of markets, technological innovation, and the rise of rational thought. While the debate goes on, it remains quite difficult to understand that most of these recent contributions implicitly follow the lead of Weberian analysis without explicitly referring to Weber's original thesis on the role of the Protestant ethic in capitalist development. This is even more curious given the fact that the issue of Protestantism is a decisive feature in Weber's sociology – and thus a key component of the intellectual legacy of modern social sciences at large.

Accordingly, the following sections elaborate on a reappraisal of Weber's related work.

The presentation proceeds as follows. The first section outlines Max Weber's research program, highlighting the sociology of capitalist development as a key concern. The second section discusses Weber's thesis of the Protestant ethics as a major factor in the genesis of Occidental capitalism. The third section provides an assessment of the intellectual context and most relevant criticism of this thesis, covering a set of issues that ranges from Weber's contemporaries to the most recent controversies. The paper concludes that the Weber thesis on the Protestant ethics has proven its relevance for further discussions on the evolution of modern capitalism – also with regard to current institutional transformations in the context of globalisation.

2. Max Weber's Sociology of Capitalist Development: An Outline

Weber's sociological approach is said to resemble a most comprehensive attempt in promoting a unified theoretical and empirical research program of the social sciences. Related attempts in reconstructing the unity of Weber's social thought address the argument that the relation between culture and social life, basically the interdependence of belief-systems and social reality, constitutes the basis of Weberian ideas in terms of a comprehensive sociology of culture. Thus, based on the Weberian social-ontological dualism, which informs his analysis of the process of rationalization, it has been suggested that Weber factually formulated a valuable comparison of historical cultures (Schroeder 1992). Concerning Weber's sociological research concepts, then, major components like the agency-structure problem as well as the conceptual implications of the multi-causality of historical development processes have been taken to the fore. The concept of ideal types excels as a tool of causal analysis in Weber's comparative-historical approach (Kalberg 1994).

In this line of reasoning, the Weberian renaissance in sociological theory has been designated to articulate the critique of structuralist and functionalist interpretations of Weberian thought, which had become prevalent in particular with Parson's approach to social theory as a theory of social systems. This basic orientation in the criticism of structuralist and functionalist positions has been stimulated most pressingly by arguments such as Tenbruck's on the role of religious aspects in Weber's theorising. Indeed, Tenbruck argues that that the centre of Weber's sociology is created by the analysis of historico-religious disenchantment and rationalisation as a universal sequence that contributed decisively to the rise of the Western World (Tenbruck 1980). Accordingly, it is the matter of changing religious belief-systems and world-views that constitutes a key concern of Weber's account of the cultural evolution of modern societies, involving its differentiated institutional architecture. In this setting, the role of the Protestant ethics in the institutional evolution of modern capitalism is set to be decisive.

However, sociological modifications of that position have been controversially pinpointing the aspect of rationalisation as a process of continuous disenchantment that shapes both individual and collective levels of social action. In particular, Schluchter identifies Western rationalisation as Weber's main concern that would result in a diversity of segmented attempts at formulating a universal history. Based on that assessment, Schluchter's analytical framework focuses on the notion of structural principles and their ethical-institutional dimensions, which allows for delimiting Weber's developmental history from accompanying strands of evolutionism and systems theory by underlining the corresponding theory of action (Schluchter 1981). Weber actually believed that capitalism generated major socio-cultural problems, which would come to hinder capitalist long-run growth. He anticipated the decline of capitalism due to the advent of an all-encompassing social bureaucratisation that would finally result from the rationalisation of socio-economic affairs and beliefs in modern capitalism. The notion of the 'iron cage' would describe this fate of modern society – thus putting Weber in line with cultural pessimists like Schumpeter, who would view the economic success of capitalism as a source of its socio-cultural decomposition (Swedberg 1998). In accounting for deterministic elements and underlying tendencies of a cultural pessimism in these arguments, an allegedly Nietzschean sociology of fate in Weberian thought has been traced as a motive in the corresponding assessment of the developmental dynamism of Occidental capitalism, pointing to the notion of the unintended consequences of social action as a characteristic of modern societies (Turner 1996). In this Weberian line of reasoning, rationalisation and secularisation are intertwined, with Protestantism and its rationalising world-view as a decisive moment in the economic and political development of the Occident. More specifically, the Protestant Ethics may be viewed both as a result as well as a further stimulus of a comprehensive rationalisation process.

Debating the intellectual status of Weberian thought, this interpretation has been subject to further controversies. Most prominently, Hennis dissents with that kind of reconstruction of Weberian thought as an analytical effort in theorising rationalisation, for he understands Weber's approach primarily as an effort in coming to terms with a specific science of man, based upon the role of ethical aspects in conditioning the cultural articulation of personality which results after all in a theory of the development of mankind (Hennis 1988). Thus, the cultural dimension of individual behaviour is taken to the fore, perceived as a historically specific manifestation of changing contextual settings. Appropriately, then, the analytical implications of that perspective as well as its methodological background are most generally supposed to resemble historist traditions in the social sciences, especially in the German tradition of the Historical School of political economy. Methodologically, this aspect is exemplified by the matter of concept formation in terms of Weber's use of the notion of ideal types and *Verstehen* as means of analysing human action, which are said to reflect the specific Neo-Kantian dimension of Weber's research methodology, especially regarding the impact of Rickert's methodological ideas. Related to these considerations, it has been concluded that Weber intended to establish a generalizing social science as a methodological complement to both historiography and the natural sciences (Burger 1987).

Weber's intellectual proximity to the Historical School is usually illustrated with reference to this attempted integration of explanatory and interpretative approaches, which points to Weber's concern with the methodological positions of contemporary scholars like Roscher and Knies as well as Rickert and Dilthey. Therefore, derived from Max Weber's fierce opposition against both the methodological positions of organicism and positivism, Weber's original research program has been convincingly portrayed as an extension of German historism (Ringer 1997). In particular Weber's approach to culture and modernity is said to reflect a sociological and philosophical discourse that is shaped by the sociological varieties of originally historist concerns, as for instance promoted in Simmel's works on the philosophy of history as an often neglected influence on Weber's theorising (Scaff 1989). Weber's intellectual relations with his academic and political contemporaries indeed involve a milieu of eminent historist German scholars such as Gustav von Schmoller and Werner Sombart, among others, but also historically-minded economists like Schumpeter (Shionoya 1997, 2005). This is also in agreement with references to his manifold political activities and public statements on political issues, as Weber has been portrayed as a specific brand of German liberal with nationalist leanings, who was open-minded for social reform (Mommsen 1989).

This historist orientation in the portrayal of the intellectual reference points of Weberian ideas has been contested by critical claims, which tend to differentiate, modify or even reject the historist content of Weber's economic and political sociology. The latter line of reasoning is most prominent with Tribe, who suggests that the decisive intellectual sources of Weberian ideas, as prevalent especially in his early works, belong primarily to the sphere of classical political theory rather than to the allegedly ill-conceived framework of German historism (Tribe 1989). Referring to a broader intellectual context, the Weber-Durkheim relation in the formation of modern sociology has been characterised by Giddens as contextual association and dissociation in terms of theoretical approaches and historical context (Giddens 1987). Swedberg accordingly portrays Max Weber as a founder and major representative of economic sociology, designed as a distinctly post-historist venture, which analyses economic institutions by means of sociological concepts that focus on the matter of rational action, while highlighting the relationship between economy, polity, law, and religion. These topics have of course remained most relevant for current research on the social embeddedness of economic life (Swedberg 1998). Weber's analysis of the role of Protestantism in the evolution of modern capitalism thus belongs to a highly relevant field of inquiry even in the context of economic sociology.

To sort out the analytical specificities of Weber's reasoning on capitalist development, his work on general economic history, based on the transcripts of lectures in 1919 and 1920, may be taken to the fore (Weber 1923/1991). This overview of social and economic history provides a comprehensive survey of economic development from ancient times to the modern capitalism. It addresses the pattern of Western economic development, by claiming that capitalist institutional forms always existed in history, yet it was only with the development of rational mechanisms like capital accounting and rational commerce, which would allow for establishing a capitalist system of market transactions and this promote the historically as well as geographically unique emergence of modern capitalism in Western Europe (Weber 1923/1991: 286-289). Weber argues against the misconceived claim that the rationalistic substance of modern capitalism involves a more accentuated outlook of economic interest than any other period in history. Instead, Weber distinguishes between proper economic interests, which can be traced in all societies past and present – be they capitalist, pre-capitalist, or non-capitalist – and a distinctly capitalist articulation of these kinds of interests, quite in line with the rational character of modern capitalism. In this setting, Weber also acknowledges that market competition, the key area of capital accumulation, is to be perceived as an interest-driven process among conflicting parties (Weber 1923/1991: 239-240).

Although Weber highlights the cultural dimension of capitalism, he does not neglect material factors as well – as both spheres co-evolve in space and time. Indeed, in Weber's view, the rise of capitalism was related to favourable changes in the distribution of economic resources. Primarily, the expansion of markets for consumer goods as well as the introduction of new technologies allowed a lowering of prices, which fuelled capitalist economic relations. The latter are coined by the specific characteristics of rationality as a socio-cultural paradigm with major behavioural connotations. Above all, this refers to the introduction of rational bookkeeping and capital accounting; two aspects, which help separating business and household capital, and thus allow for continued and organised capitalist accumulation. Also, the emergence of a rationally organized and formally free labour, which is treated like a commodity on markets, becomes a key feature of modern capitalism, paralleled by the development of rational law and administration in business firms and state administration, which heralds the expansion of bureaucracies in the public and private sectors (Weber 1923/1991: 302-4). After all, these factors of capitalist development are mainly shaped by the particular role of Protestantism – although the influence of Jewish beliefs as well as of Christianity in its Catholic and Lutheran manifestations is also to be acknowledged (Weber 1923/1991: 312-314). Accordingly, this Weber thesis on Protestant ethics as a driving force in the genesis of capitalist rationalisation is to be viewed as the most essential component of Weber's more comprehensive sociology of capitalist development.

3. The Weber Thesis: Protestant Ethics in the Evolution of Modern Capitalism

As outlined above, Weber approached the analysis of modern capitalism by means of an exploration of its institutional foundations. The study on the protestant ethic and the 'spirit of capitalism' – published under the title '*Die protestantische Ethik und der Geist des Kapitalismus*' in 1904 and 1905 – excelled within that venture, applied to modern capitalism as a historical individual, that is, as a complex of relations in historical reality which are to be subsumed categorically with regard to their cultural meaning (Weber 1904-1905/1920: 30). In this study, Weber, who was a Protestant himself, argues that the Protestant Reformation was critical to the rise of capitalism through its impact on belief systems. Christian asceticism in general, and Calvinism in particular, promoted ideas such as the necessity of proving faith in worldly productive activities, thus highlighting labour and rational conduct as manifestations of a divine 'calling'. Hence the spirit of capitalism is well described by the rational and ethical control of the drive for acquisition, as in Calvinism, which propels the systematisation of acquisitive activities (Weber 1921/1972: 378).

Weber's argument proceeds as follows. The rationalisation of labour, law, organisation and accounting is framed by the emergence of a specific capitalist spirit, which tends to shape economic and social behaviour. Basically, this capitalist spirit, which denotes the attitude of a rational conduct of life as well as a professionally rationalised mode of business operation is historically rooted in the spirit of Christian asceticism, most visibly in Protestant professional asceticism, and here in particular in the diverse Protestant sects that share inner-worldly asceticism with the belief-system of Calvinism as a specific institutional source of the capitalist genesis in Western Europe and North America (Weber 1904-1905/1920: 202-204). Related modes of economic behaviour are defined by the expectation of profit through the realisation of exchange opportunities, oriented at the capital account in a sustainably rational manner (Weber 1920a: 4-5). Thus, Weber claims that 'capitalism is identical with the striving for profit, in continuous and rational capitalist enterprise: for an always renewed profit: for "profitability"' (Weber 1920a: 4).

In explaining the rise of capitalism in the Western world, Weber accentuates that simple impulses to acquisition, the pursuit of gain, the accumulation of monetary wealth, are not necessarily associated with capitalism. Indeed, the notion of unlimited greed for gain, which has been put forward as a key facet of capitalism by both Marxists and post-historist scholars such as Sombart, is not at all identical with the rationale of modern capitalism. Viewed from a comparative historical perspective, the desire for gain has been seen in all sorts of social and economic conditions. According to Weber, even economic life of ancient Rome exhibited features of capitalism, as defined by 'pure economic content', which applies when objects of property may be exchanged on markets by private agents to the end of acquisition (Weber 1909/1924: 15). Historically unique institutional features of Western capitalism are the rational capitalist organisation of formally free labour in the setting of a rational-capitalist organisation, paralleled by the separation of business from the household and the introduction of rational bookkeeping as an accounting technique that allows for exact calculation (Weber 1920a: 7-8). Decisively, the ability to calculate is determined by the ability to rational action, unhampered by magical beliefs. At this point, religion exercises a major impact on the development of economic systems – and in the case of modern capitalism, a most crucial facilitating role is played by a capitalist spirit of rational calculation and conduct that is rooted in the ethics of Protestantism with its inner-worldly ascetics (Weber 1904-1905/1920: 61-62).

What makes Protestantism special? Weber suggests that religions may be classified according to their acceptance or rejection of the empirical world, that is, according to their degree of inner-worldly orientation. In the case of acceptance, this goes together with the question of transforming, adapting, or escaping from the world. Calvin's doctrine of predestination and the notion of the 'calling' were essential for promoting a transformational attitude toward rational conduct, productive labour, and wealth accumulation. Indeed, it is not the position Martin Luther and German Protestantism in its Lutheranian blend but that of rather radical Protestant dissenters like Calvin which represents the essence of the Protestant ethics of capitalism. According to Calvin, individuals were predestined to salvation or damnation. Professional success served as a demonstration of a basically unknown fate, possibly in line with the divine 'calling'. In effect, this would promote an 'inner-worldly asceticism' with a focus on efficiency, possibly resulting in non-ostentatious wealth.

Weber even argues that the religious belief-system of the Protestant sects actually came to fit to different professional occupations. For instance, Calvinists with their utilitarian attitude would exhibit comparative advantages in becoming entrepreneurs (Weber 1904-1905/1920: 100-103). Accordingly, Weber pinpoints the matter of entrepreneurship as a representation of the capitalist spirit and its religious underpinnings. The Weberian entrepreneur is not merely a risk-taking adventurer or explorer, as Werner Sombart and other contemporary economists and sociologists would have it. Instead, the entrepreneur represents the rational attitude of the modern professional, reflecting those aspects of the Protestant ethic which have contributed to the rationalisation of economic life and highlighting entrepreneurship as professional concern, also understood as a religious duty (Weber 1904-1905/1920: 53-54). Rational conduct of business corresponds to the rationalisation of other spheres of economic life that could lead to the establishment of an 'iron cage of serfdom', that is an all-encompassing administrative system of bureaucratic rule in which individuals were reduced to mere objects of administration – although the professional charisma of the entrepreneur might provide an institutional antidote (Weber 1918 /1924: 506-507). However, Weber did not proceed with a further elaboration on the complex motives and behavioural dimensions of entrepreneurship. Thus, it has been suggested that his notion of entrepreneurship resemble the 'character mask' of the Marxian capitalist. Mommsen thus claimed that Weber described capitalism in an almost Marxian mode of argumentation, namely as an irresistible social force coercing men to subject themselves seemingly voluntarily to its social conditions (Mommsen 1974: 55).

However, there is also a distinct organisational aspect of religious affairs to be taken into account. Weber differentiates between churches such as the Catholic or Lutheran churches, which are labelled as inclusive and voluntary organisations with a formal hierarchy in administration that is set to serve all believers within the domain of the church. Sects that are rooted in Puritanism, such as the Quakers, however, resemble exclusive and voluntary communities that summon religiously qualified believers who are governed by a peer network. The closely knit interaction within the social and economic communities of these sects has provided a level of rule-following behaviour that was most conducive to the formation of market exchange in a rational, transparent setting of legal rules and social norms (Weber 1920b). Given the relative freedom from governmental interference in North America, the local Protestant sects would thrive in their economic efforts that lay the foundations of the institutional advantages of American capitalism (Noland 2003).

Yet apart from his work on the Protestant ethics, Weber's sociology of religion also encompasses comprehensive works on Judaism, Hinduism, Buddhism, and Confucianism – with work on Islam still in progress at the time of his untimely death in 1920. As Weber follows a non-deterministic line of reasoning, the genesis of Occidental capitalism needed to be explained by complex processes, which would not prevent the formation of distinct types of capitalism in other parts of the world, and under other cultural and religious conditions. Judaism preceded the Christian religion –and its drive for a material transformation of the world had been put forward as a key ingredient of the capitalist spirit by Weber's contemporary Werner Sombart before. Weber, however, derives the relative economic success of Western European Jews from their status as a 'pariah' minority group that still lacked the spiritual connection between economic success and piety. Confucianism with its focus on harmoniously adaptive socio-natural relations was antithetical to the rational dynamics of capitalism. Taoism contradicted capitalism, because of its magic spiritualism and the encouragement of passive attitudes. While Hinduism and Buddhism promoted asceticism, their escapist 'other-worldly' asceticism also did not lend to the support of capitalist institutions (Weber 1915-1919/1920).

In summary, the relationship between the Protestant ethics and the evolution of modern capitalism remains constitutes a key component of Weber's sociology of capitalist development, which is framed by even more comprehensive efforts of providing a unified social science that contains a sociological analysis of general economic and social history of peoples and civilisations. The basic questions of Weber's research program remain highly relevant, because of two major reasons (Noland 2003). First, they have made central the question of the uniqueness of Western capitalism and its developmental pattern. Ever since the 18th century, modern economic growth has been an Occidental phenomenon, and it has been more rapid in Western Europe and its overseas colonies than in other parts of the world. It remains an open question whether and how Protestantism contributed to modern economic growth – yet it is obvious that it occurred soon after most of these parts of the world experienced the advent of Protestantism. Second, Weber has pointed to the significant role of non-economic factors in driving capitalist development. This applies in particular to the role of religion and related world-views. Whether it is the Protestant legacy or other religions such as Catholicism or Judaism may not be decisive. From an analytical point of view, these historically intertwined influences may be difficult to dissect. Decisively, however, as outlined in the following section, even the critics of the Weber thesis had to acknowledge the relevance of motivational and behavioural institutional conditions in the analysis of modern capitalism.

4. Beyond the Weber Thesis: Critical Appraisals

A critical appraisal of Max Weber's thesis on the Protestant ethics in capitalist development is well advised to take off with paying reference to Weber's intellectual context. Indeed, Weber's concerns with the evolution of capitalism in Western Europe fit well into the interests of the contemporary German Historical School in its post-Schmollerian phase of analytical orientation that was based on the concern with explaining the rise of modern capitalism, as represented most prominently by Werner Sombart. Actually, Weber's major contribution to these debates is his study on the Protestant ethic and the spirit of capitalism. In order to understand its argumentation, a reconsideration of the related work of Werner Sombart as well as of preceding efforts by Gustav von Schmoller is at hand.

Schmoller's historical perspective implied a reconsideration of institutional factors in economic development by acknowledging the plurality of individual motives that shape economic behaviour. Therefore, from the perspective of Schumpeterian economic sociology, it is said to demand an analysis of those factors that were treated as data by conventional economic theory, principally institutional features like the behaviour of social groups and individuals (Schumpeter 1926: 17-18). Schmoller is also highlighted with his arguments against attempts of tracing the origins of modern capitalism to the institutional features of certain historical periods, for he is credited with realising fundamental identities under widely different cultural forms, as exemplified by the case of merchant guilds and industrial cartels (Schumpeter 1939: 228-229). Indeed, Schmoller's institutional focus confronts materialist concepts that were prominent with Marxian theory and, according to him, seemed to exert an unwelcome influence on post-Schmollerian contributions within the German Historical School, like those of Weber and Sombart, as expressed by the use of the notion of capitalism. Schmoller actually argued that capital would indeed play a great role in the economy, but this should be explained psychologically, accounting for the cultural context of the particular actors, involving ideas and moral systems, customs and law, and other institutions (Schmoller 1903: 144). In this setting, the role of the Reformation in the development process, apart from its influence on the doctrine of natural law and the rationale of modern science, is linked to the connection between productive labour and religious piety, which is said to fuel the economic dynamism of Protestant nations – in particular the Germanic states (Schmoller 1901: 80).

While Schmoller was a senior of Weber, his most influential contemporary discussant was Werner Sombart, whose approach to capitalist development reflected Schmoller's concern with historical studies, while continuously acknowledging the complementing achievements of the Marxian perspective (Backhaus 1989). His notion of 'economic systems' should conceptualise the essential historical forms and institutional features of economic processes, addressing a coherent setting of economic spirit, organisation and technological dynamism (Sombart 1929: 14). Sombart applies this scheme to the genesis and evolution of modern capitalism in Western Europe, by doing so paralleling as well as stimulating Weber's corresponding efforts on the Protestant ethics. Indeed, Sombart pinpoints the dimension of economic spirit as a characteristic and driving force of capitalist evolution. According to Sombart, economic spirit denotes the domain of motivation in driving economic action, that is 'all the expressions of the intellect, all the characteristics that become apparent in the course of economic activities', accompanied by 'all ambitions, all value judgements, all principles' that shape the behaviour of economic agents (Sombart 1913/1988: 12).

Derived from that definition, Sombart described the capitalist spirit, which had already influenced the period of early capitalism since the 13th century, as the 'Faustian spirit: the spirit of unrest, of restlessness', for it would contribute to the decomposition of established routines, values and organic communities in favour of 'self-interest' and 'self-determination' (Sombart 1916/1987: 327). Indeed, the capitalist economic spirit should reflect ideas of acquisition, competition and rationality that were also rooted in diverse religious domains. Monetary acquisition represents the purpose of economic activity. Accompanied by an attitude of competition, it becomes boundless – as means become ends in an infinite quest for economic progress, propelling the rationalisation of economy and society (Sombart 1930: 196-197). The underlying ambiguity of the capitalist spirit is reflected by two constitutive components: an 'entrepreneurial spirit' based on a drive for unlimited acquisition, conquering and the will for power on the one hand, and a 'bourgeois spirit' of rational order, careful calculation and exact accounting on the other hand (Sombart 1916/1987: 329-330). However, in the period of 'high capitalism', entrepreneurial motivation becomes devoid of religious motives and customary bonds beyond bourgeois morals as the capitalist spirit is fully secularised (Sombart 1927/1987: 30-31). Finally, that capitalist spirit erodes completely, giving way to the rationalised atmosphere of 'bureaucratised capitalism' (Sombart 1927/1987: 806).

In this process of capitalist development, the role of religion is important as an intellectual and spiritual force that shapes the contours of the capitalist spirit. However, Sombart disagree with Weber's emphasis on Protestantism as a religious force in capitalism – also because Sombart's view of capitalism is less biased towards the matter of socio-cultural rationalisation and more open for the idea of unlimited acquisition as a motivational paradigm. Sombart's monograph on the role of the Jews in economic life is therefore meant to refute Weber's thesis on the Protestant ethics. Indeed, Sombart claims that the dominating ideas of Puritanism, which were so powerful in promoting the spirit of modern capitalism, were in fact more perfectly developed in Judaism, and were thus also of a much earlier date. Altogether, Sombart suggests that Puritan doctrines were deduced from Jewish sources that would combine the drive for an unlimited accumulation of wealth with a socially codified dynamism of inclusion (Sombart 1911). Furthermore, Sombart directly rejects the Weberian line of reasoning on Protestantism and capitalism when he states most clearly in his work '*Der Bourgeois*', which deals with the diverse intellectual sources of the capitalist spirit, that Protestant sects have historically exercised a pronounced antic-capitalist stance, while the Lutheran tradition in Germany represents a pre-capitalist, craft-based value system that exhibits a decidedly anti-capitalist orientation (Sombart 1913/1988: 244-245). In effect, then, Sombart's more encompassing view of modern capitalism also allows for a more diverse line of reasoning when it comes to the identification of its religious and ethical sources.

Joseph Schumpeter is another intellectual contemporary of Weber, who joins in the criticism of the Protestant ethics thesis, yet with a different argumentation than Sombart (Ebner 2003). Indeed, in contrast to both Weber and Sombart, Schumpeter claims that there is no distinct spirit of capitalism in the sense of a new way of thinking, which would have emerged in the context of the transformation of feudalism. Instead, every economic system is based on a variety of institutional forms that allow for its evolutionary self-transformation (Schumpeter 1954: 80-81). Capitalism thus evolved from the socio-cultural substance of preceding forms of economic organisation, based on institutional elements that were cumulatively growing in influence. Resembling the principle of historical continuity as a perspective on economic development, Schumpeter suggests that there is no logically autonomous problem of the birth of capitalism in terms of an outburst of economic activity of a new type – as claimed by Weber (Schumpeter 1939: 228). As Schumpeter defines capitalism as private property economy in which innovations are carried out by means of borrowed money, it follows that the historical dating of capitalism should depend on the emergence of institutional mechanism of credit creation, to be traced in Southern Europe at least since the 12th century (Schumpeter 1939: 223-224). Therefore Sombart's idea of the advent of a distinct capitalist spirit since the 15th century is dismissed, together with Weber's concept of a specific type of rationality, rooted in Protestant ethics, as a formula denoting the capitalist spirit (Schumpeter 1939: 228-229). This argumentation also includes a critique of the Weberian argument of a transition from an ideal typical 'feudal man' to a 'capitalist man', for this scheme seems to misrepresent the evolutionary character of the historical transition process of economies and societies (Schumpeter 1954: 80).

More specifically, with a nod to the Weberian argumentation, Schumpeter points out that the specific feature of rising capitalism lie in developing the institutional aspects of rationality in two ways. First, money becomes a unit of account and thus serves the practice of cost calculation, promoting a 'spirit of rationalist individualism'.

Second, the mental attitudes of modern science as well as the means of its exploitation are promoted by that type of rationality, fuelling scientific and technological progress as an endogenous factor in the capitalist process. Even cultural spheres are subjugated to that hegemonic rationality with its drive for quantification and rationalisation (Schumpeter 1942: 123-124). As the institutional order of capitalism is supported by pre-capitalist institutional patterns and social strata, their decomposition heralds the final decline of capitalism and its socialist transformation (Schumpeter 1942: 131-133). In this context, the matter of religion is for Schumpeter, a staunch Catholic, less important than for Weber and Sombart. This is primarily due to Schumpeter's refutation of the notion of a historically specific capitalist spirit that would be fuelled by distinct religious world-views. Moreover, when it comes to the formation of individualism and modern rationality, Schumpeter denies Protestantism a key role. Instead, he claims that individualism and rationalism began in Catholic thought, in particular with Duns Scotus and Aquinas (Schumpeter 1954: 91-92).

It is noteworthy that the international discussion on the Weberian thesis has followed a similar direction. Among the most prominent critics is R. H. Tawney, who alters Weber's argument by emphasising the declining influence of the Roman Catholic Church as a condition of capitalist rationalisation while pinpointing the aspect that Calvinist thought still obstructed market freedom in modern sense (Tawney 1926: 178-179). H. M. Robertson also stresses that capitalism emerged already in 14th-century Northern Italian city states, which were obviously Catholic areas (Robertson 1933). These concerns are echoed in later debates, as for instance in Deepak Lal's suggestion that most fundamental institutional innovations were occurring in Europe centuries well before the Reformation (Lal 1998). Randall Collins summarises this criticism with the claim that Christendom was the main Weberian revolution that created the institutional forms within which capitalism could emerge, whereas the Protestant Reformation just gave rise to another take-off (Collins 1986: 76). Accordingly, Weber is repeatedly attacked for misrepresenting both Protestantism and Catholicism, thus confusing the historical record with respect to the rise of capitalism in Catholic and Protestant areas (Kaufmann 1997, Iannaccone 1998).

Nonetheless, even though historical evidence may put some pressure on the Weberian thesis, it still stimulates major efforts in theorising on the relationship between religion and economic development. From a rational choice perspective, for instance, the Weber thesis has been reiterated by claiming that political-economic competition in Western Europe in effect created market space for new entrants – namely the Protestant reformers – who rapidly gained rationally switched allegiances (Ekelund, Hébert, and Tollison 2002). Furthermore, an interpretation of the Weber thesis in terms of evolutionary game theory comes up with the argument that the Calvinist doctrine of predestination increased the cost of contractual defection, thus driving Protestant contract compliance. The resulting spread of information networks in the Protestant lands then generated externalities that promoted the rise of industrial capitalism (Blum and Dudley 2001). This viewpoint is line with empirical observations which portray Catholicism as a 'hierarchical' religion that obstructs societal trust and comes together with less efficient judiciaries, greater corruption, lower-quality bureaucracies, lower rates of civic participation, inferior infrastructures, and higher inflation (La Porta et al., 1997: 336-337). Of course, one should be cautious about the causalities implied in these results. Yet it is commonly understood in regressions on economic performance that the hypothesis according to which the coefficients on variables of religious affiliation are jointly equal to zero can frequently be rejected, although no robust relationship between adherence to major world religions and national economic performance has been uncovered so far (Barro and McCleary 2002, 2003). Accordingly, the Weber thesis remains relevant, not only in a historical perspective, but also with regard to current economic and social affairs.

5. Conclusion

As outlined above, the Weber thesis on the Protestant ethics may be deficient with regard to its historical-empirical underpinnings, yet its concern with the institutional foundations of capitalist development remains relevant for current debates. Indeed, Weber's sociology of capitalism, with its broad historical, geographical and intellectual range, is once more central to the discussion of the past, present and future of modern capitalism. Three fields of study may be particularly relevant when it comes to applications of Weberian themes to current issues. First, the matter of globalisation and the 'clash of cultures', as Huntington had it, which is particularly relevant for Weberian concerns when it comes to the rise of China – and East Asia at large. This brings to mind Weber's dictum that Chinese capitalism may be possible, yet that it would look entirely different as compared with the Western model. Second, the socio-cultural conditions for overcoming underdevelopment may be a fruitful domain of application, given the discourse on good governance in the face of the fact that both market and state failure are endemic in the developing world. Third, the Weberian notion of rationality in the capitalist spirit may be applied to the current turmoil in the global financial markets. The financial crisis has uncovered major inefficiencies – and irrationalities – in the set-up of global markets, which seem to contradict the ethos of rational conduct that was underlined by Weber. After all, Max Weber was explicit in his position that the institutional evolution of modern capitalism was a path-dependent, undetermined process. This is also a way of stressing the relevance of the Weberian legacy in the social sciences.

References

Backhaus, J. (1989), Werner Sombarts Konjunkturtheorie, in B. Schefold (ed.) *Studien zur Entwicklung der ökonomischen Theorie*, Vol.VII, Berlin: Duncker und Humblot, pp.77-98.

Barro, R.J. and R.M. McCleary (2002), Religion and Political Economy in an International Panel, *NBER Working Paper No.8931*, Cambridge: National Bureau of Economic Research.

Barro, R.J. and R.M. McCleary (2003), Religion and Economic Growth," *NBER Working Paper No.9682*, Cambridge: National Bureau of Economic Research.

Blum, U. and L. Dudley (2001), Religion and Economic Growth: Was Weber Right?, *Journal of Evolutionary Economics*, Vol.11, No.2, pp.207–30.

Burger, T. (1987), *Max Weber's Theory of Concept Formation: History, Laws, and Ideal Types*, Durham: Duke University Press.

Collins, R. (1986), Weberian Sociological Theory, Cambridge: Cambridge University Press.

Ebner, A. (2003) The Institutional Analysis of Entrepreneurship: Historist Aspects of Schumpeter's Development Theory, in J.G. Backhaus (ed.), *Joseph Alois Schumpeter: Entrepreneurship, Style and Vision*, Boston: Kluwer, pp.117-139.

Ekelund, R.B. Jr., R.F. Hébert and R.D. Tollison (2002), An Economic Analysis of the Protestant Reformation, *Journal of Political Economy*, Vol.110, No.3, pp.646-671.

Giddens, A. (1987), Weber and Durkheim: Coincidence and Divergence, in W.J. Mommsen and J. Osterhammel (eds.), *Max Weber and His Contemporaries*, London: Allen and Unwin, pp.182-189.

Hennis, W. (1988), *Max Weber: Essays in Reconstruction*, London: Unwin Hyman.

Iannaccone, L.R. (1998), Introduction to the Economics of Religion, *Journal of Economic Literature*, Vol.36, No.3, pp.1465-1196.

Jones, Eric L. (1981), *The European Miracle: Environments, Economies, and Geopolitics in the History of Europe and Asia*, Cambridge: Cambridge University Press.

Kalberg, S. (1994), *Max Weber's Comparative-Historical Sociology*, Cambridge: Polity Press.

Kaufmann, F.-X. (1997), Religion and Modernization in Europe, *Journal of Institutional and Theoretical Economics*, Vol.153, No.1, pp.80-96.

Lal, D. (1998), *Unintended Consequences: The Impact of Factor Endowments, Culture, and Politics on Long-Run Economic Performance*, Cambridge, MA: MIT Press.

Landes, D.S. (1998), *The Wealth and Poverty of Nations*, New York: W.W. Norton and Company.

LaPorta, R., F. Lopez-de-Silanes, A. Shleifer, and R.W. Vishny (1997), Trust in Large Organizations, *American Economic Review*, Vol.87, No.2, pp.333-338.

Mokyr, J. (1990), *The Lever of Riches: Technological Creativity and Economic Progress*, New York: Oxford University Press.

Mommsen, W.J. (1974), *The Age of Bureaucracy: Perspectives on the Political Sociology of Max Weber*, Oxford: Basil Blackwell.

Mommsen, W.J. (1989), *The Political and Social Theory of Max Weber: Collected Essays*, Cambridge: Polity Press.

Noland, M. (2003), Religion, Culture, and Economic Performance, *Institute for International Economics Working Paper No. 03-8*, Washington: Institute for International Economics.

North, D. C. (2005), *Understanding the Process of Economic Change*, Princeton: Princeton University Press.

North, D. C. and R. P. Thomas (1973), *The Rise of the Western World: A New Economic History*, Cambridge: Cambridge University Press.

Ringer, F. (1997), *Max Weber's Methodology: The Unification of the Cultural and Social Sciences*, Cambridge, MA: Harvard University Press.

Robertson, H. M. (1933), Aspects of the Rise of Economic Individualism*: A Criticism of Max Weber and His School*, Cambridge: Cambridge University Press.

Rosenberg, N. and L. E. Birdzell (1986), *How the West Grew Rich: The Economic Transformation of the Industrial World*, New York: Basic Books.

Scaff, L.A. (1989), *Fleeing the Iron Cage: Culture, Politics, and Modernity in the Thought of Max Weber*, Berkeley: University of California Press.

Schluchter, W. (1981), *The Rise of Western Rationalism: Max Weber's Developmental History*, Berkeley: University of California Press.

Schmoller, G. (1901), *Grundriß der Allgemeinen Volkswirtschaftslehre*, Vol 1., Leipzig: Duncker und Humblot.

Schmoller, G. (1903), Werner Sombart: Der moderne Kapitalismus, *Jahrbuch für Gesetzgebung, Verwaltung und Volkswirtschaft im Deutschen Reich*, Vol.51, pp.349-369.

Schroeder, R. (1992), *Max Weber and the Sociology of Culture*, London: Sage.

Schumpeter, J.A. (1926), Gustav v. Schmoller und die Probleme von heute, *Schmollers Jahrbuch für Gesetzgebung, Verwaltung und Volkswirtschaft im Deutschen Reiche*, Vol.50, No.1., pp.1-52.

Schumpeter, J.A. (1939), *Business Cycles: A Theoretical, Historical and Statistical Analysis of the Capitalist Process*, Two Volumes, New York: McGraw-Hill.

Schumpeter, J.A. (1942), *Capitalism, Socialism and Democracy*, London: Allen and Unwin.

Schumpeter, J.A. (1954), *History of Economic Analysis*, New York: Oxford University Press.

Shionoya, Y. (1997), *Schumpeter and the Idea of Social Science: A Metatheoretical Study*, Cambridge: Cambridge University Press.

Shionoya, Y. (2005), *The Soul of the German Historical School: Methodological Essays on Schmoller, Weber and Schumpeter*, Berlin: Springer.

Sombart, W. (1911), *Die Juden und das Wirtschaftsleben,* Leipzig: Duncker und Humblot.

Sombart, W. (1913/1988), *Der Bourgeois: Zur Geistesgeschichte des modernen Wirtschaftsmenschen*, Reinbek: rohwolt.

Sombart, W. (1916/1987), *Der moderne Kapitalismus. Historisch-systematische Darstellung des gesamteuropäischen Wirtschaftslebens von seinen Anfängen bis zur Gegenwart*, repr. of Second Edition, Vol.1, München: dtv.

Sombart, W. (1927/1987), *Der moderne Kapitalismus. Historisch-systematische Darstellung des gesamteuropäischen Wirtschaftslebens von seinen Anfängen bis zur Gegenwart*, repr., Vol.3, München: dtv.

Sombart, W. (1929), Economic Theory and Economic History, *The Economic History Review*, Vol.2, No.1, pp. 1-19.

Sombart, W. (1930), Capitalism, in *Encyclopedia of the Social Sciences*, Vol. 3, ed. by E. Seligman, London: Macmillan, pp.195-208.

Swedberg, R. (1998), *Max Weber and the Idea of Economic Sociology*, Princeton: Princeton University Press.

Tawney, R.H. (1926), *Religion and the Rise of Capitalism*, New York: Harcourt Brace.

Tenbruck, F.H. (1980), The Problem of Thematic Unity in the Works of Max Weber, *British Journal of Sociology*, Vol.31, No.3, pp.316-351.

Tribe, K. (1989), *Reading Weber*, London and New York: Routledge.

Turner, B.S. (1996), *For Weber: Essays on the Sociology of Fate*, Revised Edition, London: Sage.

Weber, M. (1904-1905/1920), Die protestantische Ethik und der Geist des Kapitalismus, *Archiv für Sozialwissenschaft und Sozialpolitik*, Vol.XX, pp.1-54 and Vol.XXI, pp.1-110, repr. in M. Weber, *Ge-*

sammelte Aufsätze zur Religionssoziologie, Vol.1, J.C.B.Mohr, Tübingen, pp.17-206.

Weber, M. (1909/1924), Agrarverhältnisse im Altertum, *Handwörterbuch der Staatswissenschaften*, Third Edition, repr. in M. Weber, *Gesammelte Aufsätze zur Sozial- und Wirtschaftsgeschichte*, Tübingen: Mohr, pp.1-288.

Weber, M. (1915-1919/1920), Die Wirtschaftsethik der Weltreligionen, *Archiv für Sozialwissenschaft und Sozialpolitik*, Vol.41-46, repr. in M. Weber, *Gesammelte Aufsätze zur Religionssoziologie*, Vol.1, J.C.B.Mohr, Tübingen, pp. 237-573.

Weber, M. (1918/1924), Der Sozialismus, Vienna, repr. in M. Weber, *Gesammelte Aufsätze zur Soziologie und Sozialpolitik*, Tübingen: Mohr, pp.492-518.

Weber, M. (1920a), Vorbemerkung, in M. Weber, *Gesammelte Aufsätze zur Religionssoziologie*, Vol.1, J.C.B.Mohr, Tübingen, pp. 1-16.

Weber, M. (1920b), Die protestantischen Sekten und der Geist des Kapitalismus, repr. in M. Weber, *Gesammelte Aufsätze zur Religionssoziologie*, Vol.1, J.C.B.Mohr, Tübingen, pp. 207-236.

Weber, M. (1921/1972), *Wirtschaft und Gesellschaft: Grundriss der verstehenden Soziologie*, Fifth Revised Edition, Tübingen: Mohr.

Weber, M. (1923/1991), Wirtschaftsgeschichte: Abriß der universalen Sozial- und Wirtschaftsgeschichte, Berlin: Duncker und Humblot.

Comment on Erik Reinert „The Reformation and Seckendorff"

Hans Frambach

In his interesting and very rich lecture Erik Reinert touched many, and I think most of the relevant facts of the relationship between the reformation and Veit Ludwig v. Seckendorff. My intention is to stress some similarities but also point out some differences concerning such a comparison.

First of all, at the beginning of the 15th century, the reformation started with Martin Luther, who lived from 1483-1546. Seckendorff lived from 1626-1692, that means he worked about 150 years later than Luther.

In 1648 the Thirty Years War was over and the Treaty of Westphalia concluded. We have to realize that v. Seckendorff lived in an epoch where peace had started in the German countries and the quarrels of Reformation finally came to an end.

v. Seckendorff's major work, "Der Teutsche Fürstenstaat", published in 1655/56, was undoubtedly written in a Lutherian sense. We can find a clear confession to the Christian belief. Even though v. Seckendorff tries to treat the different Christian religions equally, he prefers the protestant religion in the sense of the Confession of Augsburg.[1] v. Seckendorff (1737, 287-288) distinguishes

[1] Confession written by Melanchthon and presented to Emperor Karl V. at the Imperial Diet on 1530; in 1555 the religious peace of Augsburg was concluded. It was a law which guaranteed to the followers of the Lutheran religion (the right of possessions? and freedom to practice their religion. After the Confession of Augsburg combinations of government and church gained momentum. In countries with protestant religion the governments had to support the churches and clerical schools substantially by financial means. As a result

three kinds of Christian religions: the Roman Catholic Church, the Confession of Augsburg (Lutheran) and the Reformed Church, which emerged from the Lutheran Religion.

Like Luther and other reformers, v. Seckendorff's foundations was of Christian faith. v. Seckendorff was convinced (as were the reformers anyway) that life in general and social life in particular is granted by God. The reformers and v. Seckendorff were all confined to their time and its thoughts; they lived in the monarchic system, the system of estates and guilds which they defended. They didn't criticise the prevailing systems of society, they believed that man – the poor as well as the rich and the King – are placed into their positions by God. The existing social order is regarded as a divine order given by God and therefore not to be doubted (e.g. v. Seckendorff 1737, 76). Of course, the sovereign has undisputed power, and this includes the power over the church (which also is a serious point of criticism of the Catholic Church and the papacy). The sovereign has to justify himself solely in the face of God (v. Seckendorff 1737, 282). If the sovereign loses God's grace and blessing, v. Seckendorff (1737, 144) says, then he and the entire people will be bare and helpless.

Most reformers, and to a certain extent v. Seckendorff as well, remained within the bounds of economic thoughts of scholasticism. Economic theory of scholasticism stood on the grounds of theology and followed three main principles:

1. The principle of justice (principle of equivalence, that means, prices and wages of a transaction should be appropriate).
2. The aim of an economic action is the satisfaction of one's needs —and not the maximization of profits

secular government power was increasingly mixed with ecclesiastical and spiritual matters.

3. Man is part of a whole and this whole is the community of the faithful.

A special case is the question of taking interests. While Luther had a lot of problems with interests, he went to bring himself to tolerate moderate rates under the condition that they were controlled by law. Reformers like Ulrich Zwingli (1484-1531) agreed with the execution of a rich patrician who charged extortionate interest rates. At the same time capable reformers as Johannes Calvin (1509-1564) supported free trade and allowed moderate interest rates. The way how Calvin explained interest is very interesting: The interest is a substitute for the profit a creditor refuses if he could invest his money in an alternative use. Thus, Calvin anticipated the modern concept of opportunity costs in a perfect manner.

The reformers and v. Seckendorff agreed about the ultimate purpose of all human activities: to honour God (we can the confirming passages find for example in the works of Luther as well as in v. Seckendorff's "Fürstenstaat"). While Luther described the activities of all the levels of society v. Seckendorff devoted most parts of his observations to the activities of the Prince and of the court. v. Seckendorff stressed that the Prince himself had to serve God obediently in the same way as Luther demanded obedience to God from all people. v. Seckendorff (1737, e.g. 37, 76-82) never seemed tire in emphasising the duties of the sovereigns towards God, but also towards the welfare of the people. For v. Seckendorff virtues had the same importance as for the reformers. The writings were full of Lutherian terms like 'enduring', 'perseverance', and 'persistency in the God-given place', 'honesty', 'sincerity', 'generosity', 'justice', 'hard work', 'diligence', 'modesty' etc. Highest importance had the 'virtues of the soul' like the fear of God, and devoutness (v. Seckendorff 1737, 142-143, 636).

As the best exercise for the sovereign to "preserve and increase" his mind v. Seckendorff (1737, 137) recommends hard and diligent work (calling) and the omission of useless things, for example bumptious science, foolish arts, leisure and vice – these all make people stupid, he writes. Greed for profit, luxury, excessive consumption, extravagance of clothes (a special problem at the courts), the breakdown of the matrimony and all kinds of idle activities are condemned as well (v. Seckendorff 1737, 225-226). The correspondence between Luther and v. Seckendorff regarding these points is remarkable.

Although we have heard a lot of agreements between the Reformers and v. Seckendorff, we have to realize some divergences:

1. Because most of the reformers were theologians and v. Seckendorff a civil servant, a political economist in the sense of the word and a bureaucrat par excellence, it is obvious that the contents of the writings had a different focus. The reformers quarrelled about religious contents, while v. Seckendorff thought about the organisation of religion and church in the country. This makes it difficult to compare v. Seckendorff with the reformers. v. Seckendorff (1737, 297) was not really interested in religious contents. For example, he recommended the Lutherian parishes a continuous conformity in their different ceremonies for the sake of positive representation, but which courses of the ceremonies should be chosen, was completely unimportant in v. Seckendorff's view .

2. The reformers were not willing to accept the power of the sovereign over spiritual and ecclesiastical affairs as v. Seckendorff did. The reformers accepted the worldly power as necessary, but attention had to be paid that this power would not encroach too much on "God's realm and rule", which was represented by the Church. For example (Luther, "Von weltlicher Obrigkeit, wie weit man ihr Gehorsam schuldig sei", WA 11, 247ff.): „*If a prince or any other worldly ruler commands you to follow the pope or to believe in a certain way, or to hand over books (…) you should answer: ‚Lucifer is not allowed to sit next to God. Master, I have to obey you in*

everything concerning my body and possessions. Command me in accordance with the greatness of your power on earth and I will follow. Tell me to believe or to hand over book, I will refuse to obey. Because then you are a tyrant and are going too far." v. Seckendorff supported explicitly the power of the sovereign as being higher than the one of Church. He described and summarized this power as consisting of three elements (v. Seckendorff 1737, 281-329):

a) Power to ordain laws and orders (e.g. sovereigns can decide the religion of their subject).

b) Power to punish, to pass judgements, to ordain decrees and to place a ban etc.

c) Power to build churches, to fill the positions in the church (to appoint clergyman etc.).

Referring to one last point: Following v. Seckendorffs (1737, 314) suggestions, authorities should even decide that a sermon did not last longer than an hour, that preachers are not allowed to defame other religions from the pulpit and heap invectives on other people in public. I suspect that such regimentations were against the nature of a Martin Luther or other Reformers.

References

Martin Luther. Kritische Gesamtausgabe (Weimarer Ausgabe, WA), 65 Vols., Graz: Akademische Druck- und Verlagsanstalt (Weimar: H. Böhlau), 1964-1993.

Veit Ludwig von Seckendorff, 1737. Deutscher Fürstenstaat, 1. ed. 1655/56, Aalen: Scientia 1972.

Episodes from the Life of Georg Anton Veth

Hans A. Esser†

Large historic changes and developments are always carried by single individuals. This is also true for the reformation movement. This chapter presents episodes from the life of Georg Anton Veth, who is an ancestor of Professor Jürgen Backhaus. It tells us what kind of fate a person could have, who had changed from the Catholic to the Protestant faith, after all, some 250 years past the reformation, in the second half of the eighteenth century.

The chapter is based on a report written by George Gabain, [1] a preacher of the French-reformed community in Altona,[2] which was printed in Lubbeck und published in Celle 1786. We do not know precisely why Gabain has written this report, but he gives us the following hint: he wanted to present it to a community[3] which had given one hundred Thaler to Georg Anton Veth for renovation and cultivation of a deteriorated, indebted estate in Gackenholz[4] near Celle, on which Veth had acquired a lease.[5]

In a nutshell, the life of Georg Anton Veth was as follows. Born on June 14, 1747, he was the son of a Catholic merchant's family in Trautheim, a small village southeast of Darmstadt, and he wanted

---

1 George Gabain, Veth's Leben. [Veth's Life]. Celle, 1786. Reprinted in: *Religion und Wirtschaft: Die Bedeutung der Reformation.* Ed. Jürgen Backhaus, Münster: LIT Verlag, forthcoming 2010.

2 At the time, Altona belonged to the Kingdom of Denmark.

3 Editor's note: Gabain's report is a private print. We do not know the name of the community, for which it has been written.

4 Editor's note: later known as „Gockenholz“

5 ibidem, p. 11.

to become a Catholic priest. He started out at the Seminary in Dillingen in 1764, and later went to the University of Mainz, where he studied philosophy, theology, und canonical law. In 1768 and 1769 he successfully completed his studies and received the respective degrees. In 1769 and 1770 he was ordained to priesthood as a secular priest – he was not ordained as a priest in a monastery. In 1770, his first position is with the Count Franz Maria von Müggenthal in Leybach as a chaplain of the castle. He holds this position for about one and a half years. In 1772, he gets promoted to priest in Fritzlar, which belongs to the archdiocese of Mainz.[6]

Gabain tells us that he does not suffer from poverty: “He had a very successful parish at the St. Petri Church in Fritzlar of 500 Thaler. He was very well liked as a preacher, evidence for this provides the large number of people who went to confession, and the frequency, with which he read mass. Moreover, a capital of 600 Gulden was signed to him at the Foundation of St. Petri, which he inherited as a life rent from one of his relatives for the time of his entire life.“[7]

In Fritzlar, Veth’s life changes in a decisive way. Frequently, he travels around the country and meets many people; he also gets acquainted with Lutheran and Reformed preachers. He has first doubts about his Catholic faith, and, when he becomes a close friend of Alex Ritte, the Reformed preacher of Geismar, a small village in the vicinity of Fritzlar, his doubts about his Catholic faith become even more intense. “His familiarity to scholarly Protestant preachers, the slips he oftentimes made even during sermons, occurrences of negligence when reading the mass”[8] did not escape his clerical colleagues and supervisors of the Church for long. He soon gets a citation before the archdiocesan commission of Mainz and is

---

6 The first date probably refers to his ordination to priesthood, the second to his promotion as a preacher.

7 ibidem, p. 7.

8 ibidem, p. 5.

thoroughly interrogated. His parish is searched for illicit books; and he is "monitored secretly and by daily visits." Tipped-off that he is to be arrested, he flees in the night of the January 19to 20. With the help of his friend Ritte from Geismar, he can leave Fritzlar. The authorities look for him everywhere. For his capture, a reward of 100 Louis d'or is offered. All his assets are immediately confiscated. His brother, a businessman in Fritzlar, has to take the flak for Veth's escape, as Catholics no longer bought from him, and Protestants were afraid to enter his store, because they did not want to arouse suspicion to be involved themselves.

Veth finds shelter with his friend Ritte in Geismar, but then has to move on and looks for a new occupation. He tries to find employment as a Reformed preacher in Kassel, Bremen, and even in the Dutch city of Groningen. In Groningen, he was offered the position of a missionary, but the Church wanted him to preach the "strong Doctrine of Predestination."[9] Veth did not stand behind this Doctrine and wandered back to Halle via Bremen and Minden. Despite many letters of recommendation, he did not succeed in finding employment as a preacher. In 1780, he takes up the study of theology in Halle for two more years, as well as his favorite subjects, physics and economics, [10] until he runs out of funds.

Neither in Hesse, nor in Prussia a proselyte like him can take the position of a preacher, and he feels no inclination whatsoever to work as a teacher in the school system. In order to find a new livelihood, he thinks about using a recipe that was given to him by a

---

9 ibidem, p. 8; compare also the editor's note at the end of this chapter.

10 What is meant by economics is not quite clear as it could include agriculture and cultivation, agricultural economics, or/and the cameral sciences. Adam Smith just published *The Wealth of Nations*, New York: Dutton, 1776. It is unclear whether it was widely known at the time, most likely not. In 1727, a chair had been established at Halle for cameral sciences, but not for economics.

friend, a pharmacist, when they put up chemical experiments together. The recipe was on how to produce vinegar on the basis of honey. Again, equipped with excellent letters of recommendation, he follows the advice of friends and goes from Halle to Celle[11] in order to realize this idea. In expectation of a signed tax exemption, supported by friends and with a basic credit he starts his production of vinegar.

Although his vinegar is reported to have been of excellent quality, it did not sit well with the local competition. The vinegar maker Röppe successfully claims his elder privilege for vinegar production in the local area with the local authorities. Veth has to give in. A last ditch effort to get a privilege after all is not successful. His production facilities turn into a monument.

Veth does not give up. In the fall of 1783, he gets the offer to manage a rather desolate farm in arrears, as has been mentioned above, and he takes it. With 100 Thaler he received as a donation and 50 Thaler he received as a credit he starts to rebuild the caved-in house with his own hands. He builds a fence around it, plants potatoes and vegetables, buys two oxen, and the requisite iron tools, such as plow and harrow, he orders from Eisenach. He cuts trees, plants a plantation of plum trees, and keeps 22 sheep and a cow. The cow yields more milk and butter than expected by his neighbors as he changes her diet by keeping her in the stable; and this changes the local technology of herding. A companion, Susanna, joins him. As she came from Hesse herself, and shared his Reformed faith, they were somehow put by the Hanover authorities in the same basket.

---

[11] Editor's note: In 1684, Duke Georg Wilhelm enacts an Edict of Tolerance for Celle. In consequence, a French-Refomed Community was formed in Celle, a Jewish and a Roman-Catholic community followed, and they all prospered. Therefore, moving to Celle at the time made sense to a proselyte as Georg Anton Veth, who wanted to live and work there.

Compare: http//www.celle.de/media/custom/342_12880_1.PDF

Gabain describes her as follows: "Ugly as the original sin …, but faithful and busy as a bee, she remains his companion in good and in bad days, his maid, his knight, his cook, his administrator; in short, all and everything. She harnesses, drives the cart, threshes, digs, plows, and manages the home."[12]

These are the circumstances under which Gabain meets Georg Anton Veth in his 39th year on his farm in Gackenholz. He is not only touched by the fate of this man, but also impressed by the way how he handled the blows of fate. In his message to the sponsors he reports at length with touching words.

Many a proselyte, who renounced everything, failed and were tempted to join their old church. Many a proselyte, however, grew with his challenges. The case of Georg Anton Veth may serve as an example that abilities and traits may be sharpened under the acute challenges of a reformation, which under normal circumstances would never have shown up. The individual case cannot yield generalizations. Nevertheless, the supposition prevails that the reformation could never have succeeded if in its duration not more of such characters as Georg Anton Veth would have proceeded to show up.

Editor's Note

The way the reformation developed was very different in e.g. Germany, Switzerland, Scotland, England, France, Belgium, and the Netherlands. They all changed different things in different time

[12] ibidem, pp. 14

frames, which makes it almost impossible to summarize that diverse movements.[13]

When Georg Anton Veth went to the Netherlands looking for employment, the Reformed Church in Groningen wanted him to preach the "strong Doctrine of Predestination,"[14] but Veth did not stand behind this Doctrine and wandered back to Germany. We have read in the chapter on Calvin written by Gerrit Meijer (this volume) that Calvin himself did not put the main emphasis on this doctrine. A few words inspired by a letter from Gerrit Meijer might explain what has happened.[15]

As far as Calvin (1509-1546) and Veth (born 1747) are concerned they were, of course, no contemporaries. In the meantime, in the Netherlands in 1618/19 the Synod of Dordrecht convened with participants from Scotland and parts of Germany. This Synod brought about the official Dutch bible translation which was ultimately published in 1637. (There were two competing commercial translations already, in Amsterdam and Leiden). This Synod concluded a different interpretation of the Doctrines of Selection and Salvation, the Remonstrators and Counter-Remonstrators. This was canonized in the "Dortsche Leerregels," a document a preacher had to sign. The document not only indicated what were true, but also what were false interpretations of the bible. Also, an aspiring preacher of the Dutch Reformed church had to sign the Dutch Testimony by Guido de Bres of 1563 and the Heidelberg Catechism of 1568. These three

---

[13] This has been mentioned in a letter from Peter Senn, who has also noted that, although delayed, the influence of the Reformation in the United States was great indeed: "As you probably know, to this day more Americans say they are Christians, and go to church more, than do Europeans. The majority of Americans are Protestants of one kind or another. Many American settlers came here for the religious freedom they found. Even our currency has *In God we Trust*."

[14] ibidem, p. 8

[15] Any errors, of course, remain with the editor.

documents are called the form letters of unity. The purpose was to unify teaching and preaching. The three documents are sometimes called "The Paper Pope." The older testimonies, Athanasius, Nicea, and the Twelve Articles, are still observed.

Apparently, around 1750 also Veth was requested to sign these documents. Obviously, he did not oblige, probably because of the Doctrine of Predestination, which was propagated at variance with what the Church actually taught. The Synod of Dordrecht, which tried to provide lucidity, in fact split the Church, reflecting the general political situation. In 1618, in Germany the Thirty-Years War erupted. The Netherlands had already been at war for fifty years, which is why they concluded in 1648 the Peace of Münster ending the Eighty-Years War.

References

Gabain, George. *Veth's Leben*, Celle 1786. Reprinted in: *Religion und Wirtschaft: Die Bedeutung der Reformation.* Editor: Backhaus, Jürgen, Münster: LIT Verlag, forthcoming 2010.

Smith, Adam. *The Wealth of Nations.* New York: Dutton, 1776. Online available: http://www.celle.de/media/custom/342_12880_1.PDF

List of Authors

Jürgen G. Backhaus (*1950), JSD 1976, PhD (Econ) 1985, holds the Krupp Chair in Public Finance and Fiscal Sociology at Erfurt University since November 2000. Between 1986 and 2000, he has held the chair in Public Economics at Maastricht University. In 2006 he received the Cross of the Order of Merit of the Federal Republic of Germany (Knight's Cross), in September 2004 he was awarded an honorary doctorate by the University of Thessaly (Greece). In 1994 he founded (with Frank H. Stephen) the European Journal of Law and Economics, of which he is now the only editor. He has published more than 70 books and monographs, about 200 articles in refereed journals and book chapters, more than 30 scholarly notes and 70 reviews. His research interests span economics, but also neighboring disciplines such as law, fiscal sociology and environmental sciences.

Günther Chaloupek (*1947); Dr. iur. University of Vienna 1969, M.A. (economics) University of Kansas, Lawrence, Ks., USA, 1971; Director of the economic research department of the Austrian Chamber of Labour, member of the Advisory Council for Economic and Social Affairs; vice president of the Government Debt Committee. A selection of publications includes the following *books* (author and/or editor): Gesamtwirtschaftliche Planung in Westeuropa, Frankfurt/Main 1987; Kapitalismus im 21. Jahrhundert, Vienna 2001; Österreichische Industriegeschichte 1700-1848, Vienna 2003; numerous *articles* (in German and in English) published in journals and contributions to books in the field of history of economic theory.

Alexander Ebner is Professor of Socio-Economics at Goethe University in Frankfurt am Main, Germany. He studied economics and political science at Goethe University Frankfurt, where he also received his Ph.D. in economics, which was followed by a habilitation at the University of Erfurt. Subsequently, he held professorships at Jacobs University Bremen in Germany as well as Grenoble Ecole de Management in France. International research affiliations include the University of California at Berkeley and the Institute of Southeast Asian Studies in Singapore. Prof. Ebner's main research interests address the matter of innovation, entrepreneurship, governance and economic development. His scientific contributions include numerous articles in international social science journals, accompanied by the monograph "Embedded Entrepreneurship" with Routlegde Publishers as well as the co-edited volume "Institutions of the Market" with Oxford University Press.

Hans Esser† (1934 - 2009) first trained as a typesetter, but then turned to study economics in Cologne and received his Ph.D. there on the strength of a dissertation on the methodology of the social sciences. This remained the topic for all his life, not only theoretically, but also practically. He was named a founding senator of the University of Wuppertal and became a senior lecturer there in 1974.

Hans Frambach (*1961) focuses on the factor labor in the history of economic thought. He studied at the Technical University of Dortmund economics and the social sciences, graduated there in 1988, received his Ph.D. at the University of Wuppertal in 1992 and his Habilitation there in 1999. Since 2004 he was appointed Professor of Applied Microeconomics at the Schumpeter School of Business & Economics at the University of Wuppertal. His main research focuses on institutional economics, strategic management, the theory of the firm, and the history of economic thought with the specific emphasis on labor as a factor of production.

Edward James Gay, IV (born 25 September 1967 in New Orleans, Louisiana) Shortly after attaining his Bachelor of Arts from the University of Mississippi in 1989 Gay moved to Europe, first living in London where he worked for Regis Low on the Lloyds of London insurance market and then moving to Munich where he worked briefly for Deutsche Bank. In 1992 he settled in Berlin and began his studies of the German language, history and philosophy. He is a professional language teacher and the founder of GELL (German and English Language Learning). Gay has continued his academic pursuits attaining his Magister Artium from Humboldt University in 2002 and is currently nearing completion of a dissertation at the University of Erfurt on the philosopher and political economist Eugen Dühring. Aside from linguistics his areas of specialty include the history of political economy, philosophy, German Idealism, fascism and socialism.

Gerrit Meijer (*1938) studied economics at the University of Groningen and received his Ph.D. there on the strength of a dissertation on the theory of an economic order. He was a Lecturer of Economics at the University of Amsterdam from 1967 – 1988, and moved to the University of Maastricht in 1989, where he retired as a reader in economics in 2003. His main research focuses on the theory of economic systems and the history of economic thought.

Ringa Raudla is Senior Research Fellow in the Department of Public Administration of Tallinn University of Technology. She holds a doctoral degree in economics from the Faculty of Law, Economics, and Social Sciences, University of Erfurt, Germany. She has taught courses on public administration, public finance, law and economics, and research methods, and has worked as a consultant for several government institutions in Estonia. She has published numerous articles and book chapters in areas such as constitutional political economy, social insurance reform, public procurement, public finance, and fiscal sociology. Her most recent book is *Constitution, Public Finance, and Transition* (Peter Lang 2010).

Helge Peukert (*1956) is professor at the University of Erfurt at the chair of public finance and fiscal sociology. He received Ph.D.

degrees from the University of Frankfurt, first in economics and secondly in sociology. His main research areas documented in an abundance of publications include heterodox economic theories, public sector economics, and - as a hobby - financial markets. His most recent book is on Rudolf Goldscheid, the founder of fiscal sociology (Münster: LIT, 2009).

Enrico Schöbel is a postdoctoral lecturer in Economics and Sociology at the Goethe-University of Frankfurt am Main, Internationales Studienzentrum. He was a lecturer in Socio-Economics at the University of Osnabrück from 2006 to 2009 and assistant editor of the European Journal of Law and Economics at the University of Erfurt from 2002 to 2010. He studied Economics at the Universities of Jena and Groningen (NL). His dissertation thesis on Steuerehrlichkeit [honesty in taxation], 2008, and 27 publications in refereed journals, conference volumes, and encyclopedic books span Political Economy, Public Finance, Law & Economics, and Fiscal Sociology.

Wirtschaft: Forschung und Wissenschaft

Jürgen Backhaus; Raul Eamets; Diana Eerma (Eds.)
Economics of Education
Issues of Transition and Transformation
This book is mainly a collection of selected papers presented at the International Conference on Economics of Education at the University of Tartu, Estonia. The contributions presented here illustrate the wide variety of issues as human and social capital, skills, education and research institutions, educational services, and management, accounting and compensation systems in schools and universities. This collection of studies provides information, ideas and research that should be valuable for practitioners, policy makers, academics and students.
Bd. 29, 2010, 384 S., 39,90 €, br., ISBN 978-3-643-10723-7

LIT Verlag Berlin – Münster – Wien – Zürich – London
Auslieferung Deutschland / Österreich / Schweiz: siehe Impressumsseite

Jürgen G. Backhaus

Historische Schulen

Lange Zeit galten die Historischen Schulen, insbesondere die Deutsche Historische Schule, als Sonderweg und Hemmschuh der theoretischen Entwicklung in den wirtschaftlichen Staatswissenschaften. Diese Einschätzung, die auch einer theoriegeschichtlichen Überprüfung nicht standhalten kann, wird durch die Renaissance wirtschaftlich-theoretisch-historischer Analyse tatsächlich auch Lügen gestraft. Dieser Band dokumentiert die jüngste Renaissance Historischer Schulen als einer möglichen Forschungsrichtung in den wirtschaftlichen Staatswissenschaften.

Bd. 11, 2005, 216 S., 19,90 €, br., ISBN 3-8258-8351-5

LIT Verlag Berlin – Münster – Wien – Zürich – London

Auslieferung Deutschland / Österreich / Schweiz: siehe Impressumsseite